EXODUS

KidzFirst Publications
Lenexa, Kansas (USA)

> The first Children's Bible Quiz event, created by Rev. William Young,
> was introduced with a demonstration at the
> 1968 General Nazarene Young People's Society Convention
> Kansas City, Missouri (USA).
> Three Nazarene churches sent teams for the demonstration:
> Kansas City First, Kansas City St. Paul's, and Overland Park.

KidzFirst Bible Studies for Children: Exodus

REVISED 2018-12-06

Copyright © 2019 Global Nazarene Publications

kidzfirstpublications.org

ISBN 978-1-56344-884-3

Editor for US English version: Kimberly D. Crenshaw

Editor for Global English: Leslie M. Hart

Editorial Committee: Leslie M. Hart, William J. Hart, Kathy Lewis, and Scott Stargel

Cover Art: Megan Goodwin

Published by KidzFirst Publications
an Imprint of Sunday School and Discipleship Ministries International
Church of the Nazarene
17001 Prairie Star Parkway
Lenexa, KS 66220 (USA)

This edition published by arrangement with Nazarene Publishing House, Kansas City, Missouri USA

Scriptures taken from the Holy Bible New International Version, NIV Copyright © 1973, 1978, 1984, 2011 by Biblica, Inc. Used by permission of Zondervan. All rights reserved worldwide. www.zondervan.com

CONTENTS

SUMMARY OF THE BIBLE STUDIES FOR CHILDREN SERIES / 4

TEACHER PREPARATION / 5

LESSONS / 9

MEMORY VERSE ACTIVITIES / 124

REVIEW QUESTIONS / 128

CERTIFICATE OF COMPLETION / 168

AWARD FOR EXCELLENCE / 169

ATTENDANCE SHEET / 170

CHILDREN'S QUIZZING SCORE SHEET / 171

MEMORY VERSES FOR EXODUS - PROGRESS CHART / 172

GUIDELINES, RULES, AND PROCEDURES FOR QUIZ EVENTS / 173

THE STORY BEHIND KIDZFIRST BIBLE STUDIES FOR CHILDREN AND QUIZ EVENTS / 197

WELCOME AND OVERVIEW

Welcome to the *Bible Studies for Children* series that celebrates genuine discipleship through God's transforming Word!

These studies help children, ages 6 through 12, to gain a practical understanding of the Bible. Through this series, the children view the story of God through the lives of real people and historical events. They see God's love revealed through words, actions, and miracles. They learn how God works through ordinary people, and they discover their place in God's plan to redeem the world.

Each lesson includes the Bible context, content and review activities. In addition, the lesson provides the teacher with discussion questions and review questions. Red and blue level review questions prepare children to participate in an optional Bible Quiz event.

SUMMARY OF THE *BIBLE STUDIES FOR CHILDREN* SERIES

GENESIS

This study provides the foundation for the entire series. It describes God's relationship to all creation and his desire to establish a people to worship him. The study explains how God created the world from nothing, formed a man and a woman, and created a beautiful garden for their home. It reveals how evil, sin, and shame came into the world and the consequences of bad choices. Genesis introduces the plan of God to reconcile the broken relationship that is caused by sin. It introduces Adam, Eve, Noah, Abraham, Isaac, and Jacob. It tells about the covenant God made with Abraham and how Jacob became known as Israel. Genesis tells the story of Joseph, who saves the Egyptians from famine. It ends as the Israelite people move to Egypt to escape the famine.

EXODUS

Exodus explains how God continued to keep his promise to Abraham. It describes how Pharoh enslaved the Israelites. It reveals how God used Moses to rescue the Israelites from slavery. In Exodus, God establishes his authority over the Israelites. He leads them through the priesthood, the Tabernacle, the Ten Commandments, and other laws. God prepares the Israelites to be his people and to enter the Promised Land. As Exodus ends, only a part of God's covenant with Abraham is complete.

JOSHUA, JUDGES, & RUTH

This study explains how God fulfilled his promise to Abraham. When Moses was near the end of his life, God chose Joshua to lead the Israelites. Joshua led the 12 tribes of Israel to conquer the Promised Land and to live in it. After Joshua's death the Israelites struggled to obey God. They would obey, then disobey, and then suffer the consequences of disobedience. As the people suffered by their unfaithful choices, God called judges to lead the Israelites to faithfully obey the Lord. This study focuses on the judges Deborah, Gideon, and Samson. The story of Ruth takes place during this time of suffering. Ruth, Naomi, and Boaz show God's love and compassion in the middle of difficult circumstances. God blesses their faithfulness and redeems their circumstances. Ruth becomes the great-grandmother of King David.

1 & 2 SAMUEL

The study of 1 and 2 Samuel begins with the life and ministry of Israel's last judge, Samuel. Samuel followed God as he led Israel. The Israelites demanded a king like the nations around them. With the Lord's guidance, Samuel anoints Saul as the first king of Israel. Saul begins his reign well, but then he turns away from God. Because of this, David is chosen and anointed as the next king of Israel. David trusts God to help him to do impossible things. David is dedicated to God. But David is tempted, and he chooses to sin. Unlike Saul, David mourns because of his sin. He asks God to forgive him. God restores his relationship with David, but the consequences of sin remain with David, his family, and the nation of Israel. Throughout these stories of turmoil, God's presence remains constant. King David prepared the way for a new kind of King—Jesus.

MATTHEW

This study is the focal point of the entire series. The previous studies point to Jesus as the promised Messiah and the Son of God. This study focuses on the birth, the ministry, the crucifixion, and the resurrection of Jesus. Jesus ushered in a new era. The children learn about this new era in several events: the teachings of Jesus, the mentoring of his disciples, his death, and his resurrection. Jesus teaches what it means to live in the kingdom of heaven. Through Jesus, God provides a new way for all people to have a relationship with him.

ACTS

Acts records the birth of the church and its growth, especially through the ministries of Peter and Paul. At the beginning of this study, Jesus ascends to heaven and God sends the Holy Spirit to all believers. The good news of salvation through Jesus Christ spreads to many parts of the world. The apostles preach the gospel to the Gentiles and missionary work begins. The message of the love of God transforms both the Jews and the Gentiles. A direct connection can be seen between the evangelism of Paul and Peter and the lives of people today.

TEACHER PREPARATION

It is important to prepare thoroughly for each lesson. The children are more attentive and gain a better understanding when the study is presented well. If a teacher prepares well, he or she will also present the lesson well.

LESSON ELEMENTS

Each lesson contains the following elements.

Memory verse: Each lesson includes scripture for the children to memorize. These verses support the "Truth about God." The children will know the God of the Bible through his Word.

Truths about God: These truths help the teacher to recognize and emphasize how God's actions reveal his character and love for all people. The teacher should emphasize the "truths about God" as he or she teaches the lesson.

Lesson focus and summary: This section highlights the major ideas, events, and scriptures that the lesson covers.

Bible background: This section provides the teacher more information about the Bible story. It will help the teacher to understand better the scripture passage. The information enriches the teacher's knowledge and abilities.

Did you know?: This provides an interesting fact about the context of the story.

Vocabulary: These words and definitions will help the teacher to explain the meaning of the words used in the Bible.

Story-telling: This section suggests a storytelling method to connect the children to the Bible story.

Biblical lesson: This focuses on reading the scripture and discussion questions. This will help the children to apply the story to their lives.

Memory verse practice: This activity helps the children to memorize the verse for each lesson.

Additional activities: This section provides a game, craft, or other activity to connect the children to the lesson. These activities reinforce the main points.

Activities for older children: These activities are designed to engage older children with the main point.

Practice for a Bible Quiz event: This section provides questions to review the lesson. The review questions prepare the children to participate in an optional Bible Quiz event.

PREPARATION SEQUENCE

The following steps outline the recommended preparation sequence for the teacher.

STEP 1: LESSON REVIEW

You should thoroughly read the entire lesson. Give special attention to the memory verse, truths about God, lesson focus and summary, and the biblical lesson teaching tips.

STEP 2: BIBLE PASSAGE AND BIBLICAL BACKGROUND

Study the verses in the Bible, the biblical background, and the vocabulary sections.

STEP 3: STORY-TELLING

The **bold text** in each study suggests the words for you to say to the children.

This section includes a game or other activity to prepare the children for the biblical lesson. Become familiar with the activity, the instructions, and the supplies. Prepare and bring the necessary supplies to the class. Prepare the activity before the children arrive.

STEP 4: BIBLICAL LESSON

Review the lesson and learn it well enough to tell the story so that the children will understand the major points. Learn the definitions of the vocabulary words. When the vocabulary words appear, pause to explain them. After the story, ask the discussion questions. This will help the children to understand and to apply the story to their lives.

STEP 5: MEMORY VERSE

Memorize the verse before you teach it to the children. Page 172 contains a list of the memory verses. Pages 124-127 contain suggested memory verse activities. Choose an activity to help the children to learn the memory verse. Prepare the supplies that you will bring to class. Become familiar with the activity, and practice the way you will instruct the children.

STEP 6: ADDITIONAL ACTIVITIES

The purpose of any activity is to connect children to the lesson. Be creative! Make adjustments or substitutions in games and supplies so that they fit your culture and context. The additional activities are optional. They enhance the children's study if you choose to use them. Many of these activities require additional supplies, resources, and time. Become familiar with an activity before you choose it. Read the instructions and prepare the supplies that you will bring to class.

STEP 7: PRACTICE FOR A BIBLE QUIZ

A Bible Quiz event is an optional part of Bible Studies for Children. If you choose to participate in a Bible Quiz event, you should plan enough time to prepare the children for it. Two levels of practice questions are included for each study. The red level questions prepare children for a basic level quiz event. The questions are simple. Each question offers three possible answers. The blue level questions prepare children for a more advanced quiz event. The questions provide more challenge and offer four possible answers. With their teacher's guidance, children may choose their preferred level for the quizzing event, either red or blue. Based on the number of children and the available resources, you may choose to offer only the red level or only the blue level.

Read the Scripture passage to the children before you ask the practice questions.

SUGGESTED SCHEDULE

You should plan for one to two hours of class time. The following is a suggested schedule for each lesson with options for 90 minutes and 2 hours. You may adjust the schedule as needed.

1½ hour	2 hours	
5 minutes		You should review the previous week's lesson with any children who arrive early. You may also choose to preview memory verses, stories, or vocabulary words for today's lesson.
5 minutes	10 minutes	Story-telling opening activity
10 minutes	10 minutes	Bible story
5 minutes	10 minutes	Review
10 minutes	15 minutes	Optional activity
10 minutes	15 minutes	Biblical lesson
10 minutes	15 minutes	Memory verse activity
	10 minutes	Optional activity
30 minutes	30 minutes	Bible Quiz event practice
5 minutes	5 minutes	Review of the main points and prayer

Bible Studies for Children: Exodus

SIX-YEAR CYCLE FOR BIBLE QUIZ EVENTS

The following cycle is included for those who participate in the Bible Quiz event option of Bible Studies for Children.

The annual cycle is based on the school year of each country. The World Quiz event happens every four years in June.

- **Genesis** (2019-2020)
- **Exodus** (2020-2021)*
- **Joshua, Judges, & Ruth** (2021-2022)
- **1 & 2 Samuel** (2022-2023)
- **Matthew** (2023-2024)
- **Acts** (2024-2025)*

This is the year of the World Quiz.

LESSON 1

WHAT HAPPENED?
EXODUS 1:1-22

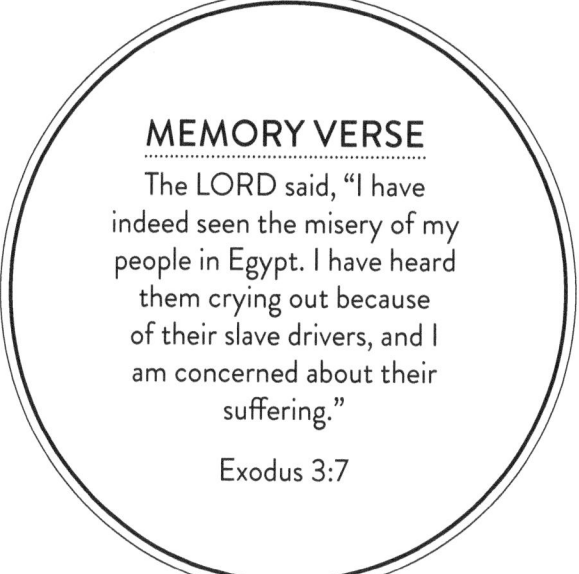

MEMORY VERSE

The LORD said, "I have indeed seen the misery of my people in Egypt. I have heard them crying out because of their slave drivers, and I am concerned about their suffering."

Exodus 3:7

TRUTHS ABOUT GOD

This lesson will teach the following truths about God. The asterisk * indicates the primary truth that you should teach to the children.

* * God showed kindness to his people in a time of trouble.
* God always keeps his promises.
* God's timetable is often different from our timetable.

LESSON FOCUS AND SUMMARY

In this study, the children will learn that God keeps his promises and provides for his chosen people.

1. The end of Genesis connects to the beginning of Exodus.
2. Exodus fulfills a portion of the promise that God made to Abraham in Genesis 15.
3. God was deeply concerned about the suffering of the Israelites caused by the Pharaoh.

 ## BIBLICAL BACKGROUND

Exodus is about obedience and disobedience, valuing and disregarding life, submission and stubborn selfishness, forgiveness and bitterness. Exodus tells the details of the life of Moses, a powerful servant of God and leader of the Israelite people. Through Moses, God led the Israelites out of slavery in Egypt, helped them become a nation, and prepared them to enter the Promised Land.

At the end of Genesis, we see the contrast between Israel and Egypt. All of Israel's sons lived in Egypt. They worshiped God and became a very large family. The Egyptians thought that their king, whom they called Pharaoh, was a god. They worshiped him. They also worshiped many other false gods and practiced dark magic. Exodus begins with a new Pharaoh. This king did not know Joseph or his God. There were many Israelites living in Egypt. Pharaoh was afraid that they would turn against him. He made the Israelites his slaves. He forced them to work very hard building cities. He would not let them leave Egypt.

Genesis ends with some unanswered questions:

- What would it take for the Israelites to become so uncomfortable that they would eagerly leave Egypt?
- How would God bring the Israelites out of Egypt to the land that he promised to Abraham four hundred years earlier?

Exodus answers those questions. Your children will learn that God is faithful. God is involved. God works to bring people to him. The God of Exodus is the God of today.

DID YOU KNOW?

The Israelites built the cities of Pithom and Rameses, called store cities, where Pharaoh stored supplies for his soldiers.

 VOCABULARY

Faith words:

To promise means to pledge that you will do something. God always does what he says that he will do. God always keeps his promises.

People:

Abraham was the ancestor of the Israelites, who were also known as the Hebrews. He is the first Hebrew patriarch.

Isaac was the son of Abraham.

Jacob, also known as **Israel**, was the son of Isaac and the grandson of Abraham.

Pharaoh was the title for the king of Egypt.

Shiphrah and **Puah** were Hebrew midwives.

Hebrews and **Israelites** are two terms that are used for the descendants of Jacob, also known as Israel.

Places:

Egypt is a country in northeast Africa. At the time of the Exodus, Egypt was a powerful nation.

Goshen was an area in northeast Egypt where the Hebrews lived.

The Nile River is the largest river in Egypt.

Terms

Descendants are a person's children, grandchildren, great-grandchildren, and all of the generations born to them.

Midwives are women who help other women give birth to babies.

STORYTELLING

Each week you will need the following items.

1. A carrier like a small travel bag
2. A storage container for each week's story items (It can be a bag, basket, or box.)

For today's story, you will need the following items.

3. Twelve similar items like crayons, marbles, or pebbles that are small enough to fit in your travel bag
4. A brick
5. A baby doll

Before class:

1. Read Exodus 1:1-22.
2. Gather today's story items. Substitute a picture for any unavailable items.
3. Place today's story items inside the travel bag. Place the travel bag in the storytelling area.

Opening activity: Follow the leader

If you have time, you can play "Follow the leader" with the children before the story time each week.

Tell the children to stand in a line, one behind the other. Choose a child to be the leader. Tell the children to watch carefully and mimic everything the leader does. The leader leads the group around the room. He or she uses different hand gestures, sounds, or means of travel for the children to imitate. For example, the leader walks with baby steps, large steps, or skips. End the game at the storytelling area.

Story time:

Read these instructions before you begin.

1. Tell the story in your own words. Remove each item from the bag as you illustrate a main point. Focus on the main points. If you are comfortable, include more details. If needed, use the script that is suggested.
2. As you tell the story, display each item in the order that it is listed. Place it where the children can see it.
3. After telling the story, place all the items inside the bag again.
4. To review the story, remove the first item. Ask a volunteer to tell what it represents. Display this item. Repeat this process until the story is retold.
5. Review the memory motion described below. Demonstrate this motion any time you mention what it represents.
6. Say, **We are on an expedition. I packed our travel bag with tools that will help us to explore the book of Exodus. Each week we will search inside the bag for the tools that we will need for our journey. Today we begin with...** Unpack the items as you tell the story.

Main points in order:

1. The twelve similar items—Hold them up. Say, **At the end of Genesis, Jacob, also known as Israel, had many sons. His son Joseph became an important leader in Egypt. During a great famine, Joseph brought his father, brothers, and their entire families to Egypt. They lived in Goshen and became a large group of people.**
2. A Brick—Say, **After Joseph died, a new king who did not know Joseph became Pharaoh. Pharaoh was afraid that all the Israelites would join his enemies and fight against Egypt. So he forced the Israelites to be his slaves. He forced them to make bricks and to build his cities.**
3. Memory motion: Chain link—Show the children how to link their two index fingers together to represent the Israelites in bondage to the Egyptians. You may also invite the children to think of another motion. Say, **As I tell the story, do this motion when you hear what it represents.**
4. Baby Doll—Say, **Even after they became slaves, God blessed the Israelites with many children. To stop their families from getting more numerous, Pharaoh commanded the Hebrew midwives to kill the Hebrew baby boys at birth. But the midwives feared God and refused to kill the baby boys. After this, Pharaoh ordered the Egyptians to**

throw all the Hebrew baby boys into the Nile River.

5. Say, **Now it is your turn to tell the story.** Return the items to the bag. Invite the children to take turns and choose an item from the bag without looking. Ask them to explain what it means or to review the memory motion. After all the items have been removed, ask the children to place them in the correct story order.

BIBLICAL LESSON

Teaching tips:

As you lead the Bible study, emphasize these ideas.

- Review Genesis 15:12-14 and 46:2-7.
- Tell in your own words how the Israelites arrived in Egypt. This will provide the context for the study of Exodus.

Read the Scripture:

Read Exodus 1:1-22 aloud.

Discussion questions:

Discuss the story and ask the children the following questions. Remember that there might not be a right or wrong answer.

1. **What happened to cause the Israelites to go to Egypt?** (Genesis 15:12-15; 46:2-7)
2. **How would you feel if you were an Israelite slave in Egypt?**
3. **Do you think the Israelites felt abandoned by God? Why?**
4. **Through whom did God work to help his suffering people? How do you think God helps suffering people today?** (Exodus 1:17-21)
5. **How do you know God consistently works in your life?**

Closing thoughts:

This is the thought that you want the children to remember.

Say, **God showed kindness to his people in a time of trouble.**

The Israelites came to Egypt as honored guests and became slaves. The Lord never forgot the Israelites or the promise that he made to give them a land of their own. The Lord showed the Israelites kindness even though terrible things happened to them. He was with them when they suffered. He saved the baby boys from being killed.

The Lord will never leave you. He sees your struggles. He is with you when bad things happen. The Lord had a plan for the Israelites, and he also has a plan for you.

MEMORY VERSE PRACTICE

The LORD said, "I have indeed seen the misery of my people in Egypt. I have heard them crying out because of their slave drivers, and I am concerned about their suffering." –Exodus 3:7

See the "Memory Verse Activities" on pages 124-127 for suggestions to help the children to learn the memory verse.

ADDITIONAL ACTIVITIES

To learn more about ancient Egypt and the culture in which the Israelites lived, consider these options.

1. Learn about Pharaohs Ahmose and Rameses II. What were they like? What are they famous for? How do they relate to Exodus?
2. Learn about ancient Egypt during the time of Rameses II. Find out what made Egypt a superpower in the ancient world.
3. Study Egyptian hieroglyphics and write a sentence in this ancient language.
4. Read Genesis 1:27-28, Genesis 2:4-24, and Exodus 1:8-22. Write a paragraph explaining the difference between God's view and Pharaoh's view of the value of people.

Build the Pyramid relay game:

Prepare the following before the lesson. You will need:

- Tape or chalk. Place tape in the shape of a triangle on the floor, or draw a triangle with the chalk. Make one triangle for each team. This represents a pyramid.
- Cut brick shapes out of paper. Cut enough bricks to fill the pyramid with rows of bricks.
- Designate a starting line two or three meters away.

Option: Make bricks by blowing into small brown paper bags, or stuffing them with crumpled paper. Gently close the open end with tape, while keeping the bag puffy. Ask the teams to try to stack these into a triangle shape against a wall or to stack them as high as they can.

Begin play:

1. Divide the children into two or more teams. Tell the children to choose a team name from one of Jacob's sons who went to Egypt. Each team will represent one of the Israelite families who are now slaves and must build cities for Pharaoh.
2. Give each team enough paper bricks, to build their pyramid.
3. Tell each team to form a line behind the starting point.
4. When the leader says to begin, one member from each team carries one paper brick to the triangle pyramid, without using their thumbs. They place the brick within the triangle in order to build their pyramid.
5. Next, they walk back and tag the next child who carries the next brick to the pyramid. Repeat this action until one team finishes building its pyramid.
6. Talk about what might make it even more difficult to build the pyramid and try the race again. Say, **What if you had to make your own bricks without any supplies or directions?** Discuss the answers. Say, **Pharaoh forced the Israelites to work very hard. He treated them cruelly. But, God was with them. Even when life was difficult, they were not alone. God blessed them and helped their families to grow during this time.**

ACTIVITY FOR OLDER CHILDREN

To Obey or Not to Obey Relay

This activity illustrates that it is difficult for us to listen to God when other messages compete for our attention.

You will need:

- A piece of paper and a pencil for each student
- Another adult

1. Divide the students into teams. Ask each team to form a line for a relay race. Explain that both you and the other adult leader will give the instructions for the race. For example: crab crawl, walk backwards, or hop. Explain to the students that they must choose to obey either you or the other leader.

2. Privately tell the adult leader that he or she should give different commands than you.

3. The team that listens to the teacher should be declared the winner even if they finish last.

4. Say, **Pharaoh told the midwives to kill the Hebrew baby boys. They refused to obey him because they feared God.** Ask, **Has someone ever tried to get you to do something you knew you should not do?** Listen to the answers. Give each student a piece of paper and a pencil. Ask the students to write about an area of their life where they need courage to obey God.

Say, **God blessed the Hebrew midwives because they did what was right. God gave them courage when they needed it. God is always with you. He will guide you to do what is right and give you the courage to do it.**

 # PRACTICE FOR BIBLE QUIZ

See the section "Review Questions" on pages 128-167 for the red and the blue practice questions for this lesson.

LESSON 2

A LEADER IS BORN
EXODUS 2:1-22

MEMORY VERSE

My shield is God Most High, who saves the upright in heart.

Psalm 7:10

TRUTHS ABOUT GOD

This lesson will teach the following truths about God. The asterisk * indicates the primary truth that you should teach to the children.

- * God was always present in Moses' life. God saved the life of Moses and helped him, even though Moses sinned.
- God protects and cares for people.
- God works in our lives, but sometimes his work is not obvious to us.

LESSON FOCUS AND SUMMARY

In this study, the children will learn that God is always at work, even when we cannot see the results.

1. To save his life, Moses' mother first hid him at home. After three months, she placed him in a basket, in the Nile River.
2. Pharaoh's daughter found the basket. She named the baby Moses and raised him as her son.
3. As an adult, Moses killed an Egyptian who was mistreating a Hebrew slave.
4. Moses escaped to Midian, married Zipporah, and had a son.

 ## BIBLICAL BACKGROUND

Moses' mother, his sister, and Pharaoh's daughter bravely defied Pharaoh's order to kill all the Hebrew baby boys. Because his life was spared, Moses was educated and trained as an Egyptian prince. God redeemed Moses' experiences and his knowledge of Egyptian government and culture.

As a young man, Moses felt a kinship with the Hebrews. He sinned when he murdered an Egyptian. He hid the body because he was afraid. When Pharaoh found out, he wanted to kill Moses. Moses fled Egypt and escaped to Midian.

In Midian, Moses continued to stand up for those who were mistreated. He protected Reuel's daughters from a group of shepherds. Reuel, also known as Jethro, invited Moses to become a member of his household, and to marry his daughter, Zipporah. Moses became a shepherd and started a new life. But he was an alien in a strange land.

God protected Moses. When Moses sinned, God did not turn away. God redeemed all that happened in Moses's life. He chose Moses to rescue the Israelites.

DID YOU KNOW?

A person's children, grandchildren, great-grandchildren, and all their children afterward are called descendants. Abraham and Sarah had a son named Jacob, also called Israel. Israel's descendants were called Israelites.

The Israelites did not have a land of their own. They were often called Hebrews, which means wanderers.

After Sarah died, Abraham married Keturah. Their son was named Midian. The Midianites descended from Abraham and Keturah. The Midianites and the Israelites, or Hebrews, were related. Read Genesis 25:2.

VOCABULARY

Faith words:

Faith is trust in God that leads a person to believe what God says, to depend on him, and to obey him.

People:

Moses was the Hebrew son of Levite slaves. His mother hid him when he was born. He was raised by Pharaoh's daughter, and he became an Egyptian prince. God chose Moses to lead the Israelites out of slavery.

Pharaoh's daughter was a member of the Egyptian royal family. She defied her father's decree to kill Hebrew babies and treated Moses as if he were her own son.

A Levite was a person born into the family of Levi. Levi was one of the sons of Jacob, who was also known as Israel. Levi was an Israelite.

Reuel was also known as Jethro. He was the high priest of Midian. He became Moses's father-in-law.

Zipporah was a shepherdess. She was the oldest daughter of Reuel. She married Moses.

Places:

Midian was located in the Arabian Peninsula along the eastern shore of the Gulf of Aqabah.

Terms:

Papyrus was an early form of paper made from the pith of the papyrus plant. The plant was once abundant in the Nile Delta. It grows to a height of two to three meters.

STORYTELLING

Each week you will need the following items.
1. The travel bag from lesson one
2. The storage container (bag, basket, or box)

For today's story, you will need the following items.
3. A basket
4. A bar of soap or a washcloth
5. Cotton balls

Bible Studies for Children: Exodus
Lesson 2

Before class:

1. Read Exodus 2:1-22.
2. Gather today's story items. Substitute a picture for any unavailable items.
3. Transfer all previous lesson items from the travel bag to the storage container. Place this beside the storytelling area.
4. Place today's story items inside the travel bag. Place the travel bag in the storytelling area.

Optional activity: Follow the leader

Tell the children to stand in a line, one behind the other. Choose a child to be the leader. Tell the children to watch carefully and mimic everything the leader does. The leader leads the group around the room. He or she uses different hand gestures, sounds, or means of travel for the children to imitate. For example, the leader walks with baby steps, large steps, or skips. End the game at the storytelling area.

Lesson review:

Ask a volunteer to select an item from the storage container and explain what it represented in a previous lesson.

Story time:

Read these instructions before you begin.

1. Tell the story in your own words. Remove each item from the bag as you illustrate a main point. Focus on the main points. If you are comfortable, include more details. If needed, use the script that is suggested.
2. As you tell the story, display each item in the order that it is listed. Place it where the children can see it.
3. After telling the story, place all the items inside the bag again.
4. To review the story, remove the first item. Ask a volunteer to tell what it represents. Display this item. Repeat this process until the story is retold.
5. Review the memory motion described below. Demonstrate this motion any time you mention what it represents.
6. Say, **We are continuing on our expedition to explore the book of Exodus. I packed our travel bag with tools that we will need. Today our journey begins with...** Unpack the items as you tell the story.

Main points in order:

1. Memory motion: Rock the baby—Show to the children how to pretend to rock a baby in their arms. This motion represents the baby Moses. You may also invite the children to think of another motion. Say, **As I tell the story, do this motion when you hear what it represents.**
2. A Basket—Say, **A Levite family had a baby boy. The mother hid him because Pharaoh said that all Hebrew baby boys must be killed. When the baby grew too big to hide, the mother made a basket out of papyrus and placed the basket in the reeds along the Nile.**
3. A Bar of soap or a washcloth—Say, **Pharaoh's daughter went to bathe in the Nile River. She saw the basket and asked her servant to bring it to her. She felt sorry for the baby and decided to adopt him as her son. She named him Moses. For a period of time, she paid Moses's mother to care for him.**
4. Cotton balls (wool)—Say, **While Moses was young, he became a member of the royal family. Although he lived and was educated like an Egyptian, he felt sorry for the Hebrews. When Moses became a young man, he saw an Egyptian who mistreated a**

Hebrew. He killed the Egyptian and hid the body. Pharaoh learned about this and wanted to kill Moses. Moses escaped to Midian. He sat down by a well where shepherds watered their flocks. He met the daughters of a man named Reuel, who gave him a place to live and a job. Moses married Reuel's daughter, Zipporah, and became a shepherd.

5. Say, **Now it is your turn to tell the story.** Return the items to the bag. Invite the children to take turns and choose an item from the bag without looking. Ask them to explain what it means or to review the memory motion. After all the items have been removed, ask the children to place them in the correct story order.

 BIBLICAL LESSON

Teaching tips:

As you lead the Bible study, emphasize these ideas.

- Remind the children that God is always working in their lives. Even if they cannot see what he is doing, God constantly works to help them. His presence is always with us.
- If possible, share a personal experience that illustrates this.

Read the Scripture:

Read Exodus 2:1-22 aloud.

Discussion questions:

Discuss the story and ask the children the following questions. Remember that there might not be a right or wrong answer.

1. **Pharaoh's decree, or order, required the people to throw baby boys into the Nile River. Did Moses's mother obey this order? Why did she respond in this way?** You may want to ask them to explain the answer.
2. **Moses grew up as a prince in an Egyptian palace. Why did he care when he saw an Egyptian beating a Hebrew?**
3. **God is not mentioned in Exodus 2. How do we know that God consistently worked to help Moses?**
4. **Imagine you knew Moses and saw these events. How would you describe the ways that the Lord protected and prepared Moses to be a great leader? Why do you think God did not do it in a different way?**
5. **Does God still prepare people to be leaders? What are some ways we see this in people's lives?**

Closing thoughts:

This is the thought that you want the children to remember.

Say, **God saved Moses's life and helped him, even when Moses sinned and killed the Egyptian.**

God worked to save Moses's life through many exciting events. Do you wonder if God works in your life? We do not often experience dramatic rescues like Moses. We cannot always see him, but God consistently works in our lives. He guides and helps us to become who he created us to be. God loves us and helps us even when we do something wrong. No problem is too big for God.

God had big plans for Moses. God has plans for you too. It may take time for you to know God's plan. As you wait, you can be certain God is always with you. He constantly works in your life!

MEMORY VERSE PRACTICE

My shield is God Most High, who saves the upright in heart. –Psalm 7:10

See the "Memory Verse Activities" on pages 124-127 for suggestions to help the children to learn the memory verse.

ADDITIONAL ACTIVITIES

To learn more about ancient Egypt and the culture in which the Israelites lived, consider these options.

1. Learn about names in ancient Egypt. Many pharaohs were named after their favorite god.
2. Research and write a short essay about Rameses's most famous military battle. With whom did he fight? What pet did he take into battle? What happened?
3. Research how the ancient Egyptians made papyrus paper out of papyrus reeds. For extra fun, search the Internet for a recipe for making your own papyrus.

"Put baby Moses in the basket," a review game

You will need:

- A basket
- 10 cotton balls
- A small doll wrapped in a cloth to represent Baby Moses

Tell the children to sit in a circle. Hand the basket to a child. Ask him or her to tell a fact from the story. If the fact is true, the child may place a cotton ball in the basket. Continue in this manner around the circle until the children have used all the cotton balls. The last child to give a true fact may add the last cotton ball and place baby Moses in the basket.

Ask the children, **Think about our Bible story. What does this basket remind us of?** Pause for the children to answer. **Moses's mother put him in a basket in the Nile to try to save his life. What do the cotton balls remind us of?** Pause for the children to answer. Moses ran away to Midian and met the shepherds and Reuel's daughters at the well. He became a shepherd and took care of Reuel's sheep. Say, **God protected Moses when he was a baby. When Moses became a man, God continue to provide for him. God loves us and provides what we need.**

ACTIVITY FOR OLDER CHILDREN

Putting it all on the line discussion

You will need:

A piece of paper and a pencil for each student

1. Give each student a piece of paper and a pencil. Ask each student to write three things that are valuable to him or her, or things that would be hard to give away or to live without. Invite the students to share what they wrote.

Bible Studies for Children: Exodus
Lesson 2

2. Ask the students, **Which one thing would be the hardest to give away?** Discuss how Moses' mother had to trust God when she put her baby in the Nile. Ask, **What fears did she have?** Then say, **God worked in the life of Moses. God protected Moses when he was a baby and a man. God provided for Moses. Do you feel afraid to trust God with something?**

3. Share an example of a time when you had to trust God to provide or to protect.

4. Ask the students, **Do you believe God will provide for you in a difficult situation?** Invite students to write about their concerns and to share with the class.

Say, **Remember, God loves you. He is always with you, even when you are afraid. He is working in your life, and he wants to prepare you for life in the future!**

 ## PRACTICE FOR BIBLE QUIZ

See the section "Review Questions" on pages 128-167 for the red and the blue practice questions for this lesson.

LESSON 3

YOU ARE STANDING ON HOLY GROUND
EXODUS 2:23-3:22

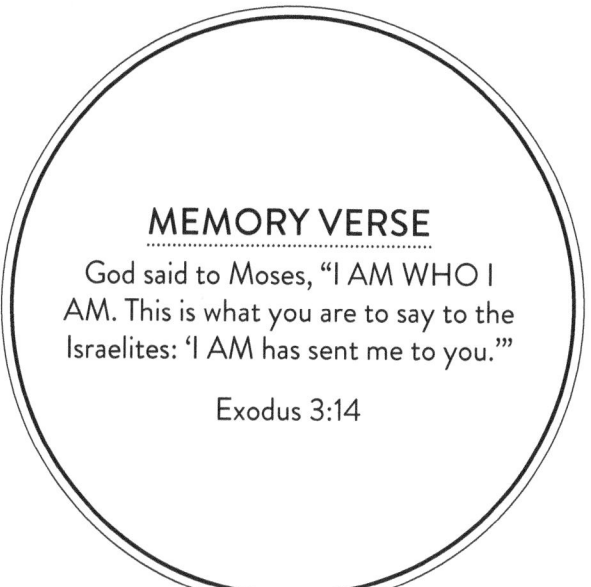

MEMORY VERSE

God said to Moses, "I AM WHO I AM. This is what you are to say to the Israelites: 'I AM has sent me to you.'"

Exodus 3:14

TRUTHS ABOUT GOD

*This lesson will teach the following truths about God. The asterisk * indicates the primary truth that you should teach to the children.*

* * God chose to work through Moses to rescue his people from slavery.
* God is a holy God.
* God cares about what happens to people.
* God chooses people to work with him to accomplish his purposes.

LESSON FOCUS AND SUMMARY

In this study, the children will learn that God accomplishes his purposes by calling people to work with him.

1. The Lord remembered his covenant with Abraham and felt concern for his enslaved people.
2. The Lord appeared to Moses in a burning bush.
3. The Lord announced his plan to rescue the Israelites.
4. The Lord told Moses to go and to deliver this message to the Israelite elders.

 ## BIBLICAL BACKGROUND

Exodus 3 helps us to understand God's character and his mission of salvation.

God pursued Moses while Moses lived an ordinary life and herded sheep. God appeared as fire in a bush and told Moses to remove his sandals. The presence of God made that ground holy. It became a sacred place, set apart for God alone.

God wants us to experience a personal relationship with him. He invites us to work with him to save all people. When Moses asked, "Who am I, that I should go to Pharaoh and bring the Israelites out of Egypt?" God responded, "I will be with you" (3:12). Moses was to rely on God's strength and not on his own strength. When God sends us, we are never alone. God always goes with us. He gives us the ability to do what he asks us to do.

In ancient cultures, names had great significance. A person's name revealed their true identity and character. In 3:13, Moses said to God, "Suppose I go to the Israelites and say to them, 'The God of

Bible Studies for Children: Exodus

your fathers has sent me to you,' and they ask me, 'What is his name?' Then what shall I tell them?" In other words, Moses asked how he should introduce God to those who did not know God.

God answered, "I AM WHO I AM. Say to the Israelites 'I AM has sent me to you.'" This emphasizes that God's presence is always here and now. God is eternal. He has no beginning. He has no end. He alone is the one who always is.

 DID YOU KNOW?

In the Bible, the Lord often reveals himself as fire.

 VOCABULARY

Faith words:

Holy means complete and pure. It also means something or someone reserved only for God. God is holy. He is different from all other beings because he alone is completely good and perfect.

People:

Jethro is also known as Reuel, the high priest of Midian. He was Moses' father-in-law.

Canaanites are the people who lived in Canaan.

I AM or **I AM WHO I AM** is God's personal name. This is the name he calls himself.

Elders are the leaders of an Israelite tribe. Elders were usually older men.

Places:

Horeb is the mountain where God appeared to Moses in the burning bush. The bush burned but was not destroyed.

Terms:

Wonders or **signs** are miracles that God performed.

STORYTELLING

Each week you will need the following items.

1. The travel bag from lesson one
2. The storage container (bag, basket, or box) with the items from the previous lessons

For today's story, you will need the following items.

3. A match or a candle
4. A small branch or a small plant
5. A sandal or a shoe
6. A piece of construction paper and a marker
7. Shiny jewelry and a small item of clothing

Before class:

1. Read Exodus 2:23—3:22.

2. Gather today's story items. Substitute a picture for any unavailable items.
3. Transfer all previous lesson items from the travel bag to the storage container. Place this beside the storytelling area.
4. Place today's story items inside the travel bag. Place the travel bag in the storytelling area.
5. Print this phrase on the construction paper: **"I AM WHO I AM."** Place this paper face down in the storytelling area.

Optional activity: Follow the leader

Tell the children to stand in a line, one behind the other. Choose a child to be the leader. Tell the children to watch carefully and mimic everything the leader does. The leader leads the group around the room. He or she uses different hand gestures, sounds, or means of travel for the children to imitate. For example, the leader walks with baby steps, large steps, or skips. End the game at the storytelling area.

Lesson review:

Ask a volunteer to select an item from the storage container and explain what it represented in a previous lesson.

Story time:

Read these instructions before you begin.

1. Tell the story in your own words. Remove each item from the bag as you illustrate a main point. Focus on the main points. If you are comfortable, include more details. If needed, use the script that is suggested.
2. As you tell the story, display each item in the order that it is listed. Place it where the children can see it.
3. After telling the story, place all the items inside the bag again.
4. To review the story, remove the first item. Ask a volunteer to tell what it represents. Display this item. Repeat this process until the story is retold.
5. Review the memory motion described below. Demonstrate this motion any time you mention what it represents.
6. Say, **We are continuing on our expedition to explore the book of Exodus. I packed our travel bag with tools that we will need. Today our journey begins with...** Unpack the items as you tell the story.

Main points in order:

1. A match or a candle and a plant or a branch—Say, **While Moses was herding sheep, he saw a bush on fire. Although it burned, it was not destroyed. Moses went to look at the strange sight.**

2. A sandal or a shoe—Say, **God called to Moses from the burning bush and said, "Do not come any closer. Take off your sandals, for the place where you are standing is holy ground" (3:5). God had seen the misery of his people in Egypt. He was concerned about their suffering. He came to rescue them and lead them into a good and spacious land. He would send Moses to Pharaoh and bring the Israelites out of Egypt.**

3. "I AM" paper sign—Say, **Moses objected to God's call. He asked, "Who am I, that I should go to Pharaoh and bring the Israelites out of Egypt?" (3:11). Moses also wanted to know what he should say if the people asked who sent him. God replied, "I AM WHO I AM. Tell the Israelites that I AM sent you to them" (3:14).**

4. Memory motion—Cup both hands at each side of your mouth. This represents that God called Moses to go. You may also invite the children to think of another motion. Say, **As I tell the story, do this motion when you hear what it represents.**

5. Gold and silver jewelry and clothing—Say, **God shared more about his rescue plan. He told Moses that they would not leave Egypt empty-handed. The Egyptians would give the Israelites gold, silver, and clothing (3:22).**

6. Say, **Now it is your turn to tell the story.** Return the items to the bag. Invite the children to take turns and choose an item from the bag without looking. Ask them to explain what it means or to review the memory motion. After all the items have been removed, ask the children to place them in the correct story order.

Bible Studies for Children: Exodus
Lesson 3

BIBLICAL LESSON

Teaching tips:

As you lead the Bible study, emphasize these ideas.

- Tell in your own words how the Lord fulfilled a promise that he made to Abraham in Genesis 15.
- Remind the children that God often works through ordinary people to accomplish his purposes.

Read the Scripture:

Read Exodus 2:23-3:22 aloud.

Discussion questions:

Discuss the story and ask the children the following questions. Remember that there might not be a right or wrong answer.

1. **What was the covenant God made with Abraham, Isaac, and Jacob?**
2. **What did God mean when he said that the ground near the burning bush was holy ground?**
3. **God said he was going to rescue the Israelites. He sent Moses to bring the people out of Egypt. Who truly rescued the Israelites?**
4. **How would you respond if God asked you to rescue an entire nation of enslaved people?**
5. **What promises did God make to Moses? If God gave you a similar job and made those promises to you, would you have the courage to do the job? Why, or why not?**

Closing thoughts:

This is the thought that you want the children to remember.

Say, **God chose to work through Moses to rescue his people from slavery.**

Have you ever wondered how God accomplishes his purposes in the world? There are times when God works alone to do something that only he can do. Many times, God includes people in his work. God could have rescued his people from Egypt without help. Nothing is too hard for him. Instead, God called Moses to work with him.

God may call you to work with him. The Bible tells many stories of how God worked through people of all ages, including children! If God calls you to do something for him, you can trust him completely. He will be with you and help you, no matter how difficult the job may seem.

MEMORY VERSE PRACTICE

God said to Moses, "I AM WHO I AM. This is what you are to say to the Israelites: 'I AM has sent me to you.'" –Exodus 3:14

See the "Memory Verse Activities" on pages 124-127 for suggestions to help the children to learn the memory verse.

ADDITIONAL ACTIVITIES

To learn more about ancient Egypt and the culture in which the Israelites lived, consider these options.

1. Learn about other times that God revealed himself through fire: firepots (Genesis 15:17); pillar of fire (Exodus 13:21); fire on Elijah's altar (1 Kings 18:38); tongues of fire (Acts 2:3).

2. Ask your pastor to talk about God's personal name, Yahweh. This is the name God used in Exodus 3:14-15.

3. In a Bible dictionary, look up information on herding sheep. Discover what shepherds did. Learn about the special meanings the word "shepherd" has in the Bible.

Burning bush cookies snack

You will need:

- 2 tree-shaped cookies for each child
- Green and orange frosting
- Plastic knives to spread the icing
- Paper towels
- Storage bags or plastic wrap to store a cookie
- Cleanup supplies

Prepare before class:

Bake two tree-shaped cookies for each child.

Allow the children to spread green frosting on their cookies. While the frosting dries, review the Bible story. Discuss the following questions.

1. What made the bush unusual?
2. Why did God tell Moses to take off his shoes?
3. How do you think God felt about his people?
4. What was God's special name? Why was it his name?
5. What would God do to convince Pharaoh to let the people go?
6. What would the Israelites take from the Egyptians?

After reviewing the story, allow the children to add orange frosting accents to make their bushes "burn." Enjoy a snack together, and eat one cookie. Ask the children to take the other cookie home and to review the Moses story with their parents.

Optional art project

You will need:

Green paper, various craft items to represent fire, and glue. Or red, yellow, and orange stamp pads or finger paint.

If cookies are not an option, give the children a piece of green paper. Tear or cut out a bush shape. Next, use a variety of red, orange, and yellow items to represent the fire. Randomly glue these items to the bush to create the fire. Some suggested materials include small squares of tissue paper, cut out small flame shapes, sequins, stamps and stamp pads, or glitter. You may allow children to place thumb prints from yellow, red, and orange washable stamp pads or finger paint. While the project dries, review the story as suggested above.

 # ACTIVITY FOR OLDER CHILDREN

Say, **God spoke to Moses through the burning bush. He told Moses his plan for saving the Israelites. God still calls people to be involved in his work. He usually doesn't do this through a burning bush.** Ask your students to think of someone who has

Bible Studies for Children: Exodus
Lesson 3

answered a call from God. Ask them why they think that this is true. Discuss questions that they would like to ask that person, and make a list. Invite one of these people or your pastor to share with the class.

Interview the people who have responded to God's call. Ask them to describe what happened.

How did they know God called them? Was it easy or hard to say yes to God? Why? How has God helped them to do his work?

Ask the students to share if they have ever felt God call them to do a particular task?

PRACTICE FOR BIBLE QUIZ

See the section "Review Questions" on pages 128-167 for the red and the blue practice questions for this lesson.

LESSON 4

MOSES...YOU CAN DO IT!
EXODUS 4:1-21, 27-31

MEMORY VERSE

Those who know your name trust in you, for you, LORD, have never forsaken those who seek you.

Psalm 9:10

TRUTHS ABOUT GOD

This lesson will teach the following truths about God. The asterisk * indicates the primary truth that you should teach to the children.

* * Moses saw God's power to keep his promises.
- God has the power to do miracles.
- God promises to help those to whom he has given a task.

LESSON FOCUS AND SUMMARY

In this study, the children will learn that God has the power to keep his promises and to do miracles.

1. The Lord called Moses to serve him and to go to Egypt.
2. The Lord gave Moses miraculous signs so that the Israelites would know that the Lord had sent him.
3. The Lord sent Aaron to help Moses.
4. In the beginning, the events in Egypt discouraged Moses and the people. God was always working out his plan.

BIBLICAL BACKGROUND

The Israelites were freed from bondage, but they still faced challenges. What would happen to them? The Lord had performed miraculous signs to reveal his presence and power. He planned to rule as God and King of the Israelite people.

In this Bible study, God creates the roles of prophet and priest to serve as his representative. Prophets speak for God. Moses, God's prophet, receives God's messages and communicates them to the people. He also performs signs and wonders. Aaron, God's priest, represents God in worship. A priest leads people to experience God's presence through worship. Today, a church's pastor or preacher is the spiritual leader.

Moses was afraid to speak for God. When Moses begged him to send someone else, God became angry (Exodus 4:13-14). It is not wrong to ask God questions. God encourages us to ask questions that are necessary to discover the truth. When our questions have been answered, we need to take action. We should not make excuses because we feel afraid.

This study reveals the reaction of the Israelites to God's message and to his messengers.

 ## DID YOU KNOW?

Moses performed signs, or miracles. Each sign had a special meaning. For example, when Moses revealed his leprous hand from his cloak, it was completely healed. God intended this to be a warning to Pharaoh that God could work powerfully through Moses, his words, and his actions.

 ## VOCABULARY

Faith words:

Obey means to do what we know God wants us to do. God wants us to obey him and to do what he tells us in the Bible.

People:

Aaron, the Levite, was Moses' older brother. The Lord said that Aaron would help Moses to speak to Pharaoh and to the people.

Terms:

The Staff of God was Moses' shepherd's crook, a tool used to guide sheep. God used this to do miraculous signs.

Leprous means a person has a skin disease called leprosy. This disease was very contagious during Bible times.

Deaf means a person is unable to hear.

Mute means a person is unable to speak.

STORYTELLING

Each week you will need the following items.

1. The travel bag from lesson one
2. The storage container (bag, basket, or box) with the items from the previous lessons

For today's story, you will need the following items.

3. A fake, rubber snake
4. A stick
5. A map, preferably of the Holy Lands
6. Magic Markers

Before class:

1. Read Exodus 4:1-21, 27-31
2. Gather today's story items. Substitute a picture for any unavailable items.
3. Transfer all previous lesson items from the travel bag to the storage container. Place this beside the storytelling area.
4. Place today's story items inside the travel bag. Place the travel bag in the storytelling area.

Optional activity: Follow the leader

Tell the children to stand in a line, one behind the other. Choose a child to be the leader. Tell the children to watch carefully and mimic everything the leader does. The leader leads the group around the room. He or she uses different hand gestures, sounds, or means of travel for the children to imitate. For example, the leader walks with baby steps, large steps, or skips. End the game at the storytelling area.

Lesson review:

Ask a volunteer to select an item from the storage container and explain what it represented in a previous lesson.

Story time:

Read these instructions before you begin.

1. Tell the story in your own words. Remove each item from the bag as you illustrate a main point. Focus on the main points. If you are comfortable, include more details. If needed, use the script that is suggested.

2. As you tell the story, display each item in the order that it is listed. Place it where the children can see it.

3. After telling the story, place all the items inside the bag again.

4. To review the story, remove the first item. Ask a volunteer to tell what it represents. Display this item. Repeat this process until the story is retold.

5. Review the memory motion described below. Demonstrate this motion any time you mention what it represents.

6. Say, **We are continuing on our expedition to explore the book of Exodus. I packed our travel bag with tools that we will need. Today our journey begins with...** Unpack the items as you tell the story.

Main points in order:

1. A rubber snake—Say, **The Lord gave Moses the ability to do miraculous signs so that the Israelites would know the Lord sent him. When Moses placed the staff on the ground, it became a snake. When he picked it up by the tail, it became a staff again. Moses's hand became leprous when placed under his cloak and then became normal. If the people still didn't believe, Moses was able to turn water into blood.**

2. A stick—Say, **Moses finally agreed to do what God called him to do. He said goodbye to Jethro, also known as Reuel, and took his wife and family with him. He also took the staff of God in his hand.** Read 4:20.

3. Memory motion—Ask the children to point their thumbs over one shoulder to represent that Moses went back to Egypt. You may also invite the children to think of another motion. Say, **As I tell the story, do this motion when you hear what it represents.**

4. Map—Say, **In the desert, Moses met Aaron, as the Lord said he would. Together they went to Egypt. In Egypt, they met with the elders of the Israelites and told them all that the Lord said. Moses showed the people the miraculous signs. The people worshiped God.**

5. Say, **Now it is your turn to tell the story.** Return the items to the bag. Invite the children to take turns choosing an item from the bag without looking. Ask them to explain what it means or to review the memory motion. After all the items have been removed, ask the children to place them in the correct story order.

BIBLICAL LESSON

Teaching tips:

As you lead the Bible study, emphasize these ideas.

- Remind the children that Moses felt afraid to return to Egypt. This was a normal, human reaction. Moses learned to trust God and God's promises to help.
- The Lord wanted to free the Israelites from a bad life and give them a good life. He was their God and King. He would protect and care for them.

Read the Scripture:

Read Exodus 4:1-21, 27-31 aloud.

Discussion questions:

Discuss the story and ask the children the following questions. Remember that there might not be a right or wrong answer.

1. **Would you obey if God asked you to go to a place where you knew people did not like you? Why or why not?**
2. **What three miracles did the Lord ask Moses to do? How would you feel if God gave you the ability to perform these miracles?**
3. **Moses said that he was "slow of speech and tongue." He did not think he was able to do what the Lord asked** him to do. **Have you ever felt anxious or afraid about doing what the Lord asked you to do? Explain your answer.**
4. **What encouragement did the Lord give to Moses in Exodus 4:11-12? How has the Lord encouraged you?**
5. Read Exodus 4:31. **What did the people do when they saw Moses perform the signs and heard that the Lord was concerned about them? How do you think they felt? Why?**

Closing thoughts:

This is the thought you want your students to remember.

Moses saw God's power to keep his promises.

Say, **Who had the power to rescue the Israelites, Moses or God? God! However, God planned to use Moses to rescue them. Moses was afraid to return to Egypt, but the Lord promised to teach and to guide him.**

God doesn't expect you to follow him without his help. He knows your strengths and your weaknesses. God helped and guided Moses. He will also help you and guide you. God called Moses when Moses was eighty years old. You are able to serve God today!

MEMORY VERSE PRACTICE

Those who know your name trust in you, for you, LORD, have never forsaken those who seek you. –Psalm 9:10

See the "Memory Verse Activities" on pages 124-127 for suggestions to help the children to learn the memory verse.

ADDITIONAL ACTIVITIES

To learn more about ancient Egypt and the culture in which the Israelites lived, consider these options.

1. Learn about the importance of the Nile River to the Egyptians. Who was the god of the Nile? Write a paragraph about your findings and share with the group.

2. Midian is most likely in modern-day Saudi Arabia. Use a map and measure how far the journey was to Egypt.

3. Research the facts about leprosy and how it is treated today.

Smile, you are on camera!

You will need:

- A video camera or a smartphone with a camera
- A copy of Exodus 4:1-21 and 27-31 for each child
- A TV or a projector
- Cords to connect the TV or projector with the camera or phone
- A highlighter

Prepare:

1. Set up the TV or projector in your classroom.
2. Prepare the video camera or phone to tape children.
3. Photocopy or print Exodus 4:1-31. Eliminate verses 22-26. Print a copy for each child.
4. With the highlighter, mark each verse or two to three verses separately on each sheet.

Hand each child a copy of the highlighted scripture passages. Explain to the children that they will read this passage aloud while they are recorded. Give every child an opportunity, but do not force them to participate. Some children may read more than one passage.

Record the children while they read their portions of the scripture. Watch the video with the children.

Options: If video recording is not an option, make an audio recording of only their voices reading a passage. Another option is to ask the children to stand in front of the room and read their passage. Shine a bright light on each reader and pretend to video record them.

Ask the children if they felt nervous while they read the scripture passage. Say, **It was difficult for you to speak into a video camera. It was also difficult for Moses. He was very afraid to do what God wanted him to do. Would you feel afraid if you had to speak to a king? God promised to help Moses. He also sent Aaron to help. Now, let us discuss what you learned from today's story.**

ACTIVITY FOR OLDER CHILDREN

You will need:

A hard-boiled egg for each student and one for the leader

Ask students to squeeze their eggs without breaking them. The eggs will break unless they know this trick. Here is the secret: Hold your egg in the palm of your hand and wrap your fingers completely around it. Applying even pressure around the shell, squeeze as hard as you like. The egg will not crack.

Say, **An egg is not very strong. But when you hold it correctly, it is stronger**

Bible Studies for Children: Exodus
Lesson 4

than you think. Moses only saw his weaknesses and his failures. The Lord saw the possibilities. At some point in our lifetime, we will feel afraid like Moses. It is easy to see what we cannot do or how we could fail. But like an egg, we are stronger when we allow the Lord to hold us in his hands. Rely on him. He provides for all our needs.

PRACTICE FOR BIBLE QUIZ

See the section "Review Questions" on pages 128-167 for the red and the blue practice questions for this lesson.

LESSON 5

A HARD JOB EVEN HARDER
EXODUS 5:1-6:9

MEMORY VERSE

Moreover, I have heard the groaning of the Israelites, whom the Egyptians are enslaving, and I have remembered my covenant.

Exodus 6:5

TRUTHS ABOUT GOD

This lesson will teach the following truths about God. The asterisk * indicates the primary truth that you should teach to the children.

* God reassured his people in a time of trouble.
- God seeks to redeem people.
- God is more powerful than human kings and rulers.

LESSON FOCUS AND SUMMARY

In this study, the children will learn that God does not always act as quickly as we would like or in the way we expect, but God always works for our best.

1. Moses and Aaron met with Pharaoh.
2. Pharaoh would not let the Israelites go.
3. As punishment, Pharaoh said the Israelites had to find their own straw and keep their brick quota.
4. The Israelites did not listen to Moses because they were discouraged.

 BIBLICAL BACKGROUND

The Israelites had not worshiped their God for hundreds of years. They listened to Aaron and Moses. They chose to believe in God and worship him. They had hope for the first time in generations. But, Pharaoh did not believe in the God of the Israelites. His response crushed their hope. His impossible demand to collect their own straw and still produce the same number of bricks discouraged Moses and the Israelites. God told Moses that Pharaoh would resist. Pharaoh's cruelty blinded the Israelites to God's promise of freedom. When people suffer, they are often discouraged and blinded to God's promises, goodness, and love.

If Pharaoh let them go after their first request, God's power and glory would not be revealed. Over time, the Israelites learned to trust God completely. God patiently shaped their character. Character, like steel, is forged over time. Both are shaped under high heat and strong pressure. God taught, guided, disciplined, cared, and encouraged the Israelites through painful difficulties. These experiences shaped them into the people of God.

Bible Studies for Children: Exodus

DID YOU KNOW?

Pharaohs often took the name of their favorite god and combined it with their own. Then they told their people that they were a god.

VOCABULARY

Faith words:

To redeem means to rescue someone from hardship or slavery and to set that person free.

People:

Foremen or **slave drivers** were Israelite and Egyptian men who were in charge of the slaves. They forced the slaves to do their work.

Places:

Canaan was a land east of Egypt. The Lord promised to give this land to the Israelites. Other people were living there at the time of Exodus.

Terms:

A quota is a fixed number of things that are required and must be done.

STORYTELLING

Each week you will need the following items.

1. The travel bag from lesson one
2. A storage container (bag, basket, or box) with the items from the previous lessons

For today's story, you will need the following items.

3. An appointment book or calendar
4. Straw or dried grass
5. A rope
6. A balloon
7. A picture of a person praying or a praying hands figurine

Before class:

1. Read Exodus 5:1-6:9.
2. Gather today's story items. Substitute a picture for any unavailable items.
3. Transfer all previous lesson items from the travel bag to the storage container. Place this beside the story telling area.
4. Place today's story items inside the travel bag. Place the travel bag in the storytelling area.

Optional activity: Follow the leader

Tell the children to stand in a line, one behind the other. Choose a child to be the leader. Tell the children to watch carefully and mimic everything the leader does. The leader leads the group around the room. He or she uses different hand gestures, sounds, or means of travel for the children to imitate. For example, the leader walks with baby steps, large steps, or skips. End the game at the storytelling area.

Lesson review:

Ask a volunteer to select an item from the storage container and explain what it represented in a previous lesson.

Story time:

Read these instructions before you begin.

1. Tell the story in your own words. Remove each item from the bag as you illustrate a main point. Focus on the main points. If you are comfortable, include more details. If needed, use the script that is suggested.

2. As you tell the story, display each item in the order that it is listed. Place it where the children can see it.

3. After telling the story, place all the items inside the bag again.

4. To review the story, remove the first item. Ask a volunteer to tell what it represents. Display this item. Repeat this process until the story is retold.

5. Review the memory motion described below. Demonstrate this motion any time you mention what it represents.

6. Say, **We are continuing on our expedition to explore the book of Exodus. I packed our travel bag with tools that we will need. Today our journey begins with...** Unpack the items as you tell the story.

Main points in order:

1. An appointment book or calendar—Say, **Moses and Aaron had their first meeting with Pharaoh. They asked Pharaoh to let the people go. Pharaoh refused.**

2. Straw or dry grass—Say, **After Moses and Aaron met with Pharaoh, Pharaoh ordered the Israelites to find their own straw. They were still required to make the same number of bricks. Pharaoh said they were lazy.**

3. Memory motion—Show the children how to shield their eyes from the sun as if they are looking for straw. You may also invite the children to think of another motion. Say, **As I tell the story, do this motion when you hear what it represents.**

4. A rope—Say, **The Israelites were slaves. They were in bondage to the Egyptians. They had to obey Pharaoh, their slave-drivers, and their foremen. If they disobeyed, they would be punished or even killed. Regardless of how unfair or cruel the circumstances were, the Israelites were forced to obey and work for no pay. They were prisoners of Pharaoh and the Egyptians.**

5. A balloon—Say, **When Moses told them God would set them free, the Israelites became excited!** Blow up the balloon, but do not tie it. Say, **Just like this balloon is filled with air, they became filled with hope.** Release some of the air from the balloon. Say, **When Pharaoh refused to let them go, they were discouraged. But when Pharaoh commanded them to get their own straw but still meet their quota, they lost all hope.** Release the rest of the air.

6. Praying picture or figurine—Say, **Moses became discouraged, too. So Moses prayed to God, and God answered his prayer. God assured Moses that he would keep his promise to free the people.**

7. Say, **Now it is your turn to tell the story.** Return the items to the bag. Invite the children to take turns and choose an item from the bag without looking. Ask them to explain what it means or to review the memory motion. After all the items have been removed, ask the children to place them in the correct story order.

 BIBLICAL LESSON

Teaching tips:

As you lead the Bible study, emphasize these ideas:

- God does not always work as quickly as we want or in the way we expect. When this happens, it is a human reaction to feel discouraged.
- When Moses was discouraged, he talked honestly to God. When we talk honestly to God, we should be ready to receive his encouragement and help.

Read the Scripture:

Read Exodus 5:1-6:9 aloud.

Discussion questions:

Discuss the story and ask the children the following questions. Remember that there might not be a right or wrong answer.

1. **If you were an Israelite, how would you feel if you suddenly had to gather your own straw but make the same number of bricks each day?**
2. **Did Moses do the right thing when he complained to God about what was happening? Why or why not?**
3. **Today's memory verse says that God heard the groaning of the Israelites. Does God hear your prayers? How do you know?**
4. **The Israelites were discouraged and did not listen to what Moses said. Would it be hard to trust God in this situation? Why or why not?**
5. **Imagine that you were Moses. Would you want to continue as God's spokesperson after what happened in today's lesson? Explain your answer.**

Conclusion:

This is the thought you want your students to remember.

Say, **God reassured his people in a difficult situation.**

Have you ever tried to do the right thing but had bad results? Moses did exactly what the Lord asked him to do. His efforts caused a bad situation to become worse. The Israelites suffered even more! Afterward, what did Moses do? He talked to God about his problems. The Lord reassured Moses that he would keep his promise. Pharaoh could not ruin God's plans.

When you serve the Lord and bad circumstances arise, do what Moses did. Talk to the Lord about the situation. You will feel his presence. He will reassure you!

 MEMORY VERSE PRACTICE

Moreover, I have heard the groaning of the Israelites, whom the Egyptians are enslaving, and I have remembered my covenant. –Exodus 6:5

See the "Memory Verse Activities" on pages 124-127 for suggestions to help the children to learn the memory verse.

ADDITIONAL ACTIVITIES

To learn more about ancient Egypt and the culture in which the Israelites lived, consider these options.

1. Research how the ancient Israelites made bricks out of mud and straw. Try to make some bricks using the same method.
2. Use the dialogue from this lesson to write a short drama. Include Pharaoh, Moses, Aaron, the Israelite foremen, and the Egyptian slave drivers as characters. Record it on video if possible.
3. Research the ancient store cities of Pithom and Rameses. What were they used for?

"A puzzling problem," a review game

You will need:

- Four large-piece puzzles, two for each team
- Place two puzzles, separately, on the table.

Create two teams of children. If you have a large group of children, divide them into more than two teams. Provide two additional puzzles for each group. Tell the groups they will race to complete their puzzles. Keep track of the time. Then disassemble each puzzle and mix together the pieces from both puzzles. Tell the teams to race once more to complete both puzzles.

Ask the children if it was easier or harder to put each puzzle together the second time? Why? Allow children to share their ideas. Ask how they would feel if they were expected to complete both puzzles as quickly as they completed one puzzle. Could they do it? Would it be easy?

Tell the children that the Israelites felt discouraged and hopeless. They were used to having the straw for their bricks provided to them. Then they had to find their own straw but make the same number of bricks each day. It was much harder and took much longer. In our study, we saw how the Israelites coped with this problem.

Other options:

Let volunteers act out the following scenes from the story, or let children choose another portion of the lesson.

- Moses and Aaron talking to Pharaoh
- Pharaoh giving cruel new directions to the foremen and slave drivers
- The Israelite slaves talking about the bad news they received
- Moses trying to encourage the foremen and the Israelites and how they reacted to him.

OR

Create a clay figure to represent someone from today's lesson. Some examples are Pharaoh rejecting Moses and Aaron's request or Moses in prayer to the Lord.

ACTIVITY FOR OLDER CHILDREN

1. Tell students that you expect them to draw a simple picture on a board or a large piece of paper. One at a time, invite the children to come to you. Blindfold the first student. Tell them you want them to draw something simple, like a vegetable or a flower, BUT they must not use their dominant hand. The dominant hand is the one we normally use to write, draw, or throw. Afterward, ask the students how they felt when they had to draw blindfolded. Then ask how they felt when they were given an additional obstacle of drawing with the non-dominate hand. Discuss how the Israelites experienced a similar situation.

2. Ask, **Have you ever believed that you obeyed God, yet things did not happen as you expected? How did you feel? What did you do? In today's Bible study, what did Moses do when he felt discouraged? What happened as a result? What would you say to other students who are discouraged and filled with doubt?**

 ## PRACTICE FOR BIBLE QUIZ

See the section "Review Questions" on pages 128-167 for the red and the blue practice questions for this lesson.

LESSON 6
STAFFS, SNAKES, AND MAGICIANS
EXODUS 6:28–7:24

MEMORY VERSE

The earth is the LORD'S, and everything in it, the world, and all who live in it.

Psalm 24:1

TRUTHS ABOUT GOD

This lesson will teach the following truths about God. The asterisk * indicates the primary truth that you should teach to the children.

* God used plagues to show his power.
- God often gives people many chances to do the right thing.
- God expects his people to obey him.

LESSON FOCUS AND SUMMARY

In this study, the children will learn how God used plagues to show his power.

1. The Lord said that Pharaoh would not listen to Moses and Aaron.
2. Aaron threw down his staff, and it became a snake.
3. When Aaron struck the water of the Nile River, the Nile and all the water in Egypt turned to blood.
4. Pharaoh's magicians also performed these two signs, but Aaron's staff swallowed up all the magicians' staffs.

 ## BIBLICAL BACKGROUND

This lesson focuses on the first two miraculous encounters between the Lord and Pharaoh. Pharaoh's sorcerers were able to duplicate the first two miracles. The magicians' ability to mimic these miracles caused Pharaoh to believe the Lord was just another local god and not the one true God.

In the first miracle, Aaron's staff became a snake. Pharaoh's magicians also turned their staffs into snakes, but Aaron's snake ate them. This proved God's miracle was more powerful than their magic. But as God predicted, Pharaoh stubbornly refused to admit that the Lord God was greater than him or his gods.

The second miracle was the first of ten plagues. Aaron struck the Nile with his staff. This caused the water to change to blood. Life in Egypt depended upon the Nile River. The Egyptian god of the Nile was named Hapi. Hapi was given credit for the greatness of the Nile. The purpose of this miracle was to prove that Hapi was inferior to the Lord God. But once again, the sorcerers were able to duplicate God's miracle with magic. Once again, Pharaoh refused to acknowledge Yahweh's superiority and authority.

DID YOU KNOW?

Hapi was the ancient Egyptian god of the Nile. The people believed that Hapi lived in a cave at the source of the Nile River. They believed that the crocodiles and the frogs fed him. In pictures, he looked like a big fat man that was covered with blue, black, or green mud from the river.

VOCABULARY

Faith words:

Worship is telling and showing God that we love Him more than anyone or anything else.

People:

Wise men, **sorcerers**, and **magicians** were men who were trained in Egyptian magic. They had knowledge of Egyptian gods.

Terms:

A prophet is someone that God has chosen to receive his messages. A prophet also shares God's messages with the people.

Secret arts are mysterious powers or activities that are sometimes called magic.

STORYTELLING

Each week you will need the following items.

1. The travel bag from lesson one
2. The storage container (bag, basket, or box) with the items from the previous lessons

For today's story, you will need the following items.

3. Hardened Play-Doh or clay
4. A rubber snake
5. Red liquid in a cup with an airtight lid
6. A stick (to represent a magician's wand)

Before class:

1. Read Exodus 6:28-7:24.
2. Gather today's story items. Substitute a picture for any unavailable items.
3. Transfer all previous lesson items from the travel bag to the storage container. Place this beside the storytelling area.
4. Place today's story items inside the travel bag. Place the travel bag in the storytelling area.

Optional activity: Follow the leader

Tell the children to stand in a line, one behind the other. Choose a child to be the leader. Tell the children to watch carefully and mimic everything the leader does. The leader leads the group around the room. He or she uses different hand gestures, sounds, or means of travel for the children to imitate. For example, the leader walks with baby steps, large steps, or skips. End the game at the storytelling area.

Lesson review:

Ask a volunteer to select an item from the storage container and explain what it represented in a previous lesson.

Story time:

Read these instructions before you begin.

1. Tell the story in your own words. Remove each item from the bag as you illustrate a main point. Focus on the main points. If you are comfortable, include more details. If needed, use the script that is suggested.

2. As you tell the story, display each item in the order that it is listed. Place it where the children can see it.

3. After telling the story, place all the items inside the bag again.

4. To review the story, remove the first item. Ask a volunteer to tell what it represents. Display this item. Repeat this process until the story is retold.

5. Review the memory motion described below. Demonstrate this motion any time you mention what it represents.

6. Say, **This week, our expedition leads us to Pharaoh himself, the king of one of the most powerful nations of that time. I have three objects in our travel bag that relate to Pharaoh, God, and the Israelites.** Unpack the items as you tell the story.

Main points in order:

1. Hardened Play-Doh or clay—Say, **The Lord said Pharaoh would not listen to Moses and Aaron and that Pharaoh's heart would harden. That is exactly what happened.**

2. A rubber snake—Say, **The Lord gave Moses the ability to do signs and wonders. He allowed Moses's brother, Aaron, to help him. When Aaron threw down his staff, it became a snake. Pharaoh's magicians also did this. Pharaoh did not listen, even when Aaron's snake ate the magicians' snakes.**

3. Memory motion—Ask the children to place their hands over their ears to represent that Pharaoh did not listen. You may also invite the children to think of another motion. Say, **As I tell the story, do this motion when you hear what it represents.**

4. Red liquid in a cup with an airtight lid—Say, **Next, Aaron struck the water of the Nile and it turned to blood.**

5. A stick—Say, **Pharaoh still did not listen because his magicians and wise men did the same thing with their secret arts.**

6. Say, **Now it is your turn to tell the story. Return the items to the bag.** Invite the children to take turns and choose an item from the bag without looking. Ask them to explain what it means or to review the memory motion. After all the items have been removed, ask the children to place them in the correct story order.

BIBLICAL LESSON

Teaching tips:

As you lead the Bible study, emphasize these ideas:

- The Lord did the miracles, not Aaron or Moses.

- The events happened exactly as the Lord said they would.
- Moses and Aaron obeyed each new instruction from God and did everything as the Lord commanded. (7:6, 20)

Read the Scripture:

Read Exodus 6:28-7:24 aloud.

Discussion questions:

Discuss the story and ask the children the following questions. Remember that there might not be a right or wrong answer.

1. Read Exodus 7:2. **Imagine that you were Moses and Aaron. Would you feel afraid to tell Pharaoh what the Lord said? How do you think that Moses and Aaron felt?**
2. **What was the first miracle that Aaron performed? What happened to show that the Lord was more powerful than the Egyptian sorcerers?**
3. **What did the Lord tell Moses in Exodus 7:14? What did this mean?**
4. **Read Exodus 7:6 and 7:20. God did the signs and wonders, but he worked through Moses and Aaron. What were they responsible to do?**
5. Read Exodus 7:22. **The sorcerers did the same things God did through Moses and Aaron. Afterward, what might Moses and Aaron have felt? Was it easier or harder for them to continue to trust God? Why?**

Closing thoughts:

This is the thought you want your students to remember.

Say, **God used plagues to show his power.**

Who was stronger, a human magician or the Lord? In the beginning, it appeared that the Egyptian magicians were as powerful as God, but they were not. Sometimes, other things or people seem to be more powerful than God, but this is an illusion. The truth is that God is bigger and more powerful. He knows more than anyone or anything. The Bible says in Exodus 7:6 and 7:20 that Moses and Aaron obeyed everything that the Lord instructed. They obeyed and trusted God.

God is able to show his power to you, too. It probably will not appear through plagues. If you trust and obey him, you will experience God's power in your life.

 MEMORY VERSE PRACTICE

The earth is the LORD'S, and everything in it, the world, and all who live in it. –Psalm 24:1

See the "Memory Verse Activities" on pages 124-127 for suggestions to help the children to learn the memory verse.

ADDITIONAL ACTIVITIES

Ask the children to draw pictures that illustrate the scenes in the Bible story. Allow the children to choose which scenes to illustrate. Here are three of the many possible options.

- Aaron's staff turning into a snake
- The magicians' staffs turning into snakes
- Aaron's staff swallowing the other snakes

Bible Studies for Children: Exodus
Lesson 6

Display the children's pictures on the classroom walls.

A hard heart is like...

You will need:

- Play-Doh in various colors
- A container with an airtight lid

Prepare:

Divide each color of Play-Doh in half. Keep half of the Play-Doh in a sealed container to keep it soft and pliable. Subdivide the other half of the Play-Doh into small balls. Make one for each child. Leave these out overnight or as long as needed so that they become hard.

Give each child a hard ball of the Play-Doh. Ask the children to try to make a heart shape. Next, give to the children the pliable Play-Doh. Ask them to mold it into the shape of a heart. Discuss which Play-Doh was easier to shape into a heart and why. Say, **The Bible says Pharaoh's heart was hard.** Ask, **How was Pharaoh's heart like this hardened Play-Doh?** Wait for children to share answers. **His heart could not be shaped or guided by anything God did. Today, we learned what happened to the Israelites when Pharaoh's heart became hard.**

ACTIVITY FOR OLDER CHILDREN

1. Tell the students, **This is a challenge to see if you can do what I do.** Do a crazy motion and have the students mimic you. Choose a student to lead the motion. Allow the students to take turns doing motions for the group to imitate.

2. Tell the students, **Pharaoh's magicians were good at duplicating what Moses and Aaron did.** Discuss what the magicians did. What did the students think when they read that Pharaoh's magicians duplicated God's miracles? Tell the students, **We cannot know how the magicians could copy God's miracles, but no power is greater than God's power. In the next lessons we will learn what happens in the contest between the one true God and the false gods of Egypt.**

PRACTICE FOR BIBLE QUIZ

See the section "Review Questions" on pages 128-167 for the red and the blue practice questions for this lesson.

LESSON 7

FROGS, GNATS, AND FLIES...OH MY!
EXODUS 7:25-8:32

MEMORY VERSE

Know that the LORD has set apart his faithful servant for himself; the LORD hears when I call to him.

Psalm 4:3

TRUTHS ABOUT GOD

This lesson will teach the following truths about God. The asterisk * indicates the primary truth that you should teach to the children.

* Through the plagues, God showed that the Egyptian gods were false gods.
- God rules over all of his creation through his power.
- God hears the prayers of his faithful servants.

LESSON FOCUS AND SUMMARY

In this study, the children will learn that God showed that the Egyptian gods were false gods.

1. The Lord sent a plague of frogs, and the magicians duplicated them.
2. The Lord sent a plague of gnats, and the magicians could not duplicate them.
3. The Lord sent a plague of flies that went only to Egypt and not to Goshen.
4. Although the Lord sent Moses and Aaron again and again to speak to Pharaoh, he would not let the Israelites go. Pharaoh's heart was hard.

 ## BIBLICAL BACKGROUND

In this lesson, we see Pharaoh begin to change his responses to Yahweh. The plague of frogs was the first plague to affect Pharaoh personally. There were frogs in the palace, frogs in his bedroom, frogs in his bed, and frogs on him! Although his sorcerers could duplicate the plague of frogs, they could not eliminate it. For the first time, Pharaoh asked Moses for help. Moses let Pharaoh choose the time for deliverance to prove God's greatness.

The plague of gnats was the first plague the sorcerers could not duplicate. They admitted that God was greater than them and all of their gods, but Pharaoh continued to resist God.

In the fourth plague, the Lord sent a massive swarm of flies to Egypt and controlled where they went. Yahweh named the exact time and place of the plague. He pointed out that the Israelites would not experience the flies. He did this to prove his power. This time, Pharaoh tried to bargain with Moses.

Bible Studies for Children: Exodus
Lesson 7

He agreed to let the Israelites worship their God in Egypt, but Moses refused. Pharaoh then agreed to let the Israelites leave Egypt for three days to worship their God and asked Moses to pray for him. But when the plague lifted, Pharaoh broke his promise.

This often happens when people who don't know God need God's help; they beg God and others for help and they promise to change. However, after they get help and the trouble passes, they break their promise and return to their old ways.

DID YOU KNOW?

In large numbers, gnats and flies are very dangerous. They eat plants and damage crops, especially wheat. They spread diseases to animals and people, and they leave behind many maggots. Maggots are worms that become gnats or flies.

VOCABULARY

Faith words:

God's power is greater and stronger than anyone or anything. God can do all things.

Terms:

Gnats are very small, flying insects that are similar to tiny flies.

A kneading trough was a large bowl that was used to mix bread dough. After the dough was mixed with yeast, it was left in the trough to swell and rise.

STORYTELLING

Each week you will need the following items.

1. The travel bag from lesson one
2. The storage container (bag, basket, or box) with items from the previous lessons

For today's story, you will need the following items.

3. Seven red candies or M&M's
4. A toy frog or plush frog
5. A fly swatter
6. A piece of clay or Play-Doh

Before class:

1. Read Exodus 7:25-8:32.
1. Gather today's story items. Substitute a picture for any unavailable items.

2. Transfer all previous lesson items from the travel bag to the storage container. Place this beside the storytelling area.
3. Place today's story items inside the travel bag. Place the travel bag in the storytelling area.

Optional activity: Follow the leader

Tell the children to stand in a line, one behind the other. Choose a child to be the leader. Tell the children to watch carefully and mimic everything the leader does. The leader leads the group around the room. He or she uses different hand gestures, sounds, or means of travel for the children to imitate. For example, the leader walks with baby steps, large steps, or skips. End the game at the storytelling area.

Lesson review:

Ask a volunteer to select an item from the storage container and explain what it represented in a previous lesson.

Story time:

Read these instructions before you begin.

1. Tell the story in your own words. Remove each item from the bag as you illustrate a main point. Focus on the main points. If you are comfortable, include more details. If needed, use the script that is suggested.
2. As you tell the story, display each item in the order that it is listed. Place it where the children can see it.
3. After telling the story, place all the items inside the bag again.
4. To review the story, remove the first item. Ask a volunteer to tell what it represents. Display this item. Repeat this process until the story is retold.
5. Review the memory motion described below. Demonstrate this motion any time you mention what it represents.
6. Say, **We are continuing on our expedition to explore the book of Exodus. I packed our travel bag with tools that we will need. Today our journey begins with...** Unpack the items as you tell the story.

Main points in order:

1. Red Candies or M & M's—Say, **In the first plague, God turned the waters of the Nile to blood.**
2. Toy or Plush Frog—Say, **Seven days after the Lord struck the Nile River, he gave Pharaoh another chance to obey him. Pharaoh refused, and God sent a plague of frogs. The frogs came out of the Nile and hopped all through the land. They were everywhere! The magicians also made frogs come out of the Nile. Pharaoh said the people could leave and told Moses to pray to God to remove the frogs. Moses obeyed, and all the frogs died right where they were. Soon the land stank. The frogs were stacked up in huge piles. Pharaoh broke his promise to let the people go.**
3. Fly swatter—Say, **After the plague of frogs, the Lord sent the plague of gnats. Aaron struck the ground and the dust became gnats. This time, the magicians could not duplicate the miracle. In amazement they said, "This is the hand of God."**
   After the gnats left, God offered Pharaoh another chance to obey him. Pharaoh refused, and God sent the plague of flies. They swarmed throughout Egypt except in the land of Goshen, where the Israelites lived. God protected the Israelites from the flies.
4. Hardened clay or Play-Doh—Say, **Pharaoh still did not listen to what Moses and Aaron said. He would not obey God's command to let the people go. Like soft clay that is exposed to the sun and wind, Pharaoh's heart had become hard.**
5. Memory motion—Show the children how to flex their arm muscles. This represents that the plagues demonstrated God's power. You may also invite the children to think of another motion. Say, **As I tell the story, do this motion when you hear what it represents.**
6. Say, **Now it is your turn to tell the story.** Return the items to the bag. Invite the children to take turns and choose an item from the bag without looking. Ask them to explain what it means or to review the memory motion. After all the items have been removed, ask the children to place them in the correct story order.

BIBLICAL LESSON

Teaching tips:

As you lead the Bible study, emphasize these ideas:

- Each plague destroyed something in Egypt and weakened the nation.
- The Egyptian magicians recognized that God's power caused the plagues.
- Pharaoh's stubbornness caused great and unnecessary suffering for him and for the Egyptians.

Read the Scripture:

Read Exodus 7:25-8:32 aloud.

Discussion questions:

Discuss the story and ask the children the following questions. Remember that there might not be a right or wrong answer.

1. **How do you think Moses felt when he prayed and the Lord stopped the plagues of frogs and flies?**
2. **Imagine that you were an Israelite. What would you think when you learned that the Egyptian magicians could not produce gnats from dust?**
3. Read Exodus 8:22. **In this plague, what did the Lord do differently for the Israelites? Why did he do this?**
4. **Imagine if millions of frogs, gnats, or flies suddenly filled your city, town, or village. What would life be like?**
5. **What would you tell Pharaoh if you were an Egyptian magician who saw God do things that you and your gods could not do?**

Conclusion:

This is the thought you want the children to remember.

Say, **Through the plagues, God showed that the Egyptian gods were false gods.**

Egypt was one of the most powerful nations on earth. They had the best army and the most money. They even thought that they had the best gods. The magicians thought that they could do anything that God did. They were surprised when they could not make dust change into gnats. Only the Lord God rules over all creation. Only he can cause it to conform to his will. When God sent the plague of gnats, the magicians realized that God was more powerful than their gods. The magicians also knew that God was more powerful than them.

When the flies swarmed only in Egypt and not in Goshen, it showed that the Lord controlled this plague. It also showed that he would protect his people. The Lord showed Pharaoh and all the Egyptians that he was the one true God. He was, is, and will always be the one true God.

MEMORY VERSE PRACTICE

Know that the LORD has set apart his faithful servant for himself; the LORD hears when I call to him. –Psalm 4:3

See the "Memory Verse Activities" on pages 124-127 for suggestions to help the children to learn the memory verse.

Bible Studies for Children: Exodus
Lesson 7

ADDITIONAL ACTIVITIES

To learn more about ancient Egypt and the culture in which the Israelites lived, consider these options.

1. If possible, research the ancient Egyptian deity Heket. Was this a god or goddess? What did he or she look like? What power did Egyptians believe that Heket had? How did the Lord show that he was more powerful than Heket? (Parents and teachers: Pre-screen Internet sites before recommending them to children.)

2. Try to discover why the plagues of gnats and flies were so harmful to Egypt. What did the gnats and flies most likely destroy? How did this affect the Egyptian economy (income)? Find out how gnats and flies affect people and crops.

Act out the plagues:

Choose three children to play the roles of Moses, Aaron, and Pharaoh. The remainder of the children will act out the role of the Egyptians. Briefly tell the story or read it from the scriptures. Invite the children to act out the parts as they are read. Help the children who are the Egyptians think of creative ways to act out each of the different plagues. Ask them how they would react to these plagues. Ask the children which of the plagues they think would be the worst for the Egyptians. Ask the children why they think God allowed the Egyptians to suffer so much. Say, **God wanted to show them that he is the one true God. He wanted them to know that he is powerful and mighty.**

Art option:

You will need:

- A framed picture of your choosing
- Drawing paper
- Crayons

Place the framed picture where children can see it. Give each child a piece of the paper and access to the crayons. Tell the children that they have two minutes to create an exact copy of this picture. Give no other explanation. Afterward, ask the children if their picture looks exactly like the framed picture. Allow the children to respond. Say, **It was impossible for you to make an exact copy of this picture. You only had crayons and paper. This week we learned that no one in Egypt could duplicate everything God did. Only God has the power to control nature.**

ACTIVITY FOR OLDER CHILDREN

You will need:

A piece of paper and a pencil for each student

Say, **God blessed Egypt when Joseph was alive. Later, the Egyptians oppressed the Israelites, and God brought plagues that took away their blessings. God showed the Egyptians that they could not rely on their gods, their water, their crops, their livestock, their health, their wealth, or their power.**

1. Ask the students to discuss what they rely on for a good life. Ask, **Are these things reliable?**

2. Ask the students to write this on a piece of paper. "God, teach me to rely on you instead of _____." Ask them to write a list of things or people that they rely on instead of God. Invite them to share their list. Then ask them

Bible Studies for Children: Exodus
Lesson 7

to continue writing about why they can trust God to care for their needs.

Say, **When we rely on God, he will care for us. When we rely on anyone or anything else, we will often be disappointed.**

 ## PRACTICE FOR BIBLE QUIZ

See the section "Review Questions" on pages 128-167 for the red and the blue practice questions for this lesson.

LESSON 8

PHARAOH! PHARAOH! LET MY PEOPLE GO!
EXODUS 9:1-35

MEMORY VERSE

A person may think their own ways are right, but the LORD weighs the heart.

Proverbs 21:2

TRUTHS ABOUT GOD

This lesson will teach the following truths about God. The asterisk * indicates the primary truth that you should teach to the children.

* * There is no one like the Lord in all the earth.
* God has power over weather, animals, and even kings.
* God has a purpose for everything he does.

LESSON FOCUS AND SUMMARY

In this study, the children will learn that God is all powerful.

1. The Lord could have instantly destroyed Egypt and everyone in it.
2. Instead, the Lord sent Moses and Aaron to ask Pharaoh's permission to leave. This recognized that Pharaoh had some earthly authority. Through the contest between Pharaoh, his magicians, and God, the Lord showed that he was all powerful.
3. Pharaoh still refused the Israelites' request to leave Egypt.
4. The Lord sent three more plagues: death of the livestock, boils, and hail.

 ## BIBLICAL BACKGROUND

Exodus 9:16 says, "But I have raised you up for this very purpose, that I might show you my power and that my name might be proclaimed in all the earth." This important verse reveals God's master plan.

Contrary to what the Egyptians believed, they were not great because of their gods or their pharaoh. Yahweh had brought success to Egypt in spite of their rejection of him. He wanted to prove to them and through them that there is no one like him in all the earth (9:14). The time had come for the world to learn that Yahweh is the supreme God. There is nothing that he cannot do. He rules over the earth and all the nations. His obedient people experience his care while his disobedient enemies face dire consequences.

Bible Studies for Children: Exodus
Lesson 8

A key verse in this lesson is Exodus 9:30. It is the first time the phrase "fear the Lord" is used in the Bible. It means to respect who God is and what he can do or face the consequences of disobedience! Pharaoh and his officials did not fear the Lord. They were proud and disobedient. The call to fear the Lord is a reminder to give God a respectful response. He deserves our worship, devotion, service, and love.

DID YOU KNOW?

Haap, also known as Apis, was the Egyptian bull god. The Egyptians chose a real bull to represent Haap. They gave this bull extra special care because they believed that Haap protected livestock. The livestock plague defeated this god.

VOCABULARY

Faith words:

Sin is disobeying God. We sin when we do something that we know God said not to do. We also sin when we do not do what God said to do.

Terms:

Boils are infected bumps under the skin that are very painful.

Soot is a dark powdery substance that remains after a fire has burned in a furnace, chimney, or fireplace.

STORYTELLING

Each week you will need the following items.

1. The travel bag from lesson one
2. The storage container (bag, basket, or box) with the items from the previous lessons

For today's story, you will need the following items.

3. A toy cow or other animal
4. A battery
5. Glue
6. A bar of soap
7. Cotton balls

Before class:

1. Read Exodus 9:1-35.
2. Gather today's story items. Substitute a picture for any unavailable items.
3. Transfer all previous lesson items from the travel bag to the storage container. Place this beside the storytelling area.
4. Place today's story items inside the travel bag. Place the travel bag in the storytelling area.

Optional activity: Follow the leader

Tell the children to stand in a line, one behind the other. Choose a child to be the leader. Tell the children to watch carefully and mimic everything the leader does.. The leader leads the group around the room. He or she uses different hand gestures, sounds, or means of travel for the children to imitate. For example, the leader walks with baby steps, large steps, or skips. End the game at the storytelling area.

Bible Studies for Children: Exodus
Lesson 8

Lesson review:

Ask a volunteer to select an item from the storage container and explain what it represented in a previous lesson.

Story time:

Read these instructions before you begin.

1. Tell the story in your own words. Remove each item from the bag as you illustrate a main point. Focus on the main points. If you are comfortable, include more details. If needed, use the script that is suggested.

2. As you tell the story, display each item in the order that it is listed. Place it where the children can see it.

3. After telling the story, place all the items inside the bag again.

4. To review the story, remove the first item. Ask a volunteer to tell what it represents. Display this item. Repeat this process until the story is retold.

5. Review the memory motion described below. Demonstrate this motion any time you mention what it represents.

6. Say, **We are continuing on our expedition to explore the book of Exodus. I packed our travel bag with tools that we will need. Today our journey begins with...** Unpack the items as you tell the story.

Main points in order:

1. Toy cow—Say, **After the plague of flies, Pharaoh broke his promise to let the Israelites go. The Lord sent a plague on the livestock. Hundreds, perhaps thousands of Egyptian cows, horses, camels, sheep, and goats died. But, not one that belonged to the Israelites died.**

2. Battery—Say, **This is a source of power. Today it represents the Lord's power. The Lord told Pharaoh, "By now I could have wiped you and your people off the earth. Instead, I raised you up so that I could show you my power"** (9:15-16).

3. Cotton balls—Say, **Next, the Lord sent a plague of boils on both people and animals. Finally, he sent a powerful hailstorm. Now Egypt's animals were dead, the people were sick from boils, and their crops were flattened by the hail.**

4. Glue—Say, **Despite these plagues, Pharaoh refused to listen. It was as if he was stuck (like glue) on one thought: "No matter what the Lord does or how bad it gets, I won't let the Israelites go."**

5. Memory motion—Ask the children to hold up three fingers. Say, **These three fingers represent that God sent three more plagues.** You may also invite the children to think of another motion. Say, **As I tell the story, do this motion when you hear what it represents.**

6. Say, **Now it is your turn to tell the story.** Return the items to the bag. Invite the children to take turns and choose an item from the bag without looking. Ask them to explain what it means or to review the memory motion. After all the items have been removed, ask the children to place them in the correct story order

BIBLICAL LESSON

Teaching tips:

As you lead the Bible study, emphasize these ideas:

- God is both powerful and merciful. God repeatedly told Pharaoh what would happen if he did not obey. God gave Pharaoh the chance to avoid disaster.
- In 9:14, the Lord suggested that the plagues would come to an end. Redemption for the Israelites was in sight.

Read the Scripture:

Read Exodus 9:1-35 aloud.

Discussion questions:

Discuss the story and ask the children the following questions. Remember that there might not be a right or wrong answer.

1. **The Lord made a distinction between the Egyptians's livestock and the Israelites' livestock. What does this teach us about the Lord's relationship with the Israelites?** (9:2-4)
2. Read Exodus 9:13-17. **What does God say about himself? Which statement impresses you the most? Why?**
3. **How does this description of God influence your faith and trust in him?**
4. **What was God's purpose in dealing with Pharaoh?** (9:15-16)
5. Read 9:33-34. **What happened when Moses spread out his hands toward the Lord? What does this say about God's power?**

Closing thoughts:

This is the thought you want your students to remember.

Say, **There is no one like the Lord in all the earth. He has power over weather, animals, and even kings.**

Sometimes, it is difficult to know or see God in our current circumstances. He can seem to be distant and disconnected. In this study, we learn that God constantly works in our lives. It was no accident that Pharaoh and Egypt became so powerful. Although it seemed like Pharaoh had control over the Israelites, this was not true. Pharaoh was a part of God's plan.

God is the same today as he was in the days of the Exodus. There is no one like the Lord! He knows more and has more power than anyone or anything. Nothing in your life is beyond his power or his reach. He can defeat your enemies.

MEMORY VERSE PRACTICE

A person may think their own ways are right, but the LORD weighs the heart. –Proverbs 21:2

See the "Memory Verse Activities" on pages 124-127 for suggestions to help the children to learn the memory verse.

Bible Studies for Children: Exodus
Lesson 8

ADDITIONAL ACTIVITIES

To learn more about ancient Egypt and the culture in which the Israelites lived, consider these options.

1. Learn about the importance of livestock in ancient Egypt. How were cows and bulls a part of Egyptian economy (buying, selling, making money)? How were cows and bulls a part of their religion? Write a paragraph telling how the plague on the livestock showed that the Lord was more powerful than the Egyptian gods.

2. Find information on hailstones. How big were the largest hailstones ever found? How can severe thunderstorms and hailstones affect houses, crops, and people?

3. Use crushed ice and water to recreate the largest hailstone ever found.

Livestock, boils, and hail review

Read the story again. Stand in a circle with the children. Begin by telling the first story fact. The child to your right shares an additional fact that comes next. Continue around the circle until you have reviewed the story. Option one: If a child cannot give a fact, he or she is out of the game. Option two: The child must repeat your fact and also add another fact to it.

Distinction

You will need:

- A clear glass pitcher or tall clear glass
- A measuring cup
- Water
- Vegetable oil
- Maple syrup
- Three containers with lids

Prepare: Measure equal amounts of water, vegetable oil, and maple syrup and pour each substance into a separate container with a lid. Place them on a table next to the clear pitcher.

Ask the children if all liquids are the same. Say, **I am going to pour this water, maple syrup, and vegetable oil into this pitcher and see what happens.** Pour equal amounts of the liquids slowly into the pitcher and do not stir them. Ask the children what happened. Tell the children there is a distinction between each liquid. **While they are all liquids, there are enough differences between them that they cannot be mixed together. In the Bible story, we discovered how the Lord made a distinction between the Egyptian people and the Israelites.**

ACTIVITY FOR OLDER CHILDREN

You will need:

- A spray bottle
- 2 sets of water proof garments. If needed, make a garment from large plastic trash bags. Cut a slit in the center of the bottom of the bag that is large enough for your head to go through and then cut two slits on the bottom of the sides for your arms.

1. Recruit two volunteers. Quietly tell one to obey all directions and the other one to disobey.

2. Create two teams from the remainder of the students. Assign one of the volunteers to each team. Say, **In two minutes, I will squirt your volunteer. You must try to convince him or her to wear the protective garments and give instructions.**

3. After the activity, compare the volunteers to the obedient and disobedient Egyptians (9:19-21). Ask the students to discuss what Moses recommended so the Egyptians' livestock would be safe during the hailstorm? Why did Pharaoh not obey? Why do we sometimes disobey God, even though it causes us to experience difficulty?

4. Lead the students in a time of prayer and commitment to obey God.

 ## PRACTICE FOR BIBLE QUIZ

See the section "Review Questions" on pages 128-167 for the red and the blue practice questions for this lesson.

LESSON 9

EGYPT IS RUINED!

EXODUS 10:1-11:10

MEMORY VERSE

Your right hand, LORD, was majestic in power. Your right hand, LORD, shattered the enemy.

Exodus 15:6

TRUTHS ABOUT GOD

This lesson will teach the following truths about God. The asterisk * indicates the primary truth that you should teach to the children.

* * God continued to give Pharaoh opportunities to yield to him.
* God has power over life and death.
* God shows his power to all people.

LESSON FOCUS AND SUMMARY

In this study, the children will learn that God has power over everything and everyone.

1. The Lord continued to speak to Pharaoh through Moses.
2. The Lord sent a plague of locusts. Nothing green remained.
3. The Lord sent a plague of darkness that lasted three days.
4. The Lord said he would send a plague on the firstborn of people and animals. They would all die.

 BIBLICAL BACKGROUND

In this lesson, Yahweh continues to demonstrate his power and authority. The plague of locusts and the plague of darkness show his power.

The Lord caused a strong wind to blow a swarm of locusts into Egypt. They completely covered the land. They ate every plant that survived the plague of hail. This eliminated Egypt's food supply. There would be no food anywhere and the people would starve. Pharaoh's officials urged Pharaoh to let the Israelites leave Egypt, but he refused. When the locusts came, Pharaoh confessed that he had sinned against the Lord and against Moses. He asked Moses to forgive him and to pray to the Lord to remove the plague. Moses prayed and God removed the locusts. Pharaoh still would not let the Israelites go.

In the ninth plague, Yahweh brought three days of darkness over the land. The Egyptians were in total darkness, but the Israelites still had light. The darkness was darker than night. It was like the darkness in a deep cave. The darkness could actually be felt. After three days of total darkness, the doom, despair, and fear felt by the Egyptians must have been overwhelming. The Egyptians and their gods were helpless before Yahweh, but Pharaoh still resisted. So God sent the tenth and final plague, the death of the firstborn.

DID YOU KNOW?

Egyptians worshiped the sun. Ra, Horus, and Osiris were Egyptian sun gods. They also believed Sekhmet, the fire goddess, could destroy Egypt's enemies by killing them with sun rays. The plague of darkness proved Yahweh's supremacy, even over the sun gods.

VOCABULARY

Faith words:

Choices are decisions we make. We make right choices when we decide to obey God. We make wrong choices when we disobey God.

People:

Pharaoh's officials were members of Pharaoh's royal court who often gave Pharaoh advice.

Places:

The Red Sea was east of Egypt.

Terms:

A locust is a type of grasshopper. Locusts travel in swarms, eating and destroying crops.

Wailing is long and loud crying because of suffering and misery.

The firstborn was the first son born in a family.

STORYTELLING

Each week you will need the following items.

1. The travel bag from lesson one
2. A storage container (bag, basket, or box) with the items from the previous lessons

For today's story, you will need the following items.

3. A piece of lined paper with the word "Memo" written at the top
4. Insect repellent
5. A flashlight
6. A baby doll and a plush toy animal

Before class:

1. Read Exodus 10:1-11:10.

2. Gather today's story items. Substitute a picture for any unavailable items.

3. Transfer all previous lesson items from the travel bag to the storage container. Place this beside the storytelling area.

4. Place today's story items inside the travel bag. Place the travel bag in the storytelling area.

Optional activity: Follow the leader

Tell the children to stand in a line, one behind the other. Choose a child to be the leader. Tell the children to watch carefully and mimic everything the leader does. The leader leads the group around the room. He or she uses different hand gestures, sounds, or means of travel for the children to imitate. For example, the leader walks with baby steps, large steps, or skips. End the game at the storytelling area.

Lesson review:

Ask a volunteer to select an item from the storage container and explain what it represented in a previous lesson.

Story time:

Read these instructions before you begin.

1. Tell the story in your own words. Remove each item from the bag as you illustrate a main point. Focus on the main points. If you are comfortable, include more details. If needed, use the script that is suggested.
2. As you tell the story, display each item in the order that it is listed. Place it where the children can see it.
3. After telling the story, place all the items inside the bag again.
4. To review the story, remove the first item. Ask a volunteer to tell what it represents. Display this item. Repeat this process until the story is retold.
5. Review the memory motion described below. Demonstrate this motion any time you mention what it represents.
6. Say, **We are continuing on our expedition to explore the book of Exodus. I packed our travel bag with tools that we will need. Today our journey begins with...** Unpack the items as you tell the story.

Main points in order:

1. "Memo" writing paper—Say, **The Lord spoke to Pharaoh through Moses. When Moses spoke to Pharaoh, it was like handing Pharaoh a memo written by God. Everything Moses told Pharaoh was a message directly from God.**
2. Insect repellent—Say, **Pharaoh refused to obey, so the Lord sent a plague of locusts. The locusts ate every crop that survived the hail. Nothing green remained. Pharaoh and his magicians could not kill the locusts. Nothing could repel them. But when Moses prayed, the Lord brought a west wind and swept the locusts out to the Red Sea. Still, Pharaoh would not obey.**
3. Flashlight—Say, **The Lord sent a plague of darkness that lasted for three days. It was so dark that it seemed that darkness could be felt. The Egyptians could not see anyone or leave their homes. But the Israelites had light. Still, Pharaoh would not let the people go. He told Moses to get out of his sight and never appear before him again.**
4. Baby doll and stuffed animal—Say, **Before Moses left Pharaoh, he gave him one more message. The Lord told Moses that he would send a plague on all the firstborn of people and animals. They would die. The other plagues ruined the land, but this plague would destroy people and animals.**
5. Memory motion—Ask the children to cover the tops of their heads to represent that locusts and darkness covered Egypt. You may also invite the children to think of another motion. Say, **As I tell the story, do this motion when you hear what it represents.**
6. Say, **Now it is your turn to tell the story.** Return the items to the bag. Invite the children to take turns and choose an item from the bag without looking. Ask them to explain what it means or to review the memory motion. After all the items have been removed, ask the children to place them in the correct story order.

BIBLICAL LESSON

Teaching tips:

As you lead the Bible study, emphasize these ideas:

- The Lord gave a reason for the plagues in 10:1-2.
- Some children may express concern about the fact that God hardened Pharaoh's heart. If so, look at the many times when Pharaoh hardened his own heart. Explain that now God was accepting and strengthening the choices Pharaoh had already firmly made. If we willingly choose to disobey God, there are consequences.

Read the Scripture:

Read Exodus 10:1-11:10 aloud.

Discussion questions:

Discuss the story and ask the children the following questions. Remember that there might not be a right or wrong answer.

1. Read Exodus 10:1-2. **What did the Lord want the Israelites to do and to know? How important is it for us to do this and know this?**
2. **During the plague of locusts, Pharaoh said that he had sinned, and he asked for forgiveness. Was he really honest with God? How do you know?** (10:16-20)
3. **How would your life change if God brought a plague of total darkness where you live?**
4. **Imagine that you were an Egyptian living in the darkness. What would you think when you discovered that the Israelites had light where they lived?**
5. **What do we learn about God's power from the three plagues discussed in this story?**

Closing thoughts:

This is the thought you want your students to remember.

Say, **God continued to give Pharaoh opportunities to yield to Him.**

God gives second chances! The story of the plagues is an example of how God gives people many opportunities to obey him. Before each plague, the Lord gave Pharaoh an opportunity to let the Israelites go. Exodus 34:6 says, "The LORD, the LORD, the compassionate and gracious God, slow to anger, abounding in love and faithfulness."

God's patience is not limitless. He wants us to know, love, and obey him. God is a gracious God, but people should accept his grace and choose his ways before it is too late.

MEMORY VERSE PRACTICE

Your right hand, LORD, was majestic in power. Your right hand, LORD, shattered the enemy. –Exodus 15:6

See the "Memory Verse Activities" on pages 124-127 for suggestions to help the children to learn the memory verse.

ADDITIONAL ACTIVITIES

To learn more about ancient Egypt and the culture in which the Israelites lived, consider these options.

1. Read about the ancient Egyptian sun gods Ra, Horus, Osiris, and the goddess Sekhmet. What were their powers? How popular were they? How did God prove he was more powerful? Draw their pictures and write a paragraph about each god.

2. Read about the type of locusts that might have swarmed ancient Egypt. Why were locusts so devastating to Egypt? You might want to searc for information on "desert locusts."

3. Completely darken a room. Stand in the room for two minutes with a dark blanket draped over your head. Afterward, read Exodus 10:1-2 and answer this question: What was the Lord's purpose in sending the plagues?

Total darkness

You'll need:

- A blindfold
- An adult-sized jacket

Prepare: Place the blindfold and jacket in your teaching area. If you want to do this activity with several children at once, prepare several blindfolds and jackets.

1. Ask for a volunteer to wear the blindfold. Say, **We will learn about the plague of darkness today. To get an idea of how dark it was for the Egyptians, this volunteer will try to wear a jacket without being able to see it.**

2. Ask the child to pick up the jacket and to put it on without any assistance. The child must fasten all buttons or zippers. Invite as many children to try this as time allows.

3. After a few attempts, ask the children, **How difficult was it to do this familiar task without being able to see? How do you think the plague of darkness affected the Egyptians?**

 ## ACTIVITY FOR OLDER CHILDREN

Ask, **Do you know what a foxhole prayer is?**

Say, **A foxhole is a pit that soldiers dug to hide from enemy gunfire. When the gunfire became intense, some soldiers who did not worship God would begin to pray in their foxholes. They promised God that they would worship and obey him if he spared their lives. God answered their prayer, but they forgot about their promise to him after the gunfire stopped.**

In the Bible story today, whose prayer reminds you of a foxhole prayer?

Ask the students if they ever prayed a foxhole prayer. Ask, **Did you keep your promise or break it? God is always working for our good. Will you commit to obey God all the time, not just when things are bad?**

Close in prayer.

PRACTICE FOR BIBLE QUIZ

See the section "Review Questions" on pages 128-167 for the red and the blue practice questions for this lesson.

LESSON 10

FREE AT LAST!

EXODUS 12:1-42

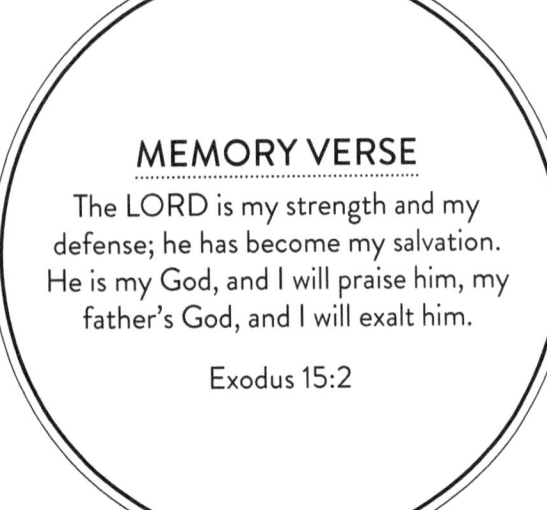

MEMORY VERSE

The LORD is my strength and my defense; he has become my salvation. He is my God, and I will praise him, my father's God, and I will exalt him.

Exodus 15:2

TRUTHS ABOUT GOD

This lesson will teach the following truths about God. The asterisk * indicates the primary truth that you should teach to the children.

* God faithfully delivered his people from slavery exactly as he promised.
- God carefully watches over his people.
- God ultimately and always defeats evil.

LESSON FOCUS AND SUMMARY

In this study, the children will learn that God keeps his promises and accomplishes his purpose.

1. God sent the last plague, the plague on the firstborn.
2. The Israelites celebrated the first Feast of Unleavened Bread, the Passover.
3. Pharaoh said the Israelites could go.
4. The Israelites left Egypt in exactly the way and at the time the Lord said they would.

 ## BIBLICAL BACKGROUND

This lesson reveals instructions for the Passover, the plague of the death of the firstborn, and Israel's exodus from Egypt. These events taught the Israelites important lessons about God and what God expected of them.

The Israelites learned that Yahweh is faithful. God promised Abraham hundreds of years earlier that he would bring Abraham's descendants out of Egypt with riches. The descendants of Abraham enslaved in Egypt did not know about God's promise to Abraham. God came to their rescue because God always keeps his promises.

The Israelites also learned that God desired their gratitude and faithfulness. If they wanted to be delivered from Pharaoh, then they had to be faithful to God. They had to observe the Passover if they wanted to be spared from the plague of death. They could not save themselves. To be saved, they had to obey God.

The Israelites learned a third lesson. They must celebrate the Passover every year. At the Passover meal, they would teach their history, their traditions, and God's goodness to the next generation.

Bible Studies for Children: Exodus
Lesson 10

Download additional resources from *kidzfirstpublications.org*

DID YOU KNOW?

Jewish people continue to celebrate the Passover today. Jewish children play a game and thoroughly search their houses for yeast.

VOCABULARY

Faith words:

Faithful means to be dependable and trustworthy. God is always faithful. He is trustworthy and always keeps his promises. God expects his people to be faithful to him and to others.

People:

The firstborn son is the first boy born into a family.

Terms:

Hyssop is a small, hairy, stemmed bush. These stems hold water well when they are bunched together with their leaves and flowers.

The Feast of Unleavened Bread is a seven-day celebration that includes Passover. At this feast, the Israelites ate only unleavened bread. This reminded them that they quickly left Egypt and did not put any yeast in the bread. This was because they could not wait for the bread to rise.

The Passover is a feast to celebrate the Israelites' deliverance from slavery in Egypt. It is a time to remember that God passed over the Israelite homes during the final plague and spared their firstborn sons from death.

An ordinance is a rule or law given by the Lord to the Israelites.

Divisions were groups of people, most likely the 12 tribes of Israel.

A vigil is a period of time when a person is watchful. The Lord kept vigil when he watched over the safety of the Israelites.

STORYTELLING

Each week you will need the following items.

1. The travel bag from lesson one
2. The storage container (bag, basket, or box) with the items from the previous lessons

For today's story, you will need the following items.

3. A "1"-shaped birthday candle
4. Pita or matzo bread
5. A piece of construction paper with "Go!" printed in green
6. A green marker
7. A Bible

Before class:

1. Read Exodus 12:1-42.
2. Gather today's story items. Substitute a picture for any unavailable items.
3. Transfer all previous lesson items from the travel bag to the storage container. Place this beside the storytelling area.
4. Place today's story items inside the travel bag. Place the travel bag in the storytelling area.

5. Print "Go!" on the construction paper with the marker. Place the sign face down in the storytelling area.

Optional activity: Follow the leader

Tell the children to stand in a line, one behind the other. Choose a child to be the leader. Tell the children to watch carefully and mimic everything the leader does. The leader leads the group around the room. He or she uses different hand gestures, sounds, or means of travel for the children to imitate. For example, the leader walks with baby steps, large steps, or skips. End the game at the storytelling area.

Lesson review:

Ask a volunteer to select an item from the storage container and explain what it represented in a previous lesson.

Story time:

Read these instructions before you begin.

1. Tell the story in your own words. Remove each item from the bag as you illustrate a main point. Focus on the main points. If you are comfortable, include more details. If needed, use the script that is suggested.
2. As you tell the story, display each item in the order that it is listed. Place it where the children can see it.
3. After telling the story, place all the items inside the bag again.
4. To review the story, remove the first item. Ask a volunteer to tell what it represents. Display this item. Repeat this process until the story is retold.
5. Review the memory motion described below. Demonstrate this motion any time you mention what it represents.
6. Say, **We are continuing on our expedition to explore the book of Exodus. I packed our travel bag with tools that we will need. Today our journey begins with...** Unpack the items as you tell the story.

Main points in order:

1. "1"-Shaped Candle—Say, **God was about to send the 10th and final plague upon the Egyptians. At midnight, the firstborn sons of the Egyptians and firstborn animals would die.**
2. Pita or matzo bread—Say, **The Lord told the Israelites to prepare a special meal. They ate unleavened bread, which is bread that has no yeast in it. They killed a lamb and put some of its blood on the doorframes of their homes. God passed over their homes, and no Israelite firstborns died. The Israelites ate the lamb and bread quickly so they would be ready to leave Egypt.**
3. Paper with the word "Go!"—Say, **After the plague of the firstborn, Pharaoh summoned Moses and Aaron. He told them to go. The Egyptians gave the Israelites gifts of gold, silver, and clothing.**
4. Bible—Say, **The Israelites left Egypt on the exact day and in the exact way the Lord promised to Abraham hundreds of years earlier.** (Genesis 15:12-14, Exodus 40-41)
5. Memory motion—Ask the children to wave their hands above their head to represent the Israelites were free! You may also invite the children to think of another motion. Say, **As I tell the story, do this motion when you hear what it represents.**
6. Say, **Now it is your turn to tell the story.** Return the items to the bag. Invite the children to take turns and choose an item from the bag without looking. Ask them to explain what it means or to review the memory motion. After all the items have been removed, ask the children to place them in the correct story order.

BIBLICAL LESSON

Teaching tips:

As you lead the Bible study, emphasize these ideas:

- The Lord planned every detail of the exodus—the timing and what provisions to take. While it may seem that the Lord was not involved at the beginning, he was actually working the whole time!

Read the Scripture:

Read Exodus 12:1-42 aloud.

Discussion questions:

Discuss the story and ask the children the following questions. Remember that there might not be a right or wrong answer.

1. **Imagine that you are an Israelite child at the first Passover. Describe your thoughts and feelings.**
2. **If you were an Israelite, how would you feel when you knew that the Lord passed over your house?**
3. **Why did God tell his people to celebrate the Feast of Passover and Unleavened Bread?**
4. **Why do you think other people left Egypt with the Israelites?**
5. **How important was it for the Israelites to remember what the Lord did? How important is this today?**

Closing thoughts:

This is the thought you want your students to remember.

Say, **God faithfully delivered his people from slavery exactly as he promised.**

Finally! The Israelites were free. Can you imagine what it was like to leave Egypt in the middle of the night? The Lord provided bread, clothes, gold, silver, and everything else they needed. The Egyptians helped them, and the Lord watched over them!

The Lord's promises can be trusted. Remember Exodus 12:28 says, "The Israelites did just what the Lord commanded." The Lord is faithful. He watches over us. It is important for us to obey him just as the Israelites did.

MEMORY VERSE PRACTICE

The LORD is my strength and my defense; he has become my salvation. He is my God, and I will praise him, my father's God, and I will exalt him. –Exodus 15:2

See the "Memory Verse Activities" on pages 124-127 for suggestions to help the children to learn the memory verse.

ADDITIONAL ACTIVITIES

To learn more about ancient Egypt and the culture in which the Israelites lived, consider these options.

Think about the Passover and the hasty departure of the Israelites.

1. Research and hold a Passover feast.

2. Develop a game or activity sheet of your own to help you remember the correct sequence of the plagues. Remember to include which plagues affected Egyptians only.

3. Imagine that you are an Israelite. Write in your journal about what it was like to live through the last plague, and then suddenly leave your home with the rest of the Israelites.

Get Ready, Get Set, Go!

You will need:

- Masking tape
- A backpack, shopping bag, or shoulder bag for each child
- A jacket or sweater for each child and leader
- Car keys for leaders

Prepare: Place jackets and bags in one corner of your room. Consider asking the children to bring their own jackets and bags from home.

Say, **Today while we work on our Bible study, we will wear jackets and carry things we might use when we travel. When I say, "Let's go," you must be ready to collect your things and follow me.** Ask the children and the leaders to put on the jackets. Give each child a backpack or bag. Give the leaders a set of keys. Move to one area of the classroom, and ask everyone to hold these items as you read the story.

Without warning say, **Let's Go! Place your books and pencils in your bags and follow me.** Travel to another part of the room or to a different room in the building. Finish a part of the lesson in the new location.

Say, **What you just did is similar to what happened to the Israelites in today's story.** Discuss what happened, why, and how the children felt.

ACTIVITY FOR OLDER CHILDREN

You will need:

- Various craft supplies for students to make a sign

1. Provide craft supplies for each student to make a door sign for his or her home or room at home. When they have finished, ask each student to share the importance of the things on his or her sign.

2. Say, **God said that the blood from the Passover Lamb was a sign on the houses of the Israelites. What happened when he saw the blood?** Discuss the answers. He passed by and no one in the house died.

3. Say, **Jesus is called the Lamb of God. How is he like the Passover lamb?** Discuss their answers. Say, **Jesus died so that we could live. Just as the firstborn survived because of the blood from the sacrifice of the Passover lamb, we can live with Jesus forever if we accept his sacrifice for our sins.**

PRACTICE FOR BIBLE QUIZ

See the section "Review Questions" on pages 128-167 for the red and the blue practice questions for this lesson.

Bible Studies for Children: Exodus
Lesson 10

LESSON 11

BE STILL! THE LORD WILL FIGHT FOR YOU!

EXODUS 13:17-14:31

MEMORY VERSE

The LORD will fight for you; you need only to be still.

Exodus 14:14

TRUTHS ABOUT GOD

This lesson will teach the following truths about God. The asterisk * indicates the primary truth that you should teach to the children.

* God fought for his people and defeated the Egyptians at the Red Sea.
- God fights for his people.
- God knows when people are strong and when they are not.

LESSON FOCUS AND SUMMARY

In this study, the children will learn that God defends his people.

1. The Lord led the Israelites with a pillar of cloud and a pillar of fire.
2. Pharaoh changed his mind and pursued the Israelites.
3. The Lord brought winds to part the Red Sea.
4. The Israelites passed through the Red Sea safely while the Egyptians drowned.

BIBLICAL BACKGROUND

This lesson focuses on the Israelites' exit from Egypt. At first, everything went well. They marched out boldly, loaded with gifts from the Egyptian people. They followed a pillar of cloud by day and a pillar of fire by night. Confident of Yahweh's total victory over Pharaoh, they were finally free from bondage and free to worship the Lord!

Then the Egyptian chariots appeared. The Israelites knew that they were no match for Pharaoh's army. Trapped against the sea, they panicked. Pharaoh still refused to let them go free, even after the tenth plague, the death of the firstborn. Could Yahweh defeat the most powerful army in the world? Would he rescue them? If God himself did not fight the battle for them, they knew that they were doomed.

At that moment, their greatest problem was not Pharaoh's army. Their greatest weakness was their lack of faith in God. Had he not proven the greatness of his power? Had he not proven the greatness of his love for them? Had he not proven his faithfulness to fulfill his promises? It was as if the sight of Pharaoh's army erased all memory of God's wondrous, miraculous works.

Had they done anything to convince Pharaoh to let them go? No. God had done it all before, and he would do it all now. They only had to be still and trust God. The battle was the Lord's. Nothing remained but to trust and obey. That is still true for God's people today.

DID YOU KNOW?

Philistines were called "people of the sea." They settled in Canaan approximately 1,100 years before Jesus was born. It is possible they originally came from the Island of Crete. The warlike Philistines became enemies of God's people.

VOCABULARY

Faith words:

To trust means to believe that God is good and always keeps his promises. People who trust God depend on him and obey him.

People:

Philistines were warlike people who lived east of Egypt, along the coast of Canaan.

Joseph was the son of Jacob, also known as Israel. Joseph became prime minister of Egypt and saved his family from famine.

The Angel of God was the Lord's messenger.

Places:

Pi Hahiroth was the last place the Israelites camped before they crossed the Red Sea. The exact location is unknown.

Terms:

A chariot was a vehicle with two or four wheels that was pulled by horses and used for battle.

STORYTELLING

Each week you will need the following items.

1. The travel bag from lesson one
2. The storage container (bag, basket, or box) with the items from the previous lessons

For today's story, you will need the following items.

3. Cotton balls
4. Matches
5. A mouse or rat trap
6. A comb
7. A broom

Before class:

1. Read Exodus 13:17-14:31.
2. Gather today's story items. Substitute a picture for any unavailable items.
3. Transfer all previous lesson items from the travel bag to the storage container. Place this beside the storytelling area.
4. Place today's story items inside the travel bag. Place the travel bag in the storytelling area.

Optional activity: Follow the leader

Tell the children to stand in a line, one behind the other. Choose a child to be the leader. Tell the children to watch carefully and mimic everything the leader does. The leader leads the group around the room. He or she uses different hand gestures, sounds, or means of travel for the children to imitate. For example, the leader walks with baby steps, large steps, or skips. End the game at the storytelling area.

Lesson review:

Ask a volunteer to select an item from the storage container and explain what it represented in a previous lesson.

Story time:

Read these instructions before you begin.

1. Tell the story in your own words. Remove each item from the bag as you illustrate a main point. Focus on the main points. If you are comfortable, include more details. If needed, use the script that is suggested.

2. As you tell the story, display each item in the order that it is listed. Place it where the children can see it.

3. After telling the story, place all the items inside the bag again.

4. To review the story, remove the first item. Ask a volunteer to tell what it represents. Display this item. Repeat this process until the story is retold.

5. Review the memory motion described below. Demonstrate this motion any time you mention what it represents.

6. Say, **We are continuing on our expedition to explore the book of Exodus. I packed our travel bag with tools that we will need. Today our journey begins with...** Unpack the items as you tell the story.

Main points in order:

1. Cotton balls and matches—Say, **The Israelites were free at last! The Lord led them by a pillar of cloud during the day and a pillar of fire by night. He did not lead them on the shortest route. Fierce warriors waited ahead. Instead, he guided them on a longer journey through the desert.**
2. A mouse or rat trap—Say, **Pharaoh changed his mind and chased the Israelites with his army. The desert was on one side. The Red Sea was on the other side, but the Egyptians were coming. The Israelites were trapped! They cried to Moses, "Why did you bring us here to die?" Moses replied, "Do not be afraid. Stand firm and you will see the deliverance the LORD will bring you today."**
3. A comb—Say, **The Lord sent a strong east wind. It blew all night long and parted the Red Sea.**
4. A broom—Say, **The Israelites walked on the dry floor of the Red Sea. Walls of water stood on their left and right. The Egyptians followed them. When the Israelites were safely across, the walls of water came crashing down. The Egyptians were swept into the sea and drowned.**
5. Memory motion—Ask the children to hold their hands up, elbows straight, with palms facing each other. This represents the space between the walls of water at the Red Sea. You may also invite the children to think of another motion. Say, **As I tell the story, do this motion when you hear what it represents.**
6. Say, **Now it is your turn to tell the story.** Return the items to the bag. Invite the children to take turns and choose an item from the bag without looking. Ask them to explain what it means or to review the memory motion. After all the items have been removed, ask the children to place them in the correct story order.

 BIBLICAL LESSON

Teaching tips:

As you lead the Bible study, emphasize these ideas.

- The Lord continually used his awesome power to protect the Israelites from new dangers.
- God told his people not to try to save themselves but to wait for him to act. When we face situations where there is nothing we can do, we must trust God and wait for his help.

Read the Scripture:

Read Exodus 13:17-14:31 aloud.

Discussion questions:

Discuss the story and ask the children the following questions. Remember that there might not be a right or wrong answer.

1. **Why did Pharaoh change his mind and pursue the Israelites?**
2. **What do you think it was like to be guided and protected by a pillar of cloud and a pillar of fire?**
3. Read Exodus 14:10. **What would you think or feel if you were an Israelite pursued by the Egyptians? Which of your recent experiences helps you to trust the Lord?**
4. **Imagine you are on the journey with the Israelites. Describe how you feel as you walk across the dry floor of the Red Sea, with the sand beneath your feet and the wall of water on both sides.**
5. **If you were a Philistine, what would you think when God guided the Israelites safely across the Red Sea and then destroyed Egypt's armies?**

Closing thoughts:

This is the thought that you want the children to remember.

Say, **God fought for His people and defeated the Egyptians at the Red Sea.**

The Israelites still faced big dangers. When the Egyptian army appeared, the Israelites panicked. They had forgotten the miracles the Lord had performed through Moses and Aaron. They would learn that God's power is not limited. He can carry out his plan regardless of how bad the situation appears. At the Red Sea, the Lord defeated the Egyptians once and for all.

What obstacles do you face? Do they scare you? Turn to God and trust him. Remember what he did in the past and wait for his help for your need.

 MEMORY VERSE PRACTICE

The LORD will fight for you; you need only to be still. –Exodus 14:14

See the "Memory Verse Activities" on pages 124-127 for suggestions to help the children to learn the memory verse.

ADDITIONAL ACTIVITIES

To learn more about ancient Egypt and the culture in which the Israelites lived, consider these options.

1. Research how much wind it would take to divide a body of water. If possible, use your research to develop a science project. Can science really explain or prove miracles? Why or why not?

2. Some people believe they have found chariot wheels in the Red Sea. Do an online search to see what you can discover. Do your findings match what the Bible says?

3. Create a graphic novel that tells the story of the Exodus. Don't worry if you're not artistic; use stick figures. At the end of your novel, add a conclusion to show what you, personally, learned from this story.

Red Sea Race

You will need:

- A backpack
- An adult-size shirt
- Chairs
- String
- A watch with a second hand

Prepare: On one side of your room, place the chairs and string in a straight line to make a narrow path. Place the shirt and backpack at the beginning of the path.

Say, **The Israelites quickly gathered their belongings and carried everything they owned across the floor of the Red Sea. They did this because the Egyptians chased them. This path is our version of the Red Sea.** Tell the children that each child will put on the shirt, pick up the backpack, and race through the path of your "Red Sea." You will record how long it takes for each child to complete the task. Afterward say, **Imagine that you were an Israelite at the Red Sea. What did you think when you saw that the Egyptians were chasing you? Did you think that escape was possible? Why, or why not?**

Team option: If you have a large number of children, duplicate the supplies that you need and make two "Red Sea" courses. Place children into teams to race against each other.

ACTIVITY FOR OLDER CHILDREN

Say, **The Israelites were trapped between the Red Sea and Pharaoh's army.** Ask, **Have you ever been in a situation where you felt trapped and helpless to change your circumstances? How did that affect you? What did you do?**

Share a personal story of a time when you needed to wait for God to help you with a difficult situation.

Say, **God told the Israelites to wait on him for a solution. Sometimes, this is what God wants us to do. When you feel anxious, remember that God is with you. He is powerful. Patiently rely on him, and he will provide a way to handle your problems.** Ask the students to discuss a difficult situation they might face. Then lead in a closing prayer and ask God for faith to trust him in difficult situations.

Bible Studies for Children: Exodus
Lesson 11

PRACTICE FOR BIBLE QUIZ

See the section "Review Questions" on pages 128-167 for the red and the blue practice questions for this lesson.

LESSON 12

BUT WHAT ABOUT ME?

EXODUS 16:1-31; 17:1-7

MEMORY VERSE

Who among the gods is like you, LORD? Who is like you—majestic in holiness, awesome in glory, working wonders?

Exodus 15:11

TRUTHS ABOUT GOD

This lesson will teach the following truths about God. The asterisk * indicates the primary truth that you should teach to the children.

* * God supplied the Israelites' needs.
* God wants people to trust him and to obey him.
* God can use ordinary things in an extraordinary way.

LESSON FOCUS AND SUMMARY

In this study, the children will learn that God wants people to know that he is faithful, to trust him, and to obey him.

1. Every time the Israelites faced a new problem, they grumbled and complained.
2. When the Israelites needed food, the Lord provided special bread called manna.
3. When the Lord provided the manna, he tested his people to see if they would obey his directions.
4. The Israelites complained about not having any water. The Lord provided water.

 ## BIBLICAL BACKGROUND

After God defeated Pharaoh's army, the issues of daily life, food, and water became the most pressing concerns. The Israelites' response to life's everyday challenges tested their faith and revealed the level of their trust in God.

When the Israelites became hungry and thirsty, they grumbled and complained. They became angry, impatient, and ungrateful. They were resentful and disrespectful toward Moses, Aaron, and God. They said that their lives as Pharaoh's slaves were better than living free under Moses and Aaron's leadership.

God mercifully refrained from punishing them. Instead, he miraculously provided quail and manna to eat. He provided water from a rock for them to drink. God proved that he would provide for their needs and that he was faithful. However, the Israelites continued to grumble, complain, and disobey. Instead of trusting God, the people trusted in their own thoughts and feelings. They were unfaithful toward God in response to God's faithfulness.

DID YOU KNOW?

According to the Bible, this is the only time manna, the bread from heaven, existed.

VOCABULARY

Faith words:

The Sabbath is the day God set aside for rest, worship, and doing good. At this point the Lord had only told the people to rest on the Sabbath. Later, he added the direction about worship. In Matthew 12:12, Jesus gives the direction to do good.

Places:

The Desert of Sin is a desert area southeast of Egypt and across the Red Sea.

Massah Meribah is the name Moses gave to the place where the Lord provided water from the rock. Massah means testing. Meribah means quarreling.

Terms:

Manna is the special bread God provided for the Israelites in the desert. Manna means, "What is it?"

Quail is a small plump bird with gray or brown feathers.

Maggots are larvae or worms that grow from fly eggs. We find maggots in rotten food.

The Glory of the Lord means the Lord's presence.

STORYTELLING

Each week you will need the following items.

1. The travel bag from lesson one
2. The storage container (bag, basket, or box) with the items from the previous lessons

For today's story, you will need the following items.

3. Construction paper and marker
4. Frosted Flakes cereal, thin crackers, or pita
5. Sealed bottle(s) of water
6. A small pillow

Before class:

1. Read Exodus 16:1-31; 17:1-7.
2. Print these words and phrases on the paper: moan, groan, grumble, whine, complain, and also the phrases "If only we had died in Egypt!" and "Why did you bring us out here to die?"
3. Gather today's story items. Substitute a picture for any unavailable items.
4. Transfer all previous lesson items from the travel bag to the storage container. Place this beside the storytelling area.
5. Place today's story items inside the travel bag. Place the travel bag in the storytelling area.

Optional activity: Follow the leader

Tell the children to stand in a line, one behind the other. Choose a child to be the leader. Tell the children to watch carefully and mimic everything the leader does. The leader leads the group around the room. He or she uses different hand gestures, sounds, or means of travel for the children to imitate. For example, the leader walks with baby steps, large steps, or skips. End the game at the storytelling area.

Lesson review:

Ask a volunteer to select an item from the storage container and explain what it represented in a previous lesson.

Story time:

Read these instructions before you begin.

1. Tell the story in your own words. Remove each item from the bag as you illustrate a main point. Focus on the main points. If you are comfortable, include more details. If needed, use the script that is suggested.

2. As you tell the story, display each item in the order that it is listed. Place it where the children can see it.

3. After telling the story, place all the items inside the bag again.

4. To review the story, remove the first item. Ask a volunteer to tell what it represents. Display this item. Repeat this process until the story is retold.

5. Review the memory motion described below. Demonstrate this motion any time you mention what it represents.

6. Say, **We are continuing on our expedition to explore the book of Exodus. I packed our travel bag with tools that we will need. Today our journey begins with...** Unpack the items as you tell the story.

Main points in order:

1. Word or phrase signs—Hand each sign to a different child. Afterward, ask each child to read their sign out loud. Say, **As they traveled through the desert, the Israelites' food was depleted. The people grumbled and complained to Moses. "If only we had died in Egypt," they said. "We had lots of food there. You have brought us into the desert to starve."**

2. Frosted Flakes—Say, **So, the Lord provided a new kind of food. Every morning, the ground was covered with thin flakes that looked like frost. The Israelites did not know what it was, so they named it manna, which means "What is it?"**

3. Small pillow—Say, **God tested the people to see if they would obey him. God said that five days a week they were to gather only enough manna to eat that day. They were not to keep any overnight. But on the sixth day, they were to gather enough for that day and the seventh day, which was the Sabbath. On the seventh day, the people were to rest and not to work. Some people obeyed God. Others did not obey.**

4. Sealed bottle of water—Say, **The Israelites' water was almost gone. They complained again. The Lord told Moses to strike a rock, and water poured out for the people to drink.**

5. Memory motion—Ask the children to rub their stomachs with their hands to represent that God gave the Israelites manna and water. You may also invite the children to think of another motion. Say, **As I tell the story, do this motion when you hear what it represents.**

6. Say, **Now it is your turn to tell the story.** Return the items to the bag. Invite the children to take turns and choose an item from the bag without looking. Ask them to explain what it means or to review the memory motion. After all the items have been removed, ask the children to place them in the correct story order.

📖 BIBLICAL LESSON

Teaching tips:

As you lead the Bible study, emphasize these ideas.

- Despite all the Lord had done for them, the Israelites still did not respond with either trust or obedience.
- When the Israelites complained about Moses and Aaron, they actually complained about God.

Read the Scripture:

Read Exodus 16:1-31 and 17:1-7 aloud.

Discussion questions:

Discuss the story and ask the children the following questions. Remember that there might not be a right or wrong answer.

1. **Was it appropriate for the Israelites to complain that they had no food or water? Why or why not?**
2. **The Israelites ran out of food and water. How did they respond? Why do you think they responded this way?**
3. **Imagine you were an Israelite and your food falls from the sky. What would you think, say, and do the first time you saw manna?**
4. **Why did the Lord want the people to gather extra food on the sixth day? Why was this command a blessing for them?**
5. **Do you think that the Israelites passed or failed the tests God gave them in the desert? Why or why not?**

Closing thoughts:

This is the thought you want the children to remember.

Say, **God supplied the Israelites' needs.**

It was not wrong for the Israelites to want food and water; everyone needs these to live and to be healthy. It was a problem that they did not trust God to care for these needs. Instead, they angrily grumbled and complained. They forgot that in the past, the Lord provided. Also, they were careless and did not always obey Him. Some people kept manna overnight, and some did not rest on the Sabbath.

You can learn from the Israelites mistakes. Trust in God's goodness, ask for his help, and obey him completely. God loves you. He is wise. He provides for your needs.

💬 MEMORY VERSE PRACTICE

Who among the gods is like you, LORD? Who is like you—majestic in holiness, awesome in glory, working wonders? –Exodus 15:11

See the "Memory Verse Activities" on pages 124-127 for suggestions to help the children to learn the memory verse.

Bible Studies for Children: Exodus
Lesson 12

ADDITIONAL ACTIVITIES

To learn more about ancient Egypt and the culture in which the Israelites lived, consider these options.

1. Read about the battle with the Amalekites in Exodus 17:8-16. Notice the mention of Joshua.
2. Make your own version of manna cakes. Do an online search of rice cake recipes. Make some for your class, or let the class make them.
3. How important is the concept of the Sabbath to the Lord? Help children research a Bible concordance to see how many times and ways the Bible mentions the Sabbath. Have them record their findings creatively.

"I am Thirsty!" a review activity

You will need:

- Crackers
- Water
- Drinking cups

Give the children the crackers to eat while you tell the story. After the story, ask if they enjoyed the crackers. Ask the children, **Did the crackers make you thirsty?** Tell the children, **The Israelites were in the desert where there was no water.** Ask the children, **If you were hot and thirsty and didn't see any water around, what would you do?** Discuss their responses. Offer the water to the children. Say, **You are thirsty after eating crackers. Can you imagine how thirsty the Israelites became in a hot, dry desert? Today we discovered what happened when the Israelites had no water in the desert.**

ACTIVITY FOR OLDER CHILDREN

Discuss these questions with the students.

- **What were God's rules about the manna?**
- **Were they hard or easy to obey? Explain.**
- **What happened when some of the people disobeyed?**
- **Why do you think God said to collect only enough manna for one day?**
- **What are some situations today when you have to rely on God for your needs?**
- **How can someone show that he or she relies on God instead of himself or herself?**

Talk with the students about what it means to rely on God. Share a personal story about a difficult situation when you had to trust God and he provided.

Say, **Some of you may struggle with difficult circumstances and you need God's help. It was difficult for the Israelites to trust God. It may be difficult for you to rely on God.** Invite the students to write a letter to God about the difficult situations they face. Invite them to also thank God for providing for their needs.

Pray and ask God to help the students to trust him to provide for their needs.

PRACTICE FOR BIBLE QUIZ

See the section "Review Questions" on pages 128-167 for the red and the blue practice questions for this lesson.

LESSON 13

A FIERY BLAZE OF GLORY

EXODUS 19:1-25

MEMORY VERSE

Now if you obey me fully and keep my covenant, then out of all nations you will be my treasured possession. Although the whole earth is mine, you will be for me a kingdom of priests and a holy nation.

Exodus 19:5-6

TRUTHS ABOUT GOD

This lesson will teach the following truths about God. The asterisk * indicates the primary truth that you should teach to the children.

- * God revealed his holiness and his power at Mount Sinai.
- God's power is greater than anyone or anything.
- God is holy, so those who have a relationship with him must respect him and obey him.

LESSON FOCUS AND SUMMARY

In this study, the children will learn that God revealed his holiness and power on Mt. Sinai and that he desires to make Israel his holy people.

1. After three months, God's people reached Mount Sinai.
2. The Lord desired to make the Israelites his treasured possession if they would obey him.
3. The Lord descended onto the mountain in fire.
4. Moses and Aaron went up the mountain to meet with God on behalf of the people.

 ## BIBLICAL BACKGROUND

The first part of Israel's journey was over. With smoke and fire, Yahweh led them to the place of the burning bush. This was where God first met with Moses. The Lord offered to enter into a covenant with the Israelites. Their acceptance of that covenant changed their relationship with God forever.

The new covenant brought new blessings and responsibilities. Israel became Yahweh's treasured possession. Through this new relationship, they could know him better and love him more. They would become a kingdom of priests. They would reflect God's character in their lives and share his teaching with the entire world. They had been set free, and they would now help to set the world free. Israel would forever be different because of their relationship with Yahweh. Through this covenant nation of Israel, the Savior of the world, Jesus Christ, would come to redeem all people.

Bible Studies for Children: Exodus
Lesson 13

 DID YOU KNOW?

In the Old Testament, a priest interceded, or stood between, the people and God. The priest spoke to God for the people. He also spoke to the people for God. In the New Testament, we learn that Jesus became our priest and intercessor. Because Jesus was human for a time, he understands how we feel. Because he is also God, when we are near to Jesus, we are close to God.

 VOCABULARY

Faith words:

A covenant is a very important agreement. It involves serious promises. In the covenant God made with the Israelites, he promised to love, bless, and protect them. They promised to love, worship, and obey him. God's covenants offer us a loving relationship with him.

People:

A priest is a person who speaks to God for people and gives people God's response. In Exodus, priests helped people to have a relationship with God.

Places:

Mount Sinai is a mountain in the desert.

Terms:

To consecrate means to make something or someone holy, or to dedicate an object or a person to serve only God.

STORYTELLING

Each week you will need the following items.

1. The travel bag from lesson one
2. The storage container (bag, basket, or box) with the items from the previous lessons

For today's story, you will need the following items.

3. A phone
4. A feather
5. Large bills of play money
6. A "Keep Out" sign (or make one out of construction paper)

Before class:

1. Read Exodus 19:1-25.
2. Gather today's story items. Substitute a picture for any unavailable items.
3. Transfer all previous lesson items from the travel bag to the storage container. Place this beside the storytelling area.
4. Place today's story items inside the travel bag. Place the travel bag in the storytelling area.

Optional activity: Follow the leader

Tell the children to stand in a line, one behind the other. Choose a child to be the leader. Tell the children to watch carefully and mimic everything the leader does. The leader leads the group around the room. He or she uses different hand gestures, sounds, or means of travel for the children to imitate. For example, the leader walks with baby steps, large steps, or skips. End the game at the storytelling area.

Lesson review:

Ask a volunteer to select an item from the storage container and explain what it represented in a previous lesson.

Story time:

Read these instructions before you begin.

1. Tell the story in your own words. Remove each item from the bag as you illustrate a main point. Focus on the main points. If you are comfortable, include more details. If needed, use the script that is suggested.

2. As you tell the story, display each item in the order that it is listed. Place it where the children can see it.

3. After telling the story, place all the items inside the bag again.

4. To review the story, remove the first item. Ask a volunteer to tell what it represents. Display this item. Repeat this process until the story is retold.

5. Review the memory motion described below. Demonstrate this motion any time you mention what it represents.

6. Say, **We are continuing on our expedition to explore the book of Exodus. I packed our travel bag with tools that we will need. Today our journey begins with...** Unpack the items as you tell the story.

Main points in order:

1. A phone—Say, **God's people finally arrived at Mount Sinai. Moses went up to the mountain. This was the same place where God spoke to him through the burning bush. God called to Moses and gave him a message for the Israelites.**

2. A feather—Say, **God reminded Moses of what he had done for the Israelites. He said, "You yourselves have seen what I did to Egypt and how I carried you on eagles' wings and brought you to myself"** (19:4).

3. Play money—Say, **God had saved the Israelites. He wanted to make them his treasured possession if they would obey his commands and keep his covenant. When Moses gave this message to the Israelites, they said, "We will do everything the LORD has said."**

4. A "Keep Out" sign—Say, **Three days later, clouds covered Mount Sinai. Thunder rumbled. Lightning flashed. The sound of a loud trumpet blasted. God came down on the mountain in fire. Moses went to the top of the mountain. God warned him that the people must not try to come up the mountain or they would die.**

5. Memory motion—Tell the children to hold their hands over their heads and touch their fingertips together to indicate that Moses went up on Mount Sinai. You may also invite the children to think of another motion. Say, **As I tell the story, do this motion when you hear what it represents.**

6. Say, **Now it is your turn to tell the story.** Return the items to the bag. Invite the children to take turns and choose an item from the bag without looking. Ask them to explain what it means or to review the memory motion. After all the items have been removed, ask the children to place them in the correct story order.

BIBLICAL LESSON

Teaching tips:

As you lead the Bible study, emphasize these ideas.

- Recognize that the holiness of God was shown on Mount Sinai.
- It was important for people to respect the holiness of God and carefully prepare before they approached him.
- In the Old Testament, God seemed unapproachable when he first taught the Israelites how to honor and to respect him as their only God. God desired a healthy relationship with his people. To make this possible, he was willing to patiently teach them.

Read the Scripture:

Read Exodus 19:1-25 aloud.

Discussion questions:

Discuss the story and ask the children the following questions. Remember that there might not be a right or wrong answer.

1. Read Exodus 19:4-5 aloud. **Why do you think the Lord said this to the Israelites?**
2. **How would you respond after hearing the Lord's command to be obedient?**
3. **The Israelites said they would do everything the Lord commanded. The remainder of the Old Testament tells the story of how well they kept their promise. Do you think they will keep it? Why or why not?**
4. **How does the description of the Lord descending on the mountain affect your image of God?**
5. **In Exodus 19:23, the Lord commands Moses to set apart the mountain as holy. What place have we set apart as a holy place to honor God?**

Closing thoughts:

This is the thought you want your students to remember.

Say, **God established his holiness and power at Mount Sinai.**

A mountain shaking! Thunder! Lightning! A loud trumpet! God is holy and powerful! We must not approach him carelessly. We also know that God loves people. So how do we get close to him?

Jesus, God's Son, made it possible for us to know God as Father. Knowing about God's holiness and power teaches us to respect him. Jesus makes it possible for us to approach God and enjoy a personal relationship with him. If you know Jesus as your Savior, thank him for what he did for you. If you don't, talk to your leader about who Jesus is and how to have a relationship with him.

MEMORY VERSE PRACTICE

Now if you obey me fully and keep my covenant, then out of all nations you will be my treasured possession. Although the whole earth is mine, you will be for me a kingdom of priests and a holy nation. –Exodus 19:5-6

See the "Memory Verse Activities" on pages 124-127 for suggestions to help the children to learn the memory verse.

ADDITIONAL ACTIVITIES

To learn more about ancient Egypt and the culture in which the Israelites lived, consider these options.

1. Read Exodus 18:13-27 to learn about the role of judges in Israel. **Who was the first judge? What was his job? How did the other judges get their jobs? Whose suggestion was it?**

2. Read Exodus 17:8-16. **What important person is mentioned for the first time? What did he do? Watch him carefully. He will become more and more important as the journey continues.**

3. **What covenants did the Lord make before this one?** Review the stories of Noah and Abraham in Genesis to see what these covenants were about.

4. Let students draw pictures to illustrate the story, then retell the story through their pictures.

Messenger Moses

You will need:

- Pieces of paper
- Envelopes
- Markers
- Small treats

With a marker, write a short message to one of the children. The message should be a simple instruction. For example, "Put your hand on your head" or "Clap your hands." Write one of the children's names on an envelope, and place the message inside. Choose another child to deliver the message to the child whose name is on the envelope. Ask the child to read the message to the class. See if the rest of the children follow the instructions or not. If some do not, use their reluctance as a teaching moment. Discuss with the children that some of the Israelites did not obey God's message when Moses delivered it.

ACTIVITY FOR OLDER CHILDREN

1. Ask students to draw a picture of something powerful but dangerous that they fear and respect. Discuss the drawings. Ask the students, **Why do you fear and respect this?** Say, **When we understand how powerful something is, we have an appropriate, respectful attitude about it. Rules for what to do around dangerous things are meant to keep us safe. Why is it good to display respectful fear for certain things? God gave us rules for following him. God does not want us to be afraid of him, but he does want us to respect him.**

2. Option: Ask a student to act out when Moses met God on Mount Sinai. Then proceed with the discussion about fear and respect.

PRACTICE FOR BIBLE QUIZ

See the section "Review Questions" on pages 128-167 for the red and the blue practice questions for this lesson.

LESSON 14

R-E-S-P-E-C-T!
EXODUS 20:1-21

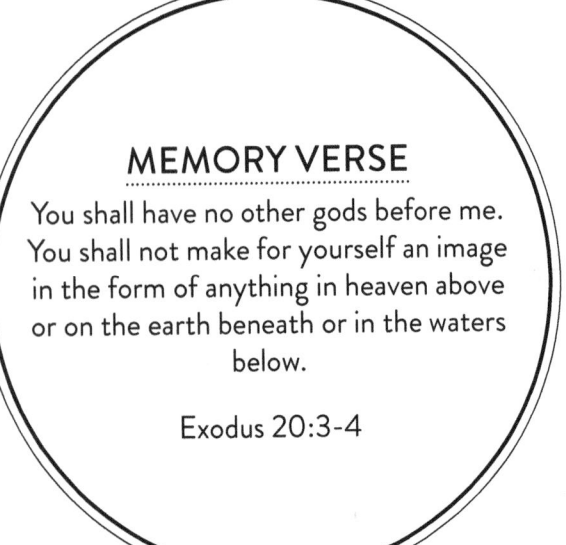

MEMORY VERSE

You shall have no other gods before me. You shall not make for yourself an image in the form of anything in heaven above or on the earth beneath or in the waters below.

Exodus 20:3-4

TRUTHS ABOUT GOD

This lesson will teach the following truths about God. The asterisk * indicates the primary truth that you should teach to the children.

* * God gave the Israelites his commands so that they could live in a covenant relationship with him.
* God wants his people to respect and obey him.
* God wants his people to treat each other well.

LESSON FOCUS AND SUMMARY

In this study, the children will learn that God provided his people the Ten Commandments so that they could live in right relationship with him and with each other.

1. God personally spoke to the Israelites.
2. God gave the Israelites commandments to help them live rightly with him and with each other.
3. The Israelites were afraid when they saw God's power.
4. Only Moses approached God.

 ## BIBLICAL BACKGROUND

Yahweh showed grace to Israel by defeating Pharaoh and his gods and rescuing the Israelites from slavery. He provided them with food and water and invited them into a covenant relationship with him. In a covenant, both parties had responsibilities to each other. Now they needed to clearly understand their responsibilities. They needed to know what God expected of them. It was time to receive God's Law, the Ten Commandments.

Yahweh wanted a holy people that he could bless. He wanted his people to be a blessing to all creation. But the Israelites had only known the teachings of Pharaoh and the Egyptians. They needed to replace their old ways of thinking and acting and to learn God's ways.

So Yahweh came near to the people and spoke. When they realized how completely holy and powerful God was, they were afraid. Moses told them that some of their fear was good. It was better to be careful and wisely keep the covenant than to be careless and foolishly break the covenant. Their respect and awe would keep them from sin.

DID YOU KNOW?

Many Jews continue to live by Exodus 16:29. Some live close enough to walk to their synagogues on the Sabbath. They do not drive on the Sabbath. Others do not even go out of their houses.

 VOCABULARY

Faith words:

A commandment is a law given by God that tells people how to live.

People:

A manservant or **a maidservant** was a trusted person who served the family with whom he or she lived.

An alien was a person who was not an Israelite.

Terms:

An idol is anything that is worshiped instead of God or loved more than God. Other nations worshiped idols and images. God's people were forbidden to make or worship them.

Jealous means to want someone to love only you. God is a jealous God because he wants us to love him more than anyone or anything.

To covet means to want something that belongs to someone else so much that a person is willing to disobey God to have it.

STORYTELLING

Each week you will need the following items.

1. The travel bag from lesson one
2. The storage container (bag, basket, or box) with the items from the previous lessons

For today's story, you will need the following items.

3. A paper with test questions
4. A ruler
5. A megaphone

Before class:

1. Read Exodus 20:1-21.
2. Gather today's story items. Substitute a picture for any unavailable items.
3. Transfer all previous lesson items from the travel bag to the storage container. Place this beside the storytelling area.
4. Place today's story items inside the travel bag. Place the travel bag in the storytelling area.
5. Print a test with common questions.

Optional activity: Follow the leader

Tell the children to stand in a line, one behind the other. Choose a child to be the leader. Tell the children to watch carefully and mimic everything the leader does. The leader leads the group around the room. He or she uses different hand gestures, sounds, or means of travel for the children to imitate. For example, the leader walks with baby steps, large steps, or skips. End the game at the storytelling area.

Lesson review:

Ask a volunteer to select an item from the storage container and explain what it represented in a previous lesson.

Story time:

Read these instructions before you begin.

1. Tell the story in your own words. Remove each item from the bag as you illustrate a main point. Focus on the main points. If you are comfortable, include more details. If needed, use the script that is suggested.

2. As you tell the story, display each item in the order that it is listed. Place it where the children can see it.

3. After telling the story, place all the items inside the bag again.

4. To review the story, remove the first item. Ask a volunteer to tell what it represents. Display this item. Repeat this process until the story is retold.

5. Review the memory motion described below. Demonstrate this motion any time you mention what it represents.

6. Say, **We are continuing on our expedition to explore the book of Exodus. I packed our travel bag with tools that we will need. Today our journey begins with…** Unpack the items as you tell the story.

Main Points:

1. A ruler—Say, **God gave the Israelites rules to tell them how to live. These were the Ten Commandments. These rules helped the Israelites to love, obey, and respect God, and to show love and respect to each other.**

2. A paper with test questions—Say, **God tested the Israelites. He wanted to know that they would remember he was their God and they were his people. He showed them his power so that they would fear and respect him.**

3. A megaphone—Say, **The people did not want God to speak to them because they feared him. Instead, they asked Moses to speak for God. So Moses went up and talked to God.**

4. Memory motion—Ask the children to hold up their hands with the ten fingers spread to indicate the Ten Commandments. You may also invite the children to think of another motion. Say, **As I tell the story, do this motion when you hear what it represents.**

5. Say, **Now it is your turn to tell the story.** Return the items to the bag. Invite the children to take turns and choose an item from the bag without looking. Ask them to explain what it means or to review the memory motion. After all the items have been removed, ask the children to place them in the correct story order.

BIBLICAL LESSON

Teaching tips:

As you lead the Bible study, emphasize these ideas.

- God did not give the Ten Commandments to make the Israelites' lives harder. God gave the commandments so that the Israelites could serve him and live well together.

- Do not over emphasize commandments that do not directly apply to the children in your group (adultery, murder). Instead, focus on applicable ones, such as honor your father and mother.

Read the Scripture:

Read Exodus 20:1-21 aloud.

Discussion questions:

Discuss the story and ask the children the following questions. Remember that there might not be a right or wrong answer.

1. **If we choose to obey God, what are some ways we must not act? What are ways we can begin to act?**
2. **What are some specific things that we should do that are not found in the Ten Commandments? What are some specific things that we should not do that are not addressed in the Ten Commandments? How does God help us to know that we should or should not do these things?**
3. **Choose one of the Ten Commandments. What are two or three ways you can obey the commandment.**
4. **The first four commandments tell us how to treat God. The last six commandments tell us how to treat others. Does the way we treat God affect how we treat others? Explain.**
5. **Why do you think the Israelites were afraid to approach God? If you were an Israelite, would you feel afraid to approach God? Why or why not?**

Closing thoughts:

This is the thought you want the children to remember.

Say, **God gave the Israelites his covenant commands.**

Everywhere we go there are rules to help us know how to act. At the swimming pool, we should not run. At the library, we should be quiet. At home, we should go to bed when it is time.

God gave us rules so that we could live in a loving, covenant relationship with him. God loves us and wants us to love him and each other. We show love when we honor and respect God and others. When we follow the Ten Commandments in our daily life, we show the world what God is like. When we all follow his rules, our lives together are a little easier and a lot more fun!

MEMORY VERSE PRACTICE

You shall have no other gods before me. You shall not make for yourself an image in the form of anything in heaven above or on the earth beneath or in the waters below. –Exodus 20:3-4

See the "Memory Verse Activities" on pages 124-127 for suggestions to help the children to learn the memory verse.

 # ADDITIONAL ACTIVITIES

To learn more about ancient Egypt and the culture in which the Israelites lived, consider these options.

1. Create a song, poem, or rhythmic pattern to help memorize the Ten Commandments. Consider a piggyback song (new words to a

familiar tune, such as "Row, Row, Row Your Boat.")

2. Study current events. Do people in your community recognize and follow the Ten Commandments? Are there people or groups who oppose seeing the Ten Commandments in public places? Make a display to show what you have discovered. Discuss this question: When people reject the Ten Commandments as guides for living, what guidelines do they use instead?

3. Make a poster listing ten ways people can show respect and honor to God.

Spinning Out of Control

You will need:

- Toy tops that spin (One for each child, if possible)
- Craft sticks (four sticks for each child, if possible)
- A table

Prepare: Place the toy tops and the craft sticks on the table in two different places.

1. Ask the children to spin their tops on the table.

2. Give each child four craft sticks and ask them to arrange them into a square shape.

3. Ask the children to spin their tops inside the square.

Option: You could demonstrate this activity for the children to watch and then discuss it together. Afterward, allow the children to try it, one at a time.

4. Discuss what happened to the top when it spun without being in the square. Did it fall off the table or bump into another top and cause it to stop working? How did the top spin when it was in the square?

Say, **Today we learned that God gave the Ten Commandments to help people know how to live in the way he created them to live. Without these commandments, people could live in a way that is not pleasing to God. This is similar to the square we created for the top. Without the appropriate boundary of the square, the top spun out of control. Sometimes a top fell off the table and could not spin. Sometimes it bumped into other tops. When that happened, neither top could spin. When we live our lives according to the boundaries of the Ten Commandments, we please God and treat others in the way we should. We enjoy life with God and each other.**

 ## ACTIVITY FOR OLDER CHILDREN

1. Bring three to five commonly used objects to class. For example, a hammer, a cell phone, a light bulb, a pair of scissors, a pencil. Hold up the hammer. Say, **I need to call my mother, but this will not work when I try to call her.** Hold it up to your ear as if to make a call. Ask, **What is wrong with this hammer? Why is it not working?** Do not wait for an answer. Repeat this scenario several more times with the other items and various mismatched tasked.

2. Discuss with the students why it is important to use these items in the way they were created to be used. Say, **You do not get the results you want or need if you use the wrong tool for the job.**

3. Ask the students why God gave the Ten Commandments to the people. Say, **The Ten Commandments help us to live in the way God created us to live. God wants us**

to become more like him by knowing him and obeying his instructions. Just as a hammer cannot be used to make a phone call, you will not fulfill God's purpose if you do not follow his directions. Discuss with the students what happens when we obey or disobey the commandments.

 ## PRACTICE FOR BIBLE QUIZ

See the section "Review Questions" on pages 128-167 for the red and the blue practice questions for this lesson.

LESSON 15

A MEAL TO SEAL THE DEAL
EXODUS 24:1-18

MEMORY VERSE

You shall not misuse the name of the LORD your God, for the LORD will not hold anyone guiltless who misuses his name. Remember the Sabbath day by keeping it holy.

Exodus 20:7-8

TRUTHS ABOUT GOD

This lesson will teach the following truths about God. The asterisk * indicates the primary truth that you should teach to the children.

* * God's people agreed to keep his covenant with them.
* God teaches people how to obey him.
* God gives us guidelines for how to worship him.

LESSON FOCUS AND SUMMARY

In this study, the children will learn that God taught his people how to live in a covenant relationship with him.

1. The people agreed to obey the Lord in a covenant ceremony.
2. The leaders of Israel went up the mountain to worship the Lord.
3. The leaders saw the God of Israel. Then, they ate a meal and enjoyed fellowship with God.
4. Moses and Joshua went up the mountain and stayed for forty days and nights.

 ## BIBLICAL BACKGROUND

In this lesson, we learn about the covenant ceremony between Yahweh and the Israelites. It began with building an altar and offering sacrifices. After the sacrifices, Moses read the Book of the Covenant to the people. Israel agreed to obey the Lord. Moses sprinkled the blood of the covenant upon the altar and upon the people to bind them to their vows. Finally, the Israelite elders joined Moses on the mountain and saw Yahweh. They shared a covenant meal to conclude the ceremony and affirm Israel's covenant with God.

Yahweh's appearance to the elders of Israel was very significant. The earthquakes, fire, lightening, dark clouds, trumpet blasts, and the Lord's warnings made the Israelites fear the mountain. But the elders were invited to see Yahweh and suffered no harm. What an amazing event it was when the Israelite elders shared a meal together in the very presence of Yahweh! This showed that God's grace and human reverence make it possible for God and his people to share a close relationship.

Bible Studies for Children: Exodus
Lesson 15

Download additional resources from *kidzfirstpublications.org*

DID YOU KNOW?

Through Old Testament sacrifices, God provided his people a way to fellowship with him, worship him, and find forgiveness for sin. After Jesus died on the cross, animal sacrifices were no longer needed.

VOCABULARY

Faith words:

An offering is a gift from people to God.

People:

Nadab and **Abihu** were Aaron's two oldest sons.

Joshua was Moses' assistant.

Terms:

The Book of the Covenant contained laws that God gave to Moses on Mount Sinai. Moses read this book to the Israelites.

An altar was a special pile of rocks consecrated to God. This is where the Israelites sacrificed animals and worshiped the Lord.

A burnt offering was an animal without defect that was sacrificed to God and burned completely. This offering showed that the person gave himself or herself completely to God.

A fellowship offering was an offering of an animal that had no defects or various kinds of bread. In this offering, people ate part of the sacrifice. This offering showed that the person wanted fellowship with God. Often this offering was given to thank God for a blessing.

STORYTELLING

Each week you will need the following items.

1. The travel bag from lesson one
2. The storage container (bag, basket, or box) with the items from the previous lessons

For today's story, you will need the following items.

3. Shaped candles for the numbers 7, 0, and 4
4. 12 small stones
5. A spray bottle
6. A lunchbox
7. A pair of spectacles or binoculars

Before class:

1. Read Exodus 24:1-18.

2. Gather today's story items. Substitute a picture for any unavailable items.

3. Transfer all previous lesson items from the travel bag to the storage container. Place this beside the storytelling area.

4. Place today's story items inside the travel bag. Place the travel bag in the storytelling area.

Optional activity: Follow the leader

Tell the children to stand in a line, one behind the other. Choose a child to be the leader. Tell the children to watch carefully and mimic everything the leader does. The leader leads the group around the room. He or she uses different hand gestures, sounds, or means of travel for the children to imitate. For example, the leader walks with baby steps, large steps, or skips. End the game at the storytelling area.

Lesson review:

Ask a volunteer to select an item from the storage container and explain what it represented in a previous lesson.

Story time:

Read these instructions before you begin.

1. Tell the story in your own words. Remove each item from the bag as you illustrate a main point. Focus on the main points. If you are comfortable, include more details. If needed, use the script that is suggested.

2. As you tell the story, display each item in the order that it is listed. Place it where the children can see it.

3. After telling the story, place all the items inside the bag again.

4. To review the story, remove the first item. Ask a volunteer to tell what it represents. Display this item. Repeat this process until the story is retold.

5. Review the memory motion described below. Demonstrate this motion any time you mention what it represents.

6. Say, **We are continuing on our expedition to explore the book of Exodus. I packed our travel bag with tools that we will need. Today our journey begins with...** Unpack the items as you tell the story.

Main points:

1. The number candles 7 and 0—Say, **God told Moses to bring Aaron, Nadab, Abihu, and seventy of the elders up Mount Sinai to see him and to worship him.**

2. The twelve small rocks—Say, **Before they left, Moses built an altar and placed twelve stone pillars at the base of the mountain. Each pillar represented one of the tribes of Israel. The young Israelite men sacrificed bulls on the altar.**

3. The spray bottle—Say, **Moses saved all of the blood from the sacrificed bulls. He sprinkled half of it on the altar and read the Book of the Covenant to the people. The people agreed to keep the covenant and obey all that the Lord had said. Then Moses sprinkled the rest of the blood on the people. He called this the blood of the covenant to remind them that keeping their covenant promise was a matter of life and death. This was a part of the covenant ceremony.**

4. The spectacles or binoculars—Say, **Moses, Aaron, Nadab, Abihu, and the 70 elders went up the mountain and saw the God of Israel.**

5. The lunchbox—Say, **God did not raise his hand against the Israelite leaders. After they saw God, they ate a meal on the mountain. This was a special fellowship with God.**

6. The number candles 4 and 0—Say, **Moses and Joshua went higher up the mountain. A cloud covered the mountain. When God called to him from the cloud, Moses went to the top of the mountain. To the Israelites below, the glory of the Lord looked like a fire on the mountain top. They wondered how Moses could survive inside a fire. Perhaps they had forgotten about how the burning bush burned but was not harmed. Moses stayed with God on the mountain for a long time: forty days and nights! Consider lighting the candles to represent the time Moses spent in God's presence.**

7. Memory motion—Ask children to shake their neighbor's hand. This motion represents that the Israelites promised to obey God's covenant. You may also invite the children to think of another motion. Say, **As I tell the story, do this motion when you hear what it represents.**

8. Say, **Now it is your turn to tell the story.** Return the items to the bag. Invite the children to take turns and choose an item from the bag without looking. Ask them to explain what it means or to review the memory motion. After all the items have been removed, ask the children to place them in the correct story order.

BIBLICAL LESSON

Teaching tips:

As you lead the Bible study, emphasize these ideas.

- Point out the differences between the Old Testament sacrificial worship and how we worship the Lord today.
- Explain that the life, death, and resurrection of Jesus changed everything. When Jesus sacrificed his life for our sins, animal sacrifices were no longer needed.

Read the Scripture:

Read Exodus 24:1-18 aloud.

Discussion questions:

Discuss the story and ask the children the following questions. Remember that there might not be a right or wrong answer.

1. Read Exodus 24:3. **Imagine you were an Israelite. How would you respond to the Lord after Moses shared God's words and laws?**
2. Read Exodus 24:7. **Do you think it was easy for the Israelites to respond with this promise to the Lord?**
3. **Moses wrote down God's law and commands. Where can we find God's written instructions for our lives?**
4. **Have you ever thought that God was telling you to do something? How did you respond?**
5. **How does God speak to his people today?**

Closing thought:

This is the thought you want your students to remember.

Say, **All of God's people agreed to keep the covenant and said, "Everything the Lord has said we will do"** (24:3). **The Israelites had suffered in Egypt. They cried out to the Lord, and now they were free, safe, and ready to serve the Lord. God answered their prayers and met all of their needs. But a covenant contains two parts. God promised to bless and protect the Israelites, and they promised to serve him and obey him. The Israelites were about to find out that it's easier to make promises than it is to keep them. Have you found that to be true for you?**

 ## MEMORY VERSE PRACTICE

You shall not misuse the name of the LORD your God, for the LORD will not hold anyone guiltless who misuses his name. Remember the Sabbath day by keeping it holy. –Exodus 20:7-8

See the "Memory Verse Activities" on pages 124-127 for suggestions to help the children to learn the memory verse.

Bible Studies for Children: Exodus
Lesson 15

ADDITIONAL ACTIVITIES

To learn more about ancient Egypt and the culture in which the Israelites lived, consider these options.

1. Read Leviticus 1:1-17, 3:1-17, 6:8-13, and 7:11-21 to learn about burnt offerings and fellowship offerings. Make a chart of the offering name, what was sacrificed, how it was done, and what it represented.

2. Draw a picture of Moses and the elders on the mountain with the Lord appearing to them. Refer to Exodus 24:9-11.

3. Create a papier-mâché model of what the Israelite camp and the mountain of God may have looked like. Create the twelve pillars (24:4), an altar (24:5), and the mountain. Save room to add the Tabernacle found in Lesson 17.

The Waiting Game

You will need:

- A small snack
- Water
- Drinking cups
- Napkins
- A helper

Serve the snack to the children. While they eat, whisper to the helper. Tell jokes or funny stories to the helper. Speak loud enough so that the class will notice the laughter, but only hear small parts of the conversation. After a few minutes, tell all the children the funny stories. Ask the children, **How did you feel when you didn't know what we said to each other? Were you curious? Did you feel jealous? When the elders went up on Mount Sinai, the rest of the Israelites had to wait before they would find out what happened. In our next lesson, we will learn what happened while the Israelites waited.**

Activity for Older Children:

You will need:

- A variety of bite-sized fruit or cheese
- Small cups
- Toothpicks

Prepare before class: Put the snack bites in paper cups, one for each student. Each cup should also be paired with a toothpick and given to each student.

Group the students in pairs. Ask one student to close his or her eyes while the other uses a toothpick to feed him or her a piece of food. After the cup is empty, have the partners change roles.

Ask the students how it felt to depend on someone else to provide something they wanted. Were they more interested in giving or receiving? Say, **Covenants involve mutual promises. God promises to bless and protect us, and we promise to trust and obey. Are we as eager to trust and obey as we are to be blessed and protected?** Discuss what this means.

PRACTICE FOR BIBLE QUIZ

See the section "Review Questions" on pages 128-167 for the red and the blue practice questions for this lesson.

LESSON 16

I WISH TO DWELL AMONG YOU
EXODUS 25:1-22

MEMORY VERSE

Honor your father and your mother, so that you may live long in the land the LORD your God is giving you.

Exodus 20:12

TRUTHS ABOUT GOD

This lesson will teach the following truths about God. The asterisk * indicates the primary truth that you should teach to the children.

* God gave instructions for his dwelling place.
- God desires to be close to his people.
- God does not force people to serve him or give to him.

LESSON FOCUS AND SUMMARY

In this study, the children will learn that God desired a dwelling place so that he could live among his people.

1. The Lord planned to live among the Israelites.
2. People were to bring valuable items to build his Tabernacle (dwelling place).
3. The Lord would accept offerings from people who gave willingly.
4. The Lord gave instructions on how to build the Ark of the Covenant.

 ## BIBLICAL BACKGROUND

After the covenant ceremony, Moses climbed the mountain to meet with Yahweh. There he received the tablets of stone. These tablets contained the laws and were written by Yahweh himself. God planned to live among the Israelites. God's instructions to prepare for his presence revealed much about God and what he expected from his covenant people.

God would actually dwell among his people! This meant that the Lord intended to close the gap that sin created between him and his covenant people. His presence would help the Israelites become more holy and assure them of his care and protection. God chose to make his presence known in the Tabernacle through the Ark of the Covenant.

As he drew nearer to Israel, Yahweh did not relax his standards or increase his tolerance for sin. Instead, his presence increased Israel's responsibilities. The rules of proper worship were intended to teach them about God. In the process, it would also increase their love and appreciation for God. It was important for God to be with his people. It was equally important that they greatly respect him and willingly serve him.

DID YOU KNOW?

The gold and silver the Israelites gave was the same gold and silver the Egyptians gave to them when they left Egypt.

VOCABULARY

Faith words:

To sacrifice means to give up something important or to do something difficult in order to please God. It can also mean a special gift given to God.

Terms:

Acacia wood is an orange-brown wood from a large, thorny tree. The wood is hard and not easily destroyed by insects.

An ephod is a special vest that the high priest wore when he served at the altar.

The Tabernacle was the tent which served as the Israelites' place of worship. God met with his people at the Tabernacle as they worshiped him.

Cherubim or a **cherub** were angels who often served as messengers for God.

A cubit was a unit of measurement in the Bible. A cubit was approximately forty-five centimeters (eighteen inches) long.

STORYTELLING

Each week you will need the following items.

1. The travel bag from lesson one
2. The storage container (bag, basket, or box) with the items from the previous lessons

For today's story, you will need the following items.

3. An offering envelope or plate
4. Directions to a game
5. A small toy chest or keepsake box
6. An angel and lion figurine or pictures of these two things

Before class:

1. Read Exodus 25:1-22.
2. Gather today's story items. Substitute a picture for any unavailable items.

3. Transfer all previous lesson items from the travel bag to the storage container. Place this beside the storytelling area.
4. Place today's story items inside the travel bag. Place the travel bag in the storytelling area.

Optional activity: Follow the leader

Tell the children to stand in a line, one behind the other. Choose a child to be the leader. Tell the children to watch carefully and mimic everything the leader does. The leader leads the group around the room. He or she uses different hand gestures, sounds, or means of travel for the children to imitate. For example, the leader walks with baby steps, large steps, or skips. End the game at the storytelling area.

Lesson review:

Ask a volunteer to select an item from the storage container and explain what it represented in a previous lesson.

Story time:

Read these instructions before you begin.

1. Tell the story in your own words. Remove each item from the bag as you illustrate a main point. Focus on the main points. If you are comfortable, include more details. If needed, use the script that is suggested.

2. As you tell the story, display each item in the order that it is listed. Place it where the children can see it.

3. After telling the story, place all the items inside the bag again.

4. To review the story, remove the first item. Ask a volunteer to tell what it represents. Display this item. Repeat this process until the story is retold.

5. Review the memory motion described below. Demonstrate this motion any time you mention what it represents.

6. Say, **We are continuing on our expedition to explore the book of Exodus. I packed our travel bag with tools that we will need. Today our journey begins with...** Unpack the items as you tell the story.

Main points in order:

1. An offering envelope or plate—Say, **God told Moses to take an offering from all the men whose hearts prompted them to give. God asked them to give precious metals, such as gold and silver, beautiful cloth, skins, and precious stones. They used the offerings to build the Tabernacle.**

2. Game directions—Say, **God gave Moses detailed directions to follow when he built the Tabernacle and the furnishings.**

3. A toy chest—Say, **God told Moses to build the Ark of the Covenant. But this ark was not a floating boat. Instead, it was a box that would hold important items from the Israelites' history and their worship. One of these items was called the Covenant. This was the stone tablet on which the Ten Commandments were written.**

4. An angel and lion figure or pictures—Say, **The people made two cherubim to place on top of the ark. No one knows what cherubim look like. Some people think they looked like a lion with wings.**

5. Memory motion—Ask the children to move one fist forward and backward, as if sawing wood to build the Ark of the Covenant. You may also invite the children to think of another motion. Say, **As I tell the story, do this motion when you hear what it represents.**

6. Say, **Now it is your turn to tell the story.** Return the items to the bag. Invite the children to take turns and choose an item from the bag without looking. Ask them to explain what it means or to review the memory motion. After all the items have been removed, ask the children to place them in the correct story order.

BIBLICAL LESSON

Teaching tips:

As you lead the Bible study, emphasize these ideas.

- The Lord wanted to live among his people. He wanted to be close to them.
- The list of things the Lord wanted for his Tabernacle may seem odd to us, but it was a list of very precious and valuable things to the Israelites. It was a big sacrifice for an Israelite to give to help to build the Tabernacle of the Lord.

Read the Scripture:

Read Exodus 25:1-22 aloud.

Discussion questions:

Discuss the story and ask the children the following questions. Remember that there might not be a right or wrong answer.

1. **Imagine you were an Israelite. How would you feel if you learned that the Lord wanted to live close to you in a special house?**
2. **What is your most valuable possession? Why is it so valuable to you?**
3. **On a scale of 1-10 (1=not at all difficult and 10=extremely difficult), how difficult would it be for you to give up your most valuable possessions to the Lord if he asked you for them?**
4. **God only wanted the gifts of the men whose hearts prompted them to give. What do you think would have happened if the Israelite men did not gladly give their offerings?**
5. **Why do you think it was so important for the Israelites to exactly follow the Lord's instructions for building the Tabernacle? How easy do you think it was for the Israelites to exactly follow the Lord's commands?**

Closing thoughts:

This is the thought you want your students to remember.

Say, **God gave instructions for his dwelling place.**

How can you serve God? Think about it! In this story, we learned that God wanted to live among his people. He wanted a closer relationship with the Israelites. He wanted them to build a house for him with their best treasures, but only if they willingly gave them. God gave specific directions for making the Tabernacle.

The Lord also desires to have a close relationship with you. You don't have to be perfect. God wants you to obey him because you love him with all your heart. God wants you to obey even if it is difficult. He will not make you obey and sacrifice something. If you love him and obey him, the Lord promises to live with you, just as he did with the Israelites.

MEMORY VERSE PRACTICE

Honor your father and your mother, so that you may live long in the land the LORD your God is giving you. –Exodus 20:12

See the "Memory Verse Activities" on pages 124-127 for suggestions to help the children to learn the memory verse.

ADDITIONAL ACTIVITIES

To learn more about ancient Egypt and the culture in which the Israelites lived, consider these options.

1. Make a "living" Ark of the Covenant. Read the description of the Ark of the Covenant in Exodus 25:1-22. Ask the children to act out each item, including the two cherubim, two poles, chest, and atonement cover. If possible, take a picture of your "living" Ark of the Covenant and post it in your classroom.

2. Make a model of the ark using the descriptions given in Exodus 25. Place it in your papier-mâché model of the Israelite camp.

3. Just how important was the Ark of the Covenant to the Israelites? Research this and the power of God associated with it. Read Joshua 3:15-17, Joshua 6:2-7, 1 Samuel 5:1-12, and 1 Chronicles 13:10. Make a booklet that describes and illustrates your findings.

4. Review all the "memory motions" from the stories thus far. Demonstrate a motion, and ask the children what it represents. Or describe what it represents and see if the children can demonstrate the motion. One at a time, allow the children to lead the activity.

Making it best

You will need:

- Large Legos or building blocks
- A table

One at a time, invite the children to help build a house with the building blocks. After the house is finished, say, **This is a good house for a small toy. How would the house need to change if it were for a fish? ...A dog? ...Or a real person? What would be different?** Discuss the answers to these questions. Then say, **God planned for the Israelites to build the Tabernacle, a place for him to live among them. So, God gave the Israelites clear directions for how to make it, the exact materials to use, and the exact size to make it. In this week's lesson, we learned about one of the special things that would go in the Tabernacle.**

ACTIVITY FOR OLDER CHILDREN

You will need:

- Large sheets of paper, one for each group
- Markers or crayons for each group

1. Organize the students into small groups. Give each group drawing materials. Ask the students to draw things that remind them of God's presence. After a few minutes, ask the groups to explain their drawings. Ask the students what the Israelites had that was a very important reminder of God's presence. The answer is the Ark of the Covenant.

2. Ask the students, **What do you know about the Ark of the Covenant? Why was it built?** Discuss that the ark was a physical reminder of God's covenant with the people. Say, **Any time the Israelites looked toward the Tabernacle, they were reminded of God's presence.** Share with the students something that reminds you of God's presence. Afterward, ask the students, **What reminds you that God is near?**

Pray and thank God for how he reminds us of his presence and his love for us.

 ## PRACTICE FOR BIBLE QUIZ

See the section "Review Questions" on pages 128-167 for the red and the blue practice questions for this lesson.

LESSON 17

SETTING UP GOD'S HOUSE
EXODUS 25:23-28:5; 30:1-10, 17-21

MEMORY VERSE:

You shall not murder. You shall not commit adultery. You shall not steal. You shall not give false testimony against your neighbor.

Exodus 20:13-16

TRUTHS ABOUT GOD

This lesson will teach the following truths about God. The asterisk * indicates the primary truth that you should teach to the children.

* * God taught his people how to worship him.
* God teaches people how to follow him.
* God gives people wisdom.

LESSON FOCUS AND SUMMARY

In this study, the children will learn that God taught people how to be his holy people.

1. God told the Israelites exactly how to build the tabernacle and all of its furnishings.
2. Aaron and his sons were to be God's priests.
3. The Holy Place and the Most Holy Place were special places for God.
4. The Ark of the Covenant Law was the only thing placed in the Most Holy Place.

 ## BIBLICAL BACKGROUND

Why was God so specific about the construction of the tabernacle, its furnishings, utensils, and the methods of worship? The Israelites knew very little about Yahweh. For hundreds of years, they had been shaped by superstition, sorcery, and idol worship. They needed so much education and training. God's instructions were designed to develop godly thought and behavior.

Israel needed to learn about God's nature and character. They needed to learn the way of holy love and healthy boundaries. They had to learn obedience, mercy, honesty, humility, forgiveness, and grace. They needed to understand how God provides and cares for his people. They needed to learn that the proper response to God's goodness is to offer ourselves and our gifts back to him. God would teach them how to give him respect. He helped them to live faithful lives that were filled with gratitude. They would learn the importance of spiritual purity and constant prayer.

They would need to relearn these lessons many times. This is still true for us today, as God continues to forgive us and reshape us in his image.

Bible Studies for Children: Exodus
Lesson 17

DID YOU KNOW?

The high priest could only enter the Most Holy Place when God instructed him to enter. If he failed to follow the Lord's instructions, he would die.

VOCABULARY

Faith words:

Wisdom is using good knowledge to make right choices. Wisdom comes from God.

People:

Eleazar and **Ithamar** were Aaron's younger sons who were priests.

Nadab and **Abihu** were Aaron's older sons who were priests.

Terms:

The Holy Place was the room in the tabernacle where the lampstand, table, and incense altar were kept. Only priests could enter the Holy Place.

The Most Holy Place was the room behind a curtain in the Holy Place. It held the Ark of the Covenant. It represented the throne room of God.

Incense is a substance that produces sweet-smelling smoke when it burns.

The Tent of the Meeting was another name for the tabernacle.

STORYTELLING ACTIVITY:

Each week you will need the following items.

You will need:

1. The Lesson One travel bag
2. The storage container (bag, basket, or box) with the items from the previous lessons

For today's story, you will need the following items.

3. A loaf of bread
4. A flashlight
5. A suit jacket
6. Hand sanitizer or soap

Before class:

1. Read Exodus 25:23-28:5 and 30:1-10, 17-21.
2. Gather today's story items. Substitute a picture for any unavailable items.
3. Transfer all previous lesson items from the travel bag to the storage container. Place this beside the storytelling area.
4. Place today's story items inside the travel bag. Place the travel bag in the storytelling area.

Opening Activity: Follow the Leader

Tell the children to stand in a line, one behind the other. Choose a child to be the leader. Tell the children to watch carefully and mimic everything the leader does. The leader leads the group around the room. He or she uses different hand gestures, sounds, or means of travel for the children to imitate. For example, the leader walks with baby steps, large steps, or skips. End the game at the storytelling area.

Bible Studies for Children: Exodus
Lesson 17

Download additional resources from *kidzfirstpublications.org*

Lesson review:

Ask a volunteer to select an item from the storage container and explain what it represented in a previous lesson.

Story Time

Read these instructions before you begin.

1. Tell the story in your own words. Remove each item from the bag as you illustrate a main point. Focus on the main points. If you are comfortable, include more details. If needed, use the script that is suggested.

2. As you tell the story, display each item in the order that it is listed. Place it where the children can see it.

3. After telling the story, place all the items inside the bag again.

4. To review the story, remove the first item. Ask a volunteer to tell what it represents. Display this item. Repeat this process until the story is retold.

5. Review the Memory Motion described below. Demonstrate this motion any time you mention what it represents.

6. Say, **We are continuing on our expedition to explore the book of Exodus. I packed our travel bag with tools that we will need. Today our journey begins with...** Unpack the items as you tell the story.

Main points in order:

1. Loaf of bread—Say, **In Exodus 25:30, God continued to give Moses directions to build the tabernacle and make the items to furnish it. He said that the bread of the Presence should be on the table at all times.**

2. Flashlight—Say, **In Exodus 25:31-40, God said to make a lampstand with six branches and seven lamps. Approximately 75 pounds of pure gold were used to make the lampstand and its wick trimmers and the trays. The lamps burned from evening until morning every day.**

3. Suit jacket—Say, **Aaron and his four sons, Nadab, Abihu, Eleazar, and Ithamar, served as priests of God. The people made special priestly garments for them to wear. These sacred garments gave the priests dignity and honor.**

4. Hand sanitizer or soap—Say, **God required Aaron and his sons to wash their hands and feet any time they went into the tabernacle or offered a sacrifice. They washed in a bronze basin that was filled with water and made for this purpose.**

5. Memory motion—Tell the children to hold their hands in front of them, fingers touching, in a tent shape to indicate the tabernacle. You may also invite the children to think of another motion. Say, **As I tell the story, do this motion when you hear what it represents.**

6. Say, **Now it is your turn to tell the story**. Return the items to the bag. Invite the children to take turns and choose an item from the bag without looking. Ask them to explain what it means or to review the Memory Motion. After all the items have been removed, ask the children to place them in the correct story order.

BIBLICAL LESSON

Teaching tips:

As you lead the Bible study, emphasize these ideas.

- Point out that the Lord gave specific instructions for building the tabernacle and also for each item that would go inside the tabernacle to be used for worship.

- If possible, provide a printout or copy of Exodus 25-30 for each child. Highlight the scripture portion for this Bible study to help the children find the answers more easily.

- Make a large drawing or find a large picture of the tabernacle. Hang it up and refer to it while teaching. Encourage the children to draw what is described.

Read the Scripture:

Exodus 25:23-30: Table, Plates, Dishes, and Bread

Exodus 25:31-32, 37: Lampstand

Exodus 27:20-21: Oil and Fire

Exodus 26:1-13: Tabernacle

Exodus 26:14-33: Tent Covering

Exodus 26:30, 34-37: Holy Place and Most Holy Place

Exodus 27:1-19: Courtyard

Exodus 28:1-5: Priestly Garments

Exodus 30:1-10: Altar of Incense

Discussion Questions:

Discuss the story and ask the children the following questions. Remember that there might not be a right or wrong answer.

1. **Why do you think the Lord gave such detailed directions for everything that involved the tabernacle?**
2. **Was the Lord being selfish to ask the people to use their best materials to make the tabernacle? Why or why not?**
3. **Which of the tabernacle furnishings sounds the most interesting to you? Why?**
4. **Why do you think the priests had to wash their hands and feet when they went into the Tent of Meeting?**
5. **The tabernacle was the dwelling place of God. Where is God's dwelling place today?**

Closing Thoughts:

This is the thought that you want your students to remember.

Say, **God taught his people how to worship him.**

Altars, lampstands, and arks! What do these things have to do with us? Think about it. The Israelites did not know how to worship the Lord. They knew much more about Egyptian gods than they knew about Yahweh. The Lord provided the tabernacle so that the Israelites had a place to meet with him and worship him. He also provided priests to lead worship.

Today church buildings are one place where we worship God. God helps us to learn how to worship through pastors and worship leaders. This week, thank the Lord for showing you how to worship and how to get closer to him.

MEMORY VERSE PRACTICE

You shall not murder. You shall not commit adultery. You shall not steal. You shall not give false testimony against your neighbor. –Exodus 20:13-16

See the "Memory Verse Activities" on pages 124-127 for suggestions to help the children to learn the memory verse.

ADDITIONAL ACTIVITIES

To learn more about ancient Egypt and the culture in which the Israelites lived, consider these options.

1. Search online Bible sites to see different ideas of what the tabernacle might have looked like.
2. Follow the detailed descriptions in Exodus to build a scale model of the tabernacle.
3. Research various ideas of what may have happened to the Ark of the Covenant. Why do you think God allowed the ark to be lost?

PB&J My Way

You will need:

- A jar of peanut butter
- A jar of jelly
- Bread
- A butter knife
- A spoon
- Paper towels
- An adult helper

Instruct your helper to follow exactly all the directions.

Ask your helper to sit in a chair in front of everyone. Tell the class that your helper needs directions for making a peanut butter and jelly sandwich. Say, **Can you tell him or her how to make the sandwich?** As the children give directions, the helper should follow them exactly. For example, if the children say, "Put the peanut butter on the bread," this should result in the helper placing the jar on top of the bread or using his or her finger instead of a knife to spread the peanut butter on the bread. Once the sandwich is finally made, discuss the need for detailed directions to make something as simple as a PB&J sandwich. Say, **Today we learned that it is important to give clear instructions. God gave the Israelites detailed directions for making his house, the tabernacle, and its furnishings.**

ACTIVITY FOR OLDER CHILDREN

Say, **God had a lot to say about the tabernacle.** Discuss why God was so specific. Say, **God wanted his people to know how holy he is and how to honor him in worship. How important is it for us to know and do this?**

Conduct a "sword drill" or contest about worship. Ask all the students to simultaneously search his or her Bible for a scripture reference when you say "go." Ask the first student to find the verse to read it aloud to the class and describe what it tells us about worship.

- Psalm 95:6, the need for humility
- Psalm 100:2, ways to worship
- John 4:24, how we must worship
- Romans 12:1-2, the need for total commitment

PRACTICE FOR BIBLE QUIZZING

See the section "Review Questions" on pages 128-167 for the red and the blue practice questions for this lesson.

LESSON 18

A REALLY BAD DECISION
EXODUS 32:1-30

MEMORY VERSE

You shall not covet your neighbor's house. You shall not covet your neighbor's wife, or his male or female servant, his ox or donkey, or anything that belongs to your neighbor.

Exodus 20:17

TRUTHS ABOUT GOD

This lesson will teach the following truths about God. The asterisk * indicates the primary truth that you should teach to the children.

- * God did not allow his people to continue to worship other gods.
- God sees what people do no matter where they are.
- God holds people accountable for their actions.

LESSON FOCUS AND SUMMARY

In this study, the children will learn that God expects his people to worship only him and to live a holy life.

1. The Israelites thought Moses and Yahweh had abandoned them in the wilderness. Before they left Egypt, they had worshiped Pharaoh's gods for many generations. In their fear and anger, they returned to the worship of false gods.
2. They demanded that Aaron lead them in worshiping idols. Aaron agreed. He built an altar and made a golden calf for them to worship.
3. The Lord told Moses what the people had done. Moses came down from the mountain.
4. When he saw that Aaron had let the people run wild, Moses took control and restored order.

 ## BIBLICAL BACKGROUND

Moses met with God on the mountain for many days and nights. While the Lord gave Moses detailed instructions for building the tabernacle, the Israelites became impatient and rebellious. They thought Moses had abandoned them, so they turned to the only gods they had known before Yahweh. Their families had worshiped Pharaoh's gods for generations. They demanded that Aaron make them an idol of the Egyptian gods. Aaron was a weak leader. He agreed to do it even though he knew it was wrong.

The punishment for breaking covenant with God was death. Yahweh told Moses he would punish those who had broken covenant. Although Moses was angry with the people, he asked God to have mercy on them. Moses did not make excuses for their sin. Instead, he confessed their sin and asked God to forgive them. Moses reminded God of his promise to Abraham. He asked God to consider that the Egyptians would claim that Yahweh had delivered the Israelites from slavery so that he could destroy them completely in the wilderness. Moses's prayers persuaded God to have mercy on Israel. God postponed their punishment long enough to give them a chance to repent. He spared those who repented but still destroyed those who refused to repent.

DID YOU KNOW?

The golden calf made by Aaron probably resembled an idol of Apis, the Egyptian bull god. Making this idol was wrong. God told them not to make any idols. Jesus is the only visible example of who God is and what he is like.

VOCABULARY

Faith words:

Evil is anything or anyone that is opposed to God. God is good, and evil is the opposite of good.

People:

Levites were people from the tribe of Levi. Moses and Aaron were Levites.

Abraham, **Isaac**, and **Jacob** (who is also known as Israel) are the men with whom God made a covenant to give the Israelites the Promised Land.

Terms:

Revelry means a wild way to celebrate that does not please God.

A laughing stock is a person whose foolish behavior causes others to mock and ridicule them.

STORYTELLING

Each week you will need the following items.

1. The travel bag from lesson one

2. The storage container (bag, basket, or box) with the items from the previous lessons

For today's story, you will need the following items.

3. A toy cow

4. Party decorations

5. A water bottle

Before class:

1. Read Exodus 32: 1-30.

2. Gather today's story items. Substitute a picture for any unavailable items.

3. Transfer all previous lesson items from the travel bag to the storage container. Place this beside the storytelling area.

4. Place today's story items inside the travel bag. Place the travel bag in the storytelling area.

Optional activity: Follow the leader

Tell the children to stand in a line, one behind the other. Choose a child to be the leader. Tell the children to watch carefully and mimic everything the leader does. The leader leads the group around the room. He or she uses different hand gestures, sounds, or means of travel for the children to imitate. For example, the leader walks with baby steps, large steps, or skips. End the game at the storytelling area.

Lesson review:

Ask a volunteer to select an item from the storage container and explain what it represented in a previous lesson.

Story time:

Read these instructions before you begin.

1. Tell the story in your own words. Remove each item from the bag as you illustrate a main point. Focus on the main points. If you are comfortable, include more details. If needed, use the script that is suggested.
2. As you tell the story, display each item in the order that it is listed. Place it where the children can see it.
3. After telling the story, place all the items inside the bag again.
4. To review the story, remove the first item. Ask a volunteer to tell what it represents. Display this item. Repeat this process until the story is retold.
5. Review the memory motion described below. Demonstrate this motion any time you mention what it represents.
6. Say, **We are continuing on our expedition to explore the book of Exodus. I packed our travel bag with tools that we will need. Today our journey begins with...** Unpack the items as you tell the story.

Main points in order:

1. A toy cow—Say, **Moses stayed on the mountain much longer than the Israelites expected. They didn't know what had happened to him. They were afraid and angry. They thought Yahweh and Moses had abandoned them, so they wanted to go back to doing what they had done before Moses introduced them to Yahweh. They wanted to worship the gods they had worshiped for generations before they left Egypt. They said to Aaron, "Come, make us gods who will go before us." Aaron did not resist or refuse. Instead, he did exactly what they wanted, even though it was evil. Aaron took their earrings and made a golden idol in the shape of a calf. They worshiped the idol and said, "These are your gods, O Israel, who brought you up out of Egypt."**

2. Party decorations—Say, **The Israelites threw a party for their Egyptian gods. They gave burnt offerings and fellowship offerings to the golden calf. Then they ate and drank and ran wild. God told Moses what had happened. When Moses went down the mountain and saw what they were doing, he threw down the stone tablets on which God had written the Ten Commandments. The tablets broke into pieces.**

3. A water bottle—Say, **Moses melted the golden calf and ground the gold into dust. He mixed the gold dust with water and made the Israelites drink it. Later, Moses prayed to God to forgive his people.**

4. Memory motion—Tell the children to pull on the lobes of their ears to indicate the Israelites pulling off their earrings to make the golden calf. You may also invite the children to think of another motion. Say, **As I tell the story, do this motion when you hear what it represents.**

5. Say, **Now it is your turn to tell the story.** Return the items to the bag. Invite the children to take turns and choose an item from the bag without looking. Ask them to explain what it means or to review the memory motion. After all the items have been removed, ask the children to place them in the correct story order.

BIBLICAL LESSON

Teaching tips:

As you lead the Bible study, emphasize these ideas.

- The Israelites broke the first two commandments when they worshiped the golden calf.
- Instead of being a strong leader like Moses, Aaron gave the people what they wanted. The consequences of his cowardice and weak leadership affected the Israelites for a long time.

Read the Scripture:

Read Exodus 32:1-30 aloud.

Discussion questions:

Discuss the story and ask the children the following questions. Remember that there might not be a right or wrong answer.

1. **Why did the people ask Aaron to make an idol?**
2. **In Exodus 25, the Israelites brought Moses offerings of gold for Yahweh. How was that offering different than this one?**
3. **Why was the worship of the golden calf so terrible?** If necessary, remind them of the information from "Did You Know" regarding the Egyptian bull god, Apis.
4. **Did Aaron give Moses good reasons or bad excuses for his actions? What do you think would have happened if Aaron had refused to give the people what they wanted?**
5. **What did Moses do with the golden calf? Why do you think he acted this way?**

Closing thoughts:

This is the thought that you want the children to remember.

Say, **God refused to allow his people to worship other gods.**

What were the Israelites thinking? The Lord had done so much for them. But when their young faith was tested, they returned to the worship of their old gods. The Israelites had to learn a difficult lesson. Following God means learning new ways and living them out. You can't follow God and hang on to old ways of thinking and acting.

The Israelites made a golden calf. However, an idol can be anything or anyone that we like, trust, or value more than God. Do you have any idols in your life? If so, confess that to God and ask the Lord to forgive your idolatry. The Lord loves you and wants a strong relationship with you. He does not want anything or anybody to come between you and him.

MEMORY VERSE PRACTICE

You shall not covet your neighbor's house. You shall not covet your neighbor's wife, or his male or female servant, his ox or donkey, or anything that belongs to your neighbor. –Exodus 20:17

See the "Memory Verse Activities" on pages 124-127 for suggestions to help the children to learn the memory verse.

ADDITIONAL ACTIVITIES

To learn more about ancient Egypt and the culture in which the Israelites lived, consider these options.

1. Who were the Levites? Read the following passages and write a paragraph telling what you learned: Genesis 29:31-34; 35:23; 49:1-2, 5-7; Exodus 2:1-2; 31:36; Numbers 1:53; 2:17; 3:1-51.

2. Create an imaginary dialogue between Moses and Joshua as they returned to the Israelite camp. What might they have said to one another?

3. Ask volunteers to identify mistakes the Israelites and Aaron made and why they behaved that way.

Golden Idols

You will need:

- Play-Doh or clay for each child.

Give each child a portion of Play-Doh or clay. Tell them to pretend it is gold, that they are the Israelites, and that you are Aaron. Ask them what the Israelites wanted Aaron to make for them. Tell them you will need some of their gold to make what they wanted. Note how generous each child is. Explain how people often seem willing to spend a great deal more on their idols than they are willing to offer to God.

ACTIVITY FOR OLDER CHILDREN

Tell students to stand in a line. Ask each one to tell a part of the story from Exodus 32. Tell the facts in order until they have shared the main points from beginning to end. Tell them to remember the portion of the story that they just shared. Then call on them out of order, but ask each to share the same thing they first shared. Say, **Did you notice how things make no sense when we get them out of order? The Israelites had worshiped Egyptian gods for many generations. Then God worked through Moses to deliver them from slavery. When they wrongly believed Moses had abandoned them, they went back to their old ways of thinking and acting instead of trusting God.** Ask the students how it felt when you called on them out of order. Were they anxious? Angry? Say, **The Israelites got into trouble when they let how they felt dictate what they believed and what they did. Instead, they needed to allow what they knew to be true about God to guide their beliefs and behaviors.**

PRACTICE FOR BIBLE QUIZ

See the section "Review Questions" on pages 128-167 for the red and the blue practice questions for this lesson.

LESSON 19

A SECOND CHANCE TO DO THE RIGHT THING
EXODUS 34:1-32

MEMORY VERSE

And he passed in front of Moses, proclaiming, "The LORD, the LORD, the compassionate and gracious God, slow to anger, abounding in love and faithfulness."

Exodus 34:6

TRUTHS ABOUT GOD

This lesson will teach the following truths about God. The asterisk * indicates the primary truth that you should teach to the children.

- * God forgave his people's sin.
- God is compassionate and gracious.
- God does not leave the guilty unpunished.

LESSON FOCUS AND SUMMARY

In this study, the children will learn that God is compassionate and forgives his people.

1. God told Moses to make two more stone tablets and to come back up the mountain.
2. The Lord came down and proclaimed his name to Moses.
3. The Lord renewed his covenant and rewrote the Ten Commandments on the stone tablets.
4. Moses's face became radiant from being in the Lord's presence.

 ## BIBLICAL BACKGROUND

Yahweh continued to meet with Moses even though Israel sinned greatly when they broke their covenant. Moses asked the Lord to forgive Israel and continue to lead them to the Promised Land. Moses also expressed a desire to know the Lord and to learn his ways. Yahweh agreed to renew his covenant with Israel and to show Moses a portion of his glory and goodness.

Yahweh revealed himself to Moses. This was an incredibly powerful event. Not only did Moses experience the reality of God's glory and goodness, Yahweh also explained it to him! God said that he is compassionate and that he cares deeply about people. God is gracious. He loves to bless his people. God is slow to anger. He is patient, understanding, and tolerant of our human limitations, even when they lead us into error. God overflows with love and faithfulness. He is loyal and devoted to his covenant people.

God forgives evil, rebellion, and sin when people sincerely confess and repent. However, even those who repent still experience consequences for their wrong behavior so that they can learn and change. God is forgiving, merciful, and just all at the same time. Exodus 32-34 tells the story of God's mercy toward the repentant Israelites. They were allowed to renew the covenant they had broken. Those who refused to repent received the appropriate penalty for their stubborn refusal. These chapters reveal that God is not mean-spirited or vengeful toward sinners, but he will not tolerate or ignore rebellion.

DID YOU KNOW?

Genesis 2:3, Exodus 20:8-11, and Exodus 34:21 all refer to the six days of creation and the seventh day of rest.

VOCABULARY

Faith words:

Gracious means to treat someone with kindness, compassion, and forgiveness or to share what you have to help others.

People:

Amorites, **Canaanites**, **Hittites**, **Perizzites**, **Hivites**, and **Jebusites** are groups of people who lived in Canaan, the Promised Land the Lord was giving to the Israelites.

Terms:

Inheritance is the money, land, or other possessions a person receives if he or she is an heir.

A treaty is a formal agreement between two or more countries or groups of people.

Asherah poles are wooden poles used in the worship of Asherah, a false goddess worshiped by the people of Canaan.

The Festival of Weeks was a one-day celebration of the harvest that happened seven weeks after Passover.

STORYTELLING

Each week you will need the following items.

1. The travel bag from lesson one
2. The storage container (bag, basket, or box) with the items from the previous lessons

For today's story, you will need the following items.

3. A hammer and a chisel
4. Construction paper and a marker
5. Paper and a pen
6. A pair of sunglasses

Before class:

1. Read Exodus 34:1-32.
2. Create a proclamation of Exodus 34:6 on the construction paper. Write, "HEAR YE, HEAR YE: "The LORD, the LORD, the compassionate and gracious God, is slow to anger, abounding in love and faithfulness."
3. Gather today's story items. Substitute a picture for any unavailable items.
4. Transfer all previous lesson items from the travel bag to the storage container. Place this beside the storytelling area.

5. Place today's story items inside the travel bag. Place the travel bag in the storytelling area.

Optional activity: Follow the leader

Tell the children to stand in a line, one behind the other. Choose a child to be the leader. Tell the children to watch carefully and mimic everything the leader does. The leader leads the group around the room. He or she uses different hand gestures, sounds, or means of travel for the children to imitate. For example, the leader walks with baby steps, large steps, or skips. End the game at the storytelling area.

Lesson review:

Ask a volunteer to select an item from the storage container and explain what it represented in a previous lesson.

Story time:

Read these instructions before you begin.

1. Tell the story in your own words. Remove each item from the bag as you illustrate a main point. Focus on the main points. If you are comfortable, include more details. If needed, use the script that is suggested.

2. As you tell the story, display each item in the order that it is listed. Place it where the children can see it.

3. After telling the story, place all the items inside the bag again.

4. To review the story, remove the first item. Ask a volunteer to tell what it represents. Display this item. Repeat this process until the story is retold.

5. Review the memory motion described below. Demonstrate this motion any time you mention what it represents.

6. Say, **We are continuing on our expedition to explore the book of Exodus.**

I packed our travel bag with tools that we will need. Today our journey begins with... Unpack the items as you tell the story.

Main points in order:

1. A hammer and a chisel—Say, **God told Moses to chisel out two new stone tablets and come up on Mount Sinai again.**

2. The proclamation—Say, **God proclaimed to Moses his name and what kind of God he is. This is what he learned.** Read your proclamation. **"The LORD, the LORD, the compassionate and gracious God, is slow to anger, abounding in love and faithfulness." Moses worshiped the Lord.**

3. Paper and a pen—Say, **The Lord repeated the covenant he had made with the Israelites. Moses wrote down all of God's commands. God again wrote the Ten Commandments on the tablets of stone.**

4. Sunglasses—Say, **When Moses came back down to camp, his face was so radiant from being in God's presence that Aaron and the Israelites were afraid to approach him.**

5. Memory motion—Tell the children to hold up one hand with two fingers extended, representing the second set of the Ten Commandments. You may also invite the children to think of another motion. Say, **As I tell the story, do this motion when you hear what it represents.**

6. Say, **Now it is your turn to tell the story.** Return the items to the bag. Invite the children to take turns and choose an item from the bag without looking. Ask them to explain what it means or to review the memory motion. After all the items have been removed, ask the children to place them in the correct story order.

Bible Studies for Children: Exodus
Lesson 19

BIBLICAL LESSON

Teaching tips:

As you lead the Bible study, emphasize these ideas.

- Help the children discover that the Lord related to the Israelites in a way that was consistent with his character.
- Despite the Israelites' sin, God honored his covenant and prepared the people to enter the Promised Land.

Read the Scripture:

Read Exodus 34:1-32 aloud.

Discussion questions:

Discuss the story and ask the children the following questions. Remember that there might not be a right or wrong answer.

1. Read 34:6. **Discuss some examples of how the Lord showed these characteristics in his relationship with the Israelites.**
2. **How do you think Moses felt when the Lord told Moses that he would do wonders among the Israelites?**
3. **Moses stayed with the Lord 40 days and 40 nights, the same amount of time as his previous visit. How did the people respond differently to Moses' absence this time?**
4. **Why do you think Moses' face was radiant after speaking with the Lord?**
5. **Do you think the Israelites deserved a second chance? How are we like the Israelites?**

Closing thoughts:

This is the thought that you want the children to remember.

Say, **God forgave his people's sin.**

Did the Israelites deserve a second chance? They made a big mistake when they disobeyed the Lord. Did you notice the Lord's response? He held them accountable for their sin, and they experienced the consequences of their actions. He also forgave them and did not reject them. They continued to be his treasured people.

This is good to know. Sometimes we find it difficult to obey, especially when people around us make bad choices and do the things we know are wrong. This story shows us that God hates sin. But if we disobey the Lord and then repent, he is still gracious, loving, and forgiving.

MEMORY VERSE PRACTICE

And he passed in front of Moses, proclaiming, "The LORD, the LORD, the compassionate and gracious God, slow to anger, abounding in love and faithfulness." –Exodus 34:6

See the "Memory Verse Activities" on pages 124-127 for suggestions to help the children to learn the memory verse.

ADDITIONAL ACTIVITIES

To learn more about ancient Egypt and the culture in which the Israelites lived, consider these options.

1. Make a poster to visually depict how the Lord describes himself in 34:6-7. Use Scripture references from the entire study to support the adjectives in 34:6-7. For example, represent "compassionate" with a large painted heart.

2. Search online for "Asherah" and "Asherah poles" to learn more about the pagan gods the Israelites would encounter in Canaan.

The Best Path

You will need:

- 10 m. length of rope
- Index cards
- A pen
- Masking tape
- A small bell

Choose a section of your classroom where there are two tall posts somewhat close together. For example, consider a doorframe. Crisscross the rope between the posts to create a web. Choose a place that will be unused by the children until it is time to do the activity. Make an opening large enough for the children to crawl through it. Also make smaller openings that would be very difficult to crawl through. On the index cards, write the following words: "Don't make treaties," "Snares," "Don't worship any other gods," and "Obey what I command." Tape the "Obey what I command" card just above the largest hole and the remaining cards on the smaller holes.

Tell the children, **In the lesson today, the Lord prepared the Israelites to live in the Promised Land. The Lord cautioned them to do certain things and not to do other things. Our job is to work together to crawl through this web and not ring the bell.** Tell the children to use the cards to help the one crawling to find the best path to take. Have the children work as a team to get through the web. If someone tries to crawl through a small space, ring the bell.

Ask, **Was it easy or hard to choose the right path? Did the directions help you to choose which path to take? How?** Discuss the children's answers. Say, **Today we learned that the Lord tried to help the Israelites to choose the right path as they prepared to enter the Promised Land.**

ACTIVITY FOR OLDER CHILDREN

You will need paper and pencils

Say, **Because the Israelites sinned, God was very angry with them. Moses had to pray and make atonement for them.** Read Exodus 33:31-32 and 34:5-10. Discuss how God's response reflects his character. Reread verses 6 and 7. Say, **Although God is quick to forgive, sin is serious, and sin has severe consequences. Because the people repented, God was merciful to them and renewed the covenant with them.** Challenge the students to consider if there is anything they have done that they need to repent of. Pray with the students and ask God for discernment, humility, and courage.

Give each student an index card. Ask each person to write a thought of devotion to God based on what they have learned in this lesson. Challenge the students to share their thoughts with their family this week.

PRACTICE FOR BIBLE QUIZ

See the section "Review Questions" on pages 128-167 for the red and the blue practice questions for this lesson.

LESSON 20

GOD DWELLS IN THE TABERNACLE
EXODUS 40:1-38

MEMORY VERSE

Then the LORD said, "I am making a covenant with you. Before all your people I will do wonders never before done in any nation in all the world."

Exodus 34:10

TRUTHS ABOUT GOD

This lesson will teach the following truths about God. The asterisk * indicates the primary truth that you should teach to the children.

* * God came in glory to live among his people.
* God helps people finish the work he calls them to do.
* God always does what he says he will do.

LESSON FOCUS AND SUMMARY

In this study, the children will learn that God came to live among the Israelites. He is faithful to keep his promises.

1. The Lord told Moses to set up the tabernacle and anoint Aaron and his sons as priests.
2. Moses did everything the Lord commanded him to do and finished his work.
3. The glory of the Lord came and filled the Tabernacle.
4. As the Israelites traveled, God's presence went with them.

 BIBLICAL BACKGROUND

The Book of Exodus ends well. When it begins, the Israelites are hopeless slaves in a foreign land. When it ends, they are God's people on an amazing journey to the Promised Land. The trip was certainly not without its challenges. Because of their impatience and disobedience, God nearly eliminated everyone except Moses and vowed to choose others to be his people. But through Moses's intercession and God's mercy, forgiveness, and grace, those who repented were spared.

After experiencing the painful consequences of breaking covenant, the people were exceedingly grateful when Yahweh chose to renew their covenant and remain with them. When Moses asked the people to donate materials to build the tabernacle, they responded willingly and generously. Their attitudes had changed. They no longer grumbled and complained. In fact, they were so generous that Moses told them to stop donating because the builders had more than they needed! The Israelites also showed their covenant faithfulness by making the tabernacle exactly as Yahweh had commanded.

Bible Studies for Children: Exodus
Lesson 20

Download additional resources from *kidzfirstpublications.org*

Their response pleased the Lord. When the tabernacle was completed, God filled it with his glory so powerfully that even Moses, who had met with God many times, could not enter it. God declared that there would be a relationship between Yahweh and Israel forever. The breach between them was closed, and a new life together had begun.

DID YOU KNOW?

Joshua was Moses's personal assistant. He would become the next Israelite leader.

VOCABULARY

Faith words:

Consecrate means to set apart an object or a person to serve God alone.

Terms:

A tunic is a loose, sleeveless garment.

To anoint means to place oil on a person's head to show that God has chosen them to do something important for him. In the Bible, kings, priests, and prophets were anointed.

Sacred means something or someone that is consecrated to God, which makes it holy.

STORYTELLING

Each week you will need the following items.

1. The travel bag from lesson one
2. The storage container (bag, basket, or box) with the items from the previous lessons

For today's story, you will need the following items.

3. A large letter "T" cut from construction paper
4. Olive oil
5. A small bag of matches and rice
6. A towel
7. Cotton balls

Before class:

1. Read Exodus 40.
2. Gather today's story items. Substitute a picture for any unavailable items.
3. Prepare the letter "T."
4. Transfer all previous lesson items from the travel bag to the storage container. Place this beside the storytelling area.
5. Place today's story items inside the travel bag. Place the travel bag in the storytelling area.

Optional activity: Follow the leader

Tell the children to stand in a line, one behind the other. Choose a child to be the leader. Tell the children to watch carefully and mimic everything the leader does. The leader leads the group around the room. He or she uses different hand gestures, sounds, or means of travel for the children to imitate. For example, the leader walks with baby steps, large steps, or skips. End the game at the storytelling area.

Lesson review:

Ask a volunteer to select an item from the storage container and explain what it represented in a previous lesson.

Story time:

Read these instructions before you begin.

1. Tell the story in your own words. Remove each item from the bag as you illustrate a main point. Focus on the main points. If you are comfortable, include more details. If needed, use the script that is suggested.

2. As you tell the story, display each item in the order that it is listed. Place it where the children can see it.

3. After telling the story, place all the items inside the bag again.

4. To review the story, remove the first item. Ask a volunteer to tell what it represents. Display this item. Repeat this process until the story is retold.

5. Review the memory motion described below. Demonstrate this motion any time you mention what it represents.

6. Say, **We are continuing on our expedition to explore the book of Exodus. I packed our travel bag with tools that we will need. Today our journey begins with...** Unpack the items as you tell the story.

Main points in order:

1. Letter "T"—Say, **The tabernacle was completed at last! Everything had been made. Now it was time to set up the Tabernacle.**

2. Olive oil—Say, **God told Moses to anoint Aaron and his sons for their new task as priests. They wore their sacred garments for the first time.**

3. Bag of matches and rice—Say, **Moses completely followed God's instructions. After he set up the altar of burnt offering, he sacrificed burnt offerings and grain offerings near the entrance to the tabernacle.**

4. Towel—Say, **On the day of their anointing, Aaron and his sons washed their hands and feet in the bronze basin. They did this each time they went into the tabernacle or approached the altar.**

5. Cotton balls—Say, **After Moses had finished his work, a cloud covered the Tent of Meeting, and the glory of the Lord filled the tabernacle. God's glory was so great that even Moses could not enter the tabernacle. From that day on, God lived among the Israelites in a cloud by day and fire by night. The journey from slavery to freedom had ended, but their adventure with God had just begun!**

6. Memory motion—Tell the children to lift their arms over their heads, palms outward, then slowly bring them down to their sides to indicate God's glory filling the Tabernacle. You may also invite the children to think of another motion. Say, **As I tell the story, do this motion when you hear what it represents.**

7. Say, **Now it is your turn to tell the story.** Return the items to the bag. Invite the children to take turns and choose an item from the bag without looking. Ask them to explain what it means or to review the memory motion. After all the items have been removed, ask the children to place them in the correct story order.

BIBLICAL LESSON

Teaching tips:

As you lead the Bible study, emphasize these ideas.

- Explain to the children that the Lord lived close to his people through his presence in the tabernacle. Today he is even closer through his Holy Spirit within us.
- Moses had completed much of his work, but he continued to lead God's people. Eventually, his assistant, Joshua, would become the leader of the Israelites.
- Today's memory verse leads us to the next study, Bible Studies for Children: Joshua, Judges, and Ruth. As they learn about the conquest of Canaan, children will see that God kept his promise to do wonders never before seen. God always keeps his promises.

Read the Scripture:

Read Exodus 40:1-38 aloud.

Discussion questions:

Discuss the story and ask the children the following questions. Remember that there might not be a right or wrong answer.

1. **Moses precisely followed the Lord's commands. Why was this important?**
2. **How does God live among us now?**
3. **The Israelites watched what the cloud was doing so they would know what God wanted them to do. How easy or hard is it to give attention to God and follow him today?**
4. **Imagine you were an Israelite. Describe how you felt when you saw the cloud of God's glory fill the Tabernacle.**
5. **The Israelites followed God by following the cloud. How do we follow God?**

Conclusion:

This is the thought that you want the children to remember.

Say, **God came in glory to live among his people.**

The glory of the Lord filled the tabernacle. What a journey! In the past, the Israelites served in Egypt as slaves. Now their God, the God of the universe, lived among them and would always be with them. Through many difficulties, the Israelites learned to trust the Lord completely. God gave them freedom, food, water, and safety. He forgave them! They still struggled to obey. But by the end of Exodus, God was living among them in his tabernacle.

Today God's presence is not limited to the tabernacle. When Jesus came to earth, it changed everything. Matthew 1:22 tells us Jesus is called Emmanuel, which means "God with us." When we ask Jesus to be our Savior, God lives in us.

Ask the children, **Would anyone would like Jesus to be their Savior? If so, it's as easy as ABC:**

Admit that you have sinned.

Believe that Jesus is the Son of God who came to save us from our sins.

Confess Jesus as Lord of your life.

If any children express interest, pray with the children and lead them through these steps in a prayer of salvation. Tell those who responded, **If you accepted Jesus as your savior, God is now living in you through his Holy Spirit! Be sure to tell your parents the good news!**

MEMORY VERSE PRACTICE

Then the LORD said, "I am making a covenant with you. Before all your people I will do wonders never before done in any nation in all the world." –Exodus 34:10

See the "Memory Verse Activities" on pages 124-127 for suggestions to help the children to learn the memory verse.

 ADDITIONAL ACTIVITIES

To learn more about ancient Egypt and the culture in which the Israelites lived, consider these options.

1. Do research on the curtain, called the temple veil in the New Testament. What was the purpose of the curtain? What did it look like? Who made it? How was it and the tabernacle transported when the cloud moved? Read Exodus 26:31-35, 31:1-11, 40:17-23, and Numbers 4:1-20.

2. What happened to the veil at the very moment Jesus died on the Cross? Read Mark 15:37-39, Luke 23:44-47, Hebrews 6:19-20, and 10:19-22.

3. How is the death and resurrection of Jesus related to the tabernacle? Read Hebrews 10:1-39.

A Perfect Fit

You will need:

- A clear glass jar
- Small rocks (or marbles)
- Uncooked rice
- Paper cups

*Read all the instructions before starting the project.

Prepare these items before the class begins. Nearly fill the jar with rocks. Next, pour in rice while shaking the jar until it is completely filled. Be sure to place the rocks in before the rice. Empty the jar and separate the rocks from the rice. Place rice and rocks in separate paper cups. Set these aside until you need them.

To begin, ask the children if they think you can fit all of the rice and all of the rocks into the jar. Discuss their answers.

1. Pour the rice into the jar.
2. Place the rocks in the jar. They will not fit.
3. Tell the students you will try again. Empty the jar and return the items to their separate cups.
4. Place the rocks in the jar first.
5. Pour the rice into the jar. They will fit when placed in this order.

Say, **When I put the rocks in first, the rice fit perfectly, filling up the empty space between the rocks. It does not work when you pour the rice in first. You must keep things in the right order. We must also order our lives in the right way to experience God's presence. In today's lesson, we learned that the Lord intentionally designed the tabernacle for his presence among his people. When** the Israelites were disobedient, they had no room in their lives for God. They were too full of themselves. But when they humbled themselves, confessed their sin, and received God's forgiveness, his presence filled all the empty spaces in their hearts. God's presence fits perfectly in God's people.

ACTIVITY FOR OLDER CHILDREN

You will need:

- Paper and pencils

1. Play a modified version of "Simon Says." Continually speed up the game. This will eliminate those who cannot keep up until there is only one student left. Give the last student a small treat.

2. Say, **Seeing hard work pay off feels great, doesn't it?** Ask the students, **What did the Israelites accomplish through hard work and closely following instructions? How were they rewarded?** Discuss the answers. **The Israelites finished the tabernacle, and the Lord filled it with his glory. When we are faithful to God, his love fills us. That is a good feeling. To be aware of God's love within us is a reward for obeying him.**

3. Share about an area in your life for which you would like to develop obedience. Perhaps this is a new habit you would like to start.

4. Ask the students to think about areas of their life where they need to develop more obedience to God. Give the students a pencil and paper. Ask them to write down these goals as a reminder during the week.

5. Pray for the class, and ask for each one to have the strength needed to remain faithful.

PRACTICE FOR BIBLE QUIZ

See the section "Review Questions" on pages 128-167 for the red and the blue practice questions for this lesson.

MEMORY VERSE ACTIVITIES

MISSING WORDS

You will need a chalkboard, white board or paper for this activity. You will also need chalk, marker, and eraser.

Write the memory verse on a chalkboard or marker board. Ask the children to recite the verse. Choose a volunteer to erase one word. Lead the children as they recite the verse again (include the missing word). Continue this until all the words disappear. If a chalkboard or marker board is not available, write each word of the verse on a separate piece of paper, and ask the children to remove one word at a time.

BIBLE WAVE

Ask the children to sit in a straight line. Tell the first child to stand, to say the first word of the verse, to wave both hands excitedly in the air, and to sit down. Ask the second child to stand, to say the second word of the verse, to wave both hands excitedly in the air, and to sit down. Continue until the verse is complete. If a child forgets a word or says the wrong word, let the other children tell the correct word. Encourage the children to say the verse quickly so that their motions look like an ocean wave.

BIBLE PASS

You will need a Bible and a source of music for this activity.

Have the children sit in a circle. Give one child the Bible. When the music starts, tell the children to pass the Bible around the circle. When the music stops, the child holding the Bible says the Bible verse. Strategically stop the music so each child has an opportunity to say the verse.

BIBLE VERSE RACE

Before the lesson, write each word or phrase of the Bible verse and the reference on a piece of paper. Make two sets.

Divide the class into two teams. Scramble the cards so that the words are out of order. Place a set of word cards on the floor in front of each team. At your signal, the first child on each team will find the first word of the verse and run to a goal line. He or she places the card on the floor and races back to the second player. The second child finds the second word of the verse and races with it to the goal line, placing it in order next to the first word. Continue until one team completes the verse in perfect order. Allow time for the second team to complete its verse. Then have both teams recite the verse together.

MEMORY VERSE ACTIVITIES

BIBLE VERSE LINE

Before the lesson, write each word or phrase of a Bible verse on a separate piece of paper.

Distribute the words to different children, and scatter them throughout the room. Choose one child to arrange the words in order by tagging each individual child holding the words. Then have the class read the verse together.

HIDE AND SEEK

Before the lesson, write each word or phrase of a Bible verse on a separate piece of paper. Then hide the pieces of paper around the room before the children arrive.

Have the children search the room for the pieces of paper and bring them back to the front. Have the children arrange the words in order, and then ask the class to recite the verse together.

STAND UP VERSES

Arrange the children in a circle, and have everyone sit down. Ask one child to stand and say the first word of the verse and then sit down. The next child stands and says the second word and then sits down. Continue until the children complete the verse. Play the game several times, encouraging the children to finish faster than the previous time.

CHAMPION & CHALLENGER

Choose two children who think that they know the memory verse. Stand them back to back in front of the group. One child will start by saying the first word of the verse. Then, the other child will say the second word. Continue back and forth until one child makes a mistake. The other child is the "champion." Ask the whole class to say the memory verse. Then, select a new "challenger," and repeat the game. Soon, both children will be able to complete the memory verse without error.

BLINDFOLD CHALLENGE

You will need a blindfold for this activity. Ask the children to stand and arrange themselves in a large circle.

Select one child to stand in the center of the circle. Place a blindfold on this child. Ask the children in the circle to join hands and walk around the circle as they repeat the phrase, "God's Word helps me each day" a few times. This will prevent the child in the middle from remembering where each child in the circle stood. Stop the children and ask the child in the middle to point to a child in the circle. The child will recite the verse in a disguised voice (high pitch voice, squeaky voice, low voice, etc.). The child in the center then tries to guess who said the verse. If the child fails to guess correctly, he or she will point to another child who will say the verse. Continue until the child in the center guesses the correct child or the child guesses wrong three times. Then choose another child to go into the center.

MEMORY VERSE ACTIVITIES

MEMORY VERSE TOSS

You will need a small ball for this activity. Ask the children to stand and arrange them in a large circle.

Tell the children that whoever catches the ball has to say the next word in the memory verse. Toss the ball to one child to start. He or she recites the first word and then tosses the ball to another child until the entire verse is recited correctly. Repeat the game and encourage the children to complete the verse faster each time.

WORD IN ACTION

Before the lesson, write a different action on separate pieces of paper or index cards, such as "turn in a circle," "lie on the floor," "pat your head," "stand one foot," "skip," "stand in a corner," "whisper," and so on.

Ask each child to choose one of the index cards and to do the activity listed on it while he or she recites the memory verse.

THE REPEATER

Before the lesson, write one or two words of the verse on a small piece of paper. Make more than one set if you want to work in groups, one set per group.

Instruct students to sit in a circle, and distribute the papers around the circle in the correct verse order. The student with the first word of the verse says the first word. Then the next student says the first word and the new word. The third student says the first, second, and third words. Repeat this process, adding a new word each time. After you complete the verse, have students pass their card to the person on their left and begin the game again.

SPIDER WEB REVIEW

You will need a ball of yarn for this activity.

Instruct the children to stand in a circle. Toss the ball of yarn to one child and ask him or her to say the first word of the verse. The child will wrap the yarn around his or her hand and toss the ball of yarn to another child across the circle. This child will say the second word of the verse and wrap the yarn around his finger. Continue playing and saying words of the verse until every child has a turn. The back and forth motion of the yarn will produce a spider web.

BALLOON POP

You will need balloons, a permanent marker, and tape.

Blow up the balloons. Write one word of the Bible verse on each balloon. Attach the balloons to the wall in correct order. Let the children read the verse together. Select one child to pop one balloon. Have the children recite the verse again, and remember to say the missing word. Select another child to pop a balloon. Let the children say the verse again. Continue until all the balloons are gone, and the children can recite the verse from memory.

HAPPY FACES MEMORY GAME

Write each word or phrase of a Bible verse on a paper plate or a circular piece of paper.

Distribute the plates to the children, and ask them to draw a happy face on the blank side of the plate (circle). Attach the plates to the wall so the children can see the words of the verse. Read the verse together. Select one child to turn over one of the plates so the happy face shows. Then have the children read the verse. Select another child to turn over another plate. Say the verse again. Continue until all of the plates show happy faces, and children can recite the verse from memory.

BIBLE VERSE UNSCRAMBLE

Write each word or phrase of a Bible verse on a piece of paper or index card.

Distribute the word cards in mixed order. Let the children arrange themselves in a circle in the correct order according to the portion of the verse they received. Have the children say the verse together. Then ask one child to turn the card around, so the other children cannot see his or her word. Have the children say the verse again. Continue in this manner until all the cards are turned around and no words are visible.

This could also be played as a race between two or more teams to see which one is the first to arrange themselves with the words of the verse in the correct order.

BIBLE QUIZ REVIEW QUESTIONS—EXODUS

LESSON 1—QUESTIONS FOR RED LEVEL REVIEW

1. What happened after Joseph and his generation died? (1:8-9)

1. A new king came into power who did not know Joseph.
2. The new king became afraid of the Israelites.
3. **Both answers are correct.**

2. How many Israelites lived in Egypt when the new king came to power? (1:7)

1. **So many that they filled the land.**
2. About 100
3. None because they had all died.

3. What did the new king believe that the Israelites would do if war broke out? (1:10)

1. They would make weapons for the enemy.
2. **They would join Egypt's enemies and leave Egypt.**
3. They would stop working and hide until the war was over.

4. What did the king do to stop the Israelites from joining his enemies and leaving Egypt? (1:11)

1. He forced them to build store cities for Pharaoh.
2. He appointed slave masters over them.
3. **Both answers are correct.**

5. What happened the more the Israelites were oppressed? (1:12)

1. They fought the Egyptians.
2. **They multiplied and spread.**
3. They all died.

6. What command did the king give to the midwives? (1:16)

1. Kill all the Hebrew babies.
2. Do not help the Hebrew women in childbirth.
3. **Kill the baby boys but let the baby girls live.**

7. What were the names of the Hebrew midwives? (1:15)

1. Puah and Rachel
2. **Shiphrah and Puah**
3. Shiphrah and Rebekah

8. Why did the midwives let the Hebrew baby boys live? (1:17)

1. **They feared God.**
2. They misunderstood the king's command.
3. Both answers are correct.

9. What happened when the midwives let the baby boys live? (1:20-21)

1. Pharaoh gave the order to kill the midwives.
2. **God was kind to the midwives and gave to them families of their own. The people became even more numerous.**
3. Pharaoh stopped the Hebrew women from having any babies.

10. What order did Pharaoh give to all his people? (1:22)

1. Throw the baby boys into the Nile.
2. Let the baby girls live.
3. **Both answers are correct.**

BIBLE QUIZ REVIEW QUESTIONS—EXODUS

LESSON 1—QUESTIONS FOR BLUE LEVEL REVIEW

1. Who went from Canaan to Egypt? (1:1-5)

1. Jacob, the sons of Israel, and their families
2. The slave masters, who were looking for jobs
3. Pharaoh's magicians, wise men, and sorcerers
4. Jethro and his daughters

2. What changed in Egypt after Joseph and all his generation died? (1:7-10)

1. A new king came to power.
2. The Israelites became so numerous that they filled the land.
3. The new king did not trust the Israelites.
4. All of the above

3. What did the new king believe that the Israelites would do? (1:10)

1. Steal all the wealth of Egypt
2. Join his enemies, fight against Egypt, and leave
3. Kill all the Egyptian boy babies
4. The Bible does not say.

4. How did Pharaoh deal with the Israelites? (1:11)

1. He appointed Hebrews to rule in Joseph's place.
2. He told them to go back to Canaan.
3. He appointed slave masters over them.
4. He ignored them.

5. How did the slave drivers treat the Hebrews? (1:11-14)

1. They gave them very little work and plenty of rest.
2. They made their lives bitter with hard labor.
3. They made them work hard but they paid them well.
4. All of the above.

6. What cities did the Israelites build for Pharaoh? (1:11)

1. Thebes and Cairo
2. Pithom and Rameses
3. Bethel and Jezreel
4. All of the above

7. What order did Pharaoh give to the Hebrew midwives? (1:15-16)

1. Kill the baby boys but let the baby girls live.
2. Send the baby boys to Canaan but keep the baby girls in Egypt.
3. Kill the baby girls but let the baby boys live.
4. Kill all the Hebrew babies, boys and girls.

8. What did Shiphrah and Puah, the Hebrew midwives, do about Pharaoh's order to kill the Hebrew boy babies? (1:17)

1. They feared God.
2. They did not do what Pharaoh said.
3. They let the Hebrew boy babies live.
4. All of the above

9. What did the Lord do for Shiphrah and Puah? (1:20-21)

1. He said "Thank you for saving the baby boys."
2. He helped them escape from Egypt.
3. He was kind to them and gave them families of their own.
4. The Bible does not say.

10. What did Pharaoh order all his people to do? (1:22)

1. Rejoice because the Hebrew boys are dead!
2. Throw every Hebrew baby boy into the Nile, but let the girls live.
3. Report anyone sheltering Hebrew boys.
4. The Bible does not say.

BIBLE QUIZ REVIEW QUESTIONS—EXODUS

LESSON 2—QUESTIONS FOR RED LEVEL REVIEW

1. What did the Levite woman do when she could no longer hide her baby boy? (2:3)

1. She coated a papyrus basket with tar and pitch.
2. She placed the basket among the reeds along the bank of the Nile.
3. **Both answers are correct.**

2. Who watched from a distance to see what would happen to the child in the basket? (2:4)

1. **The child's sister**
2. The child's mother
3. The child's brother

3. What did Pharaoh's daughter do when she saw the basket? (2:5)

1. She lifted it out of the river.
2. **She sent her slave girl to retrieve it.**
3. She sent her slave girl to destroy it.

4. Who did Pharaoh's daughter pay to nurse baby Moses? (2:8-9)

1. An Egyptian woman
2. One of her attendants
3. **His own mother**

5. What did Moses see when he watched his people at their hard labor? (2:11)

1. **An Egyptian beating a Hebrew**
2. The Hebrews building a pyramid
3. Both answers are correct

6. What did Pharaoh do when he heard that Moses had killed the Egyptian? (2:15)

1. He made Moses a slave too.
2. **He tried to kill Moses.**
3. He sent Moses to jail.

7. Where did Moses go when he fled from Pharaoh? (2:15)

1. Goshen
2. Canaan
3. **Midian**

8. Who did Moses meet at the well in Midian? (2:16, 18)

1. Soldiers from Pharaoh's army
2. His brother Aaron
3. **The seven daughters of Reuel, the priest of Midian**

9. What happened at the well in Midian? (2:16-17)

1. **Moses rescued Reuel's daughters from some shepherds.**
2. Moses decided to return to Egypt.
3. Some shepherds drove Moses away.

10. What also happened while Moses was in Midian? (2:21-22)

1. He married Zipporah.
2. He had a son named Gershom.
3. **Both answers are correct**

BIBLE QUIZ REVIEW QUESTIONS—EXODUS

LESSON 2—QUESTIONS FOR BLUE LEVEL REVIEW

1. Why did Moses's mother hide him for three months? (2:2)

1. She was ashamed of him.
2. **She saw that he was a fine child.**
3. She saw that he was a sick child.
4. She wanted a girl instead of a boy.

2. What happened after Moses's mother hid him for three months? (2:3-4)

1. She could not hide him any longer.
2. She put him in a papyrus basket on the bank of the Nile.
3. Moses' sister stood at a distance and watched.
4. **All of the above**

3. How did Pharaoh's daughter respond when she opened the basket and the baby was crying? (2:6)

1. **She felt sorry for the baby.**
2. She felt angry with his mother for placing him in a basket.
3. She felt sorry that she had rescued him.
4. She felt angry with him for crying.

4. Who raised Moses? (2:7-10)

1. An Egyptian nanny in Pharaoh's palace
2. Pharaoh's daughter, beginning on the day she found him
3. **First his mother, then Pharaoh's daughter when he grew older**
4. All of the above

5. Why did Moses kill the Egyptian? (2:11-12)

1. The Egyptian started a fight with Moses.
2. **The Egyptian was beating a Hebrew.**
3. The Egyptian stole his money.
4. The Egyptian had killed many Hebrew slaves.

6. What did Moses do with the body of the dead Egyptian? (2:12)

1. He threw it into the Nile.
2. He burned it.
3. **He hid it in the sand.**
4. He did nothing and walked away.

7. Why did Moses leave Egypt and go to Midian? (2:15)

1. Moses discovered that he was really a Midianite.
2. The Hebrews chased him out of Egypt.
3. **Pharaoh tried to kill him.**
4. All of the above

8. What happened at the well in Midian? (2:15-18)

1. Moses sat by the well.
2. Reuel's daughters came to water their father's flock.
3. Moses rescued Ruel's daughters from the shepherds.
4. **All of the above.**

9. What does Exodus 2 tell us about Reuel? (2:16)

1. He had seven daughters.
2. He was the priest of Midian.
3. He had a flock of sheep.
4. **All of the above**

10. What did Moses name his first son? (2:22)

1. Reuel, which meant, "Shepherd of God."
2. **Gershom and said, "I have become a foreigner in a foreign land."**
3. Gershom and said, "A new life has begun."
4. None of the above

Bible Studies for Children: Exodus
Bible Quiz Review Questions

BIBLE QUIZ REVIEW QUESTIONS—EXODUS

LESSON 3—QUESTIONS FOR RED LEVEL REVIEW

1. Who died while Moses was in Midian? (2:23)

1. Jethro, Moses's father-in-law
2. The king of Egypt
3. Both answers are correct

2. What did God do when he heard the Israelites groaning? (2:24-25)

1. He remembered his covenant with Abraham, Isaac, and Jacob.
2. He was concerned about them.
3. **Both answers are correct**

3. What job did Moses do for his father-in-law, Jethro? (3:1)

1. He fought Jethro's enemies.
2. **He tended Jethro's flock.**
3. Both answers are correct.

4. What did God say to Moses from the burning bush? (3:5)

1. **"The place where you are standing is holy ground."**
2. "Why did you kill the Egyptian?"
3. "Are you happy in Midian?"

5. Why did the Lord say he had come down? (3:7-8)

1. To help the Midianites
2. To punish Moses for running away
3. **To rescue his people from the hand of the Egyptians**

6. What did Moses say to God about going to Egypt? (3:11)

1. "I will never go back to Egypt."
2. **"Who am I, that I should go to Pharaoh and bring the Israelites out of Egypt?"**
3. Both answers are correct

7. What sign would prove to Moses that God had sent him to Pharaoh? (3:12)

1. **He would return with the people and worship God on this mountain.**
2. The Nile would dry up.
3. The Midianites would help the Israelites.

8. What did God say when Moses asked for his name? (3:14)

1. "I am the Lord God Almighty."
2. **"I AM WHO I AM."**
3. "I am the One True God."

9. What did God say he would do in Egypt? (3:20)

1. He would command the Midianites to fight the Egyptians.
2. **He would stretch out his hand, strike the Egyptians, and perform wonders.**
3. He would make slaves of the Egyptians.

10. What would the Israelites receive from the Egyptians? (3:22)

1. Silver and gold
2. Clothing
3. **Both answers are correct.**

BIBLE QUIZ REVIEW QUESTIONS—EXODUS

LESSON 3—QUESTIONS FOR BLUE LEVEL REVIEW

1. What happened in Egypt while Moses was in Midian? (2:23)

1. The king of Egypt died.
2. The Israelites groaned in their slavery.
3. God heard the Israelites groaning.
4. **All of the above**

2. Where did Moses take Jethro's flock? (3:1)

1. **To Mount Horeb, the mountain of God**
2. To the oasis in the desert
3. To the well for water
4. To Egypt as a gift for Pharaoh

3. When Moses noticed the burning bush, what did he do? (3:2-3)

1. He thought, "I must be crazy."
2. **He thought, "I will go over and see this strange sight."**
3. He moved the flock a safe distance away.
4. All of the above

4. As Moses approached the burning bush, what did God say? (3:4-5)

1. "This bush is dangerous. Leave quickly."
2. "Find your brother Aaron. I must speak to both of you."
3. **"Do not come any closer. Take off your sandals."**
4. All of the above

5. What message did the Lord give Moses? (3:7-8)

1. He had seen the misery of his people.
2. He was concerned about their suffering.
3. He came to rescue them from the Egyptians.
4. **All of the above**

6. How did Moses reply when God said he was sending Moses to Egypt? (3:11)

1. "I cannot go. My family needs me."
2. "I never want to set foot in Egypt again."
3. **"Who am I, that I should go to Pharaoh and bring the Israelites out?"**
4. All of the above

7. What promise did God make to Moses? (3:12)

1. "You can do it, Moses. I believe in you."
2. **"I will be with you."**
3. "You will succeed with the help of a large army."
4. "If you do this, I will make you famous."

8. How was Moses to answer when the Israelites asked who had sent him? (3:14-15)

1. "The God of the universe has sent me to you."
2. "Jethro, the high priest of Midian, has sent me to you."
3. **"I AM WHO I AM. I AM has sent me to you."**
4. "The angel of God has sent me to you."

9. What was the Lord going to do to the Egyptians? (3:20-21)

1. Strike the Egyptians
2. Perform wonders among them
3. Make them favorably disposed toward the Israelites
4. **All of the above**

10. What would the Israelites have when they left Egypt? (3:21-22)

1. **They would have silver, gold, and clothing.**
2. They would never leave Egypt.
3. They would leave with nothing but their clothes.
4. All of the above

BIBLE QUIZ REVIEW QUESTIONS—EXODUS

LESSON 4—QUESTIONS FOR RED LEVEL REVIEW

1. What did the Lord tell Moses to throw on the ground? (4:2-3)

1. His robe
2. His sandals
3. **His staff**

2. What was the first sign the Lord gave to Moses to show the Israelites? (4:2-4)

1. His hand turned into a snake, and then back to normal.
2. **His staff turned into a snake and then back into a staff.**
3. He became blind, and then he could see.

3. What was the second sign the Lord gave to Moses to show the Israelites? (4:6-7)

1. His hand fell off and then grew back again.
2. He became blind and then could see again.
3. **His hand became leprous, and then became like the rest of his skin.**

4. What did Moses say he was slow of? (4:10)

1. **Speech and tongue**
2. Understanding and wisdom
3. Both answers are correct.

5. As Moses was speaking to God, who was on his way to meet him? (4:14)

1. Pharaoh, the king of Egypt
2. **Aaron, Moses's brother**
3. Gershom, Moses's son

6. How did the Lord say he would help Moses and Aaron? (4:15)

1. Help both of them to speak
2. Teach them what to do
3. **Both answers are correct.**

7. What good news did God give to Moses in Midian? (4:19)

1. **"All the men who wanted to kill you are dead."**
2. "Don't worry. Pharaoh cannot find you."
3. "All the men who wanted to kill you have left Egypt."

8. Whom did Moses and Aaron gather together in Egypt? (4:29)

1. Pharaoh and all the Egyptians
2. **The Israelite elders**
3. The Hebrew army

9. What did the elders find out about the Lord? (4:31)

1. That He was concerned about them
2. That He had seen their misery
3. **Both answers are correct.**

10. What did the elders do after they heard that the Lord was concerned about them? (4:31)

1. **They bowed down and worshiped.**
2. They started shouting for joy.
3. Both answers are correct.

BIBLE QUIZ REVIEW QUESTIONS—EXODUS

LESSON 4—QUESTIONS FOR BLUE LEVEL REVIEW

1. What did Moses ask the Lord about going to Egypt? (4:1)

1. "What if I cannot do the two signs again?"
2. **"What if they do not believe me or listen to me?"**
3. "What if Pharaoh tries to kill me?"
4. All of the above

2. What happened when Moses took his hand out of his cloak? (4:6)

1. His cloak caught on fire but did not burn.
2. His staff turned into a snake.
3. The Nile turned to blood.
4. **His hand was leprous.**

3. What was Moses to do if the people did not believe the first two signs? (4:9)

1. Show them again, but more slowly this time
2. Pray that they would understand and believe
3. **Pour water from the Nile on the dry ground**
4. All of the above

4. What excuse did Moses use to explain why he was unable to do what the Lord asked? (4:10)

1. "Pharaoh is trying to kill me."
2. "I cannot abandon my family. They need me."
3. **"I have never been eloquent. I am slow of speech and tongue."**
4. All of the above

5. How did the Lord say he would help Moses? (4:12)

1. "I will raise up an army among the Israelites."
2. "I will start a rebellion among the Egyptians and they will overthrow Pharaoh."
3. "I will send Jethro to help you."
4. **"I will help you to speak and teach you what to say."**

6. What did God say Moses would use to perform miraculous signs? (4:17)

1. Moses's book of the Law
2. **Moses's staff**
3. Moses's sandals
4. All of the above

7. What good news did God give to Moses in Midian? (4:19)

1. "Midianite soldiers can defeat Pharaoh's army."
2. **"All those who wanted to kill you are dead."**
3. "The new Pharaoh will welcome you back."
4. All of the above

8. How did Aaron know to meet Moses in the desert? (4:27)

1. Aaron escaped from Egypt and met him by accident.
2. Moses sent him a message from Midian.
3. **The Lord told Aaron to go.**
4. All of the above

9. What did the elders learn about God from Moses and Aaron? (4:31)

1. **God saw their misery and was concerned about them.**
2. God had a whole host of angel warriors to help them.
3. God was going to strike Pharaoh with a plague that would kill him.
4. All of the above

10. What did the elders do when they saw the signs and learned that God cared about them? (4:30-31)

1. They went to Pharaoh and said, "We are all leaving."
2. **They bowed down and worshiped God.**
3. They formed an army and attacked Pharaoh.
4. All of the above

BIBLE QUIZ REVIEW QUESTIONS—EXODUS

LESSON 5—QUESTIONS FOR RED LEVEL REVIEW

1. What message from God did Moses and Aaron give to Pharaoh? (5:1)

1. "Obey Moses and Aaron Now!"
2. **"Let my people go."**
3. "Moses and Aaron are going back to Midian."

2. What was Pharaoh's answer to the Lord's message? (5:2)

1. "I do not know the Lord."
2. "I will not let Israel go."
3. **Both answers are correct.**

3. What did Moses and Aaron ask Pharaoh to let them do? (5:3)

1. Take a trip to the mountains
2. **Take a three-day journey into the wilderness**
3. Take a river boat down the Nile

4. What did Pharaoh say the foremen could not give to the people anymore? (5:7)

1. **Straw for making bricks**
2. More helpers
3. Places to live

5. Where did the Israelites go to gather stubble to use for straw? (5:12)

1. All over Canaan
2. **All over Egypt**
3. All over Babylon

6. What did the slave drivers expect the people to do? (5:13)

1. **Complete the required work for each day**
2. Work both day and night
3. Gather double the amount of straw each day

7. What happened when the foremen did not meet their quota of bricks? (5:14)

1. They were killed.
2. **They were beaten.**
3. They were put in prison.

8. After the Israelite foremen complained, what did the Lord tell Moses? (6:1)

1. "Now you will see what I will do to Pharaoh."
2. "Because of my mighty hand he will let them go."
3. **Both answers are correct.**

9. What was the Lord going to do for the Israelite people? (6:7-8)

1. Make them into a strong army to fight against Pharaoh
2. **Take them as his people and bring them to the land he promised**
3. Both answers are correct.

10. Why didn't the Israelites listen to Moses? (6:9)

1. **Because of their discouragement and cruel bondage**
2. Because they were tired
3. Because they were angry

Bible Studies for Children: Exodus
Bible Quiz Review Questions

BIBLE QUIZ REVIEW QUESTIONS—EXODUS

LESSON 5—QUESTIONS FOR BLUE LEVEL REVIEW

1. What message did God give to Moses and Aaron for Pharaoh? (5:1)

1. "Let my people build a temple for me in Goshen."
2. "Let my people build their own city."
3. **"Let my people go, so that they may hold a festival to me in the desert."**
4. "Let my people go to the land of Midian."

2. How did Pharaoh respond to Moses and Aaron's message from the Lord about the festival in the desert? (5:1-2)

1. "Who is the Lord, that I should obey him?"
2. "Who is the Lord, that I should let Israel go?"
3. "I do not know the Lord and I will not let Israel go."
4. **All of the above**

3. What happened after the first meeting with Pharaoh? (5:7-8)

1. Pharaoh told the foremen to help the people find straw.
2. **The people had to gather their own straw and make the same number of bricks.**
3. The people had to make more bricks than before.
4. The people made enough bricks with less straw.

4. Where did the Israelites go to gather stubble to use for straw? (5:12)

1. **All over Egypt**
2. Only in Goshen
3. Into the desert
4. All the way to Midian

5. What did Pharaoh tell the Israelite foremen? (5:17-18)

1. That they could make fewer bricks because it was hard to find straw
2. That he would give them more straw
3. **That they were lazy and needed to get to work**
4. That they were making bad bricks

6. What did Moses ask the Lord after he met with the foremen? (5:22)

1. "Lord, didn't you say you were going to free them?"
2. **"O Lord, why have you brought trouble upon this people?"**
3. "Why didn't Pharaoh let the people go?"
4. "Lord, can I go home to Midian?"

7. How did the Lord answer Moses? (6:1, 7)

1. "Now you will see what I will do to Pharaoh."
2. "Because of my mighty hand he will let them go."
3. "Because of my mighty hand, he will drive them out of his country."
4. **All of the above**

8. What did God remember when he heard the groaning of the Israelites? (6:5)

1. His strength and power to do miracles
2. **His covenant with Abraham, Isaac, and Jacob**
3. His anger toward Pharaoh
4. His plans for Moses

9. What was Moses to tell the people? (6:6, 8)

1. The Lord would free them from being slaves.
2. The Lord would redeem them with an outstretched arm.
3. The Lord would bring them to the land He swore to give to Abraham, Isaac, and Jacob.
4. **All of the above**

10. What was the Israelites' response to the message Moses gave them from the Lord? (6:9)

1. They asked for a sign from God.
2. They believed and were encouraged.
3. **They were discouraged and did not listen.**
4. They wanted to talk to Aaron.

BIBLE QUIZ REVIEW QUESTIONS—EXODUS

LESSON 6—QUESTIONS FOR RED LEVEL REVIEW

1. What was Moses to tell Pharaoh? (6:28-29)

1. That he would no longer speak to Pharaoh about the Lord
2. **Everything the Lord told him**
3. That he was leaving Egypt

2. What did Moses say when the Lord asked him to speak to Pharaoh? (6:30)

1. **"Since I speak with faltering lips, why would Pharaoh listen to me?"**
2. "Pharaoh didn't listen to me the first time."
3. "Pharaoh does not like me."

3. What did the Lord tell Moses and Aaron to do when Pharaoh asked them to perform a miracle? (7:8-9)

1. To strike Moses's hand, which would make it leprous
2. To tell the water of the Nile River to turn into blood
3. **To throw down Aaron's staff, which would become a snake**

4. What did Aaron's staff do to the magicians' staffs? (7:12)

1. Turned them to stone
2. **Swallowed them**
3. Nothing

5. How did Pharaoh feel at the end of the first miracle? (7:13)

1. He was amazed and listened carefully.
2. **His heart became hard and he would not listen to Moses and Aaron.**
3. He felt afraid and angry.

6. What did the Lord say about Pharaoh? (7:14)

1. "Pharaoh's heart continues to be hard."
2. "He refuses to let the people go."
3. **Both answers are correct.**

7. What would happen when God turned the water of the Nile into blood? (7:17-18)

1. The fish would die.
2. The Nile would stink and the Egyptians would not be able to drink its water.
3. **Both answers are correct.**

8. What did Aaron do in the presence of Pharaoh and his officials? (7:20)

1. He poured the water into the Nile.
2. **He raised his staff and struck the water of the Nile.**
3. He dug along the Nile.

9. Why was Pharaoh's heart hardened again? (7:22)

1. **The magicians did the same things by their secret arts.**
2. The magicians could not do the same things.
3. He was angry with the magicians.

10. Where did Pharaoh go after this? (7:23)

1. To the city
2. To the temple
3. **To his palace**

BIBLE QUIZ REVIEW QUESTIONS—EXODUS

LESSON 6—QUESTIONS FOR BLUE LEVEL REVIEW

1. What did the Lord say when He spoke to Moses in Egypt? (6:28-29)

1. "Moses, quit giving me excuses!"
2. "It is time to do the miracles I taught you."
3. **"I am the Lord. Tell Pharaoh, king of Egypt, everything I tell you."**
4. "Moses you can go back to Midian now."

2. What question did Moses ask the Lord? (6:30)

1. **"Since I speak with faltering lips, why would Pharaoh listen to me?"**
2. "Since I am uneducated, how can I talk to Pharaoh?"
3. "Since I feel sick, can someone else go to Pharaoh?
4. "Since I am getting old, why do you want me to go?"

3. What did God say Moses and Aaron would be? (7:1)

1. Moses would be a prophet to Pharaoh, and Aaron would be his servant.
2. **Moses would be like God to Pharaoh, and Aaron would be his prophet.**
3. Moses would be a magician to Pharaoh, and Aaron would be his helper.
4. Moses would be a king to Pharaoh, and Aaron would be his advisor.

4. What would happen to Pharaoh's heart even though the Lord would multiply his signs and wonders? (7:3)

1. It would become soften.
2. It would become weak.
3. **It would become hard.**
4. It would become dead.

5. What would Pharaoh ask Moses and Aaron to do when they delivered the Lord's message to him? (7:9)

1. He would ask what the Lord's name was.
2. **He would ask them to perform a miracle.**
3. He would ask exactly where the Israelites were planning to go.
4. All of the above

6. What was the first miracle Aaron did? (7:9)

1. **His staff became a snake.**
2. His staff became a lizard.
3. His staff turned to stone.
4. His staff turned to gold.

7. What happened to the staffs of the magicians? (7:12)

1. They broke.
2. They did not turn into snakes.
3. **They became snakes and were swallowed by Aaron's staff.**
4. The Bible does not say.

8. What was the first plague the Lord would send? (7:17)

1. All the men would become leprous.
2. **The water of the Nile would turn to blood.**
3. A great sandstorm would bury Egypt.
4. The Nile would dry up.

9. When the Nile turned to blood, what would happen? (7:18)

1. The fish would die.
2. The river would stink.
3. The Egyptians would not be able to drink the water.
4. **All of the above**

10. What happened after the Nile turned to blood? (7:22-24)

1. **The magicians did the same thing by their secret arts.**
2. The Egyptians got sick.
3. Pharaoh finally realized how powerful the Lord is.
4. All of the above

BIBLE QUIZ REVIEW QUESTIONS—EXODUS

LESSON 7—QUESTIONS FOR RED LEVEL REVIEW

1. What plague came seven days after the Lord struck the Nile? (7:25; 8:2)

1. Frogs
2. Gnats
3. Flies

2. What happened when the magicians tried to make frogs come up on the land? (8:7)

1. They were not able to make frogs come up.
2. They were able to make frogs come up.
3. Their frogs were all red.

3. When did the frogs leave and die? (8:12-13)

1. Seven days later
2. After Moses cried out to the Lord
3. After Pharaoh cried out to the Lord

4. What happened to the dust when Aaron struck the ground with his staff? (8:17)

1. The dust turned to mud.
2. The dust became rats.
3. The dust became gnats.

5. When the magicians used their secret arts to produce gnats, what happened? (8:18-19)

1. Millions of gnats appeared
2. They could not produce gnats
3. They produced frogs instead

6. Where did the Lord say the flies would be? (8:21-22)

1. The flies would be in Egypt but not in Goshen.
2. The flies would be in Egypt and in Goshen.
3. Both answers are correct.

7. What happened to Egypt because of the flies? (8:24)

1. The Nile turned red.
2. The land was ruined.
3. The land was improved.

8. What did Pharaoh want Moses to do? (8:28)

1. Not go very far
2. Pray for him
3. Both answers are correct.

9. What happened when Moses prayed to the Lord about the flies? (8:30-31)

1. The flies left Pharaoh but did not leave his people.
2. No flies remained after Moses prayed.
3. Moses did not pray about the flies.

10. What happened after the flies left? (8:32)

1. Pharaoh hardened his heart.
2. Pharaoh would not let the people go.
3. Both answers are correct.

BIBLE QUIZ REVIEW QUESTIONS—EXODUS

LESSON 7—QUESTIONS FOR BLUE LEVEL REVIEW

1. What happened seven days after the Lord struck the Nile? (7:25—8:2)

1. Moses went to Pharaoh again.
2. Moses told Pharaoh to let the people go.
3. Moses said that frogs would plague Egypt if Pharaoh did not let the people go.
4. **All of the above.**

2. How did the magicians respond to the plague of frogs? (8:7)

1. They ran and hid because they believed frogs were evil.
2. **They also made frogs come up on the land.**
3. They could not make frogs come up on the land.
4. They killed all the frogs.

3. What did Pharaoh tell Moses and Aaron to do about the plague of frogs? (8:8)

1. To catch all the frogs
2. To kill all the frogs
3. **To pray to the Lord to take the frogs away**
4. To turn their staffs into snakes to eat the frogs

4. What happened when the frogs died? (8:14-15)

1. They were piled into heaps.
2. The land reeked of them.
3. Pharaoh hardened his heart.
4. **All of the above.**

5. What happened as part of the plague of gnats? (8:17-19)

1. Aaron threw handfuls of dust in the air.
2. The magicians also produced gnats.
3. **The magicians could not produce gnats.**
4. The gnats swarmed on animals but not on the people.

6. How did Pharaoh respond when the magicians could not produce gnats? (8:19)

1. He said the Israelites could sacrifice to God in Egypt.
2. **His heart was hard and he would not listen.**
3. He listened to the magicians.
4. He killed the magicians.

7. How was the plague of flies different from the first three plagues? (8:22)

1. The Lord would deal differently with Goshen, where his people lived.
2. There would be no swarms of flies in Goshen.
3. The Lord would make a distinction between his people and Pharaoh's people.
4. **All of the above**

8. How did the plague of flies affect Egypt? (8:24)

1. Flies covered the Nile.
2. Flies filled just the temples of Egypt.
3. **Flies ruined the land.**
4. Flies killed all the livestock.

9. How did Pharaoh react to the plague of flies? (8:28)

1. **He said the Israelites could go to offer sacrifices to the Lord in the desert but not very far.**
2. He said the Israelites could go to the mountains but not to the desert.
3. He said they could only take a two-day journey.
4. He said he didn't care how far they went.

10. What happened when Moses prayed about the flies? (8:30-31)

1. The flies left Pharaoh but not his officials.
2. The flies left Pharaoh and his officials but not his people.
3. Pharaoh softened his heart and let the people go.
4. **The Lord did what Moses asked.**

BIBLE QUIZ REVIEW QUESTIONS—EXODUS

LESSON 8—QUESTIONS FOR RED LEVEL REVIEW

1. What happened during the plague on the livestock? (9:4, 6)

1. The Egyptian livestock died.
2. The Israelite livestock did not die.
3. **Both answers are correct.**

2. When Pharaoh sent men to investigate the plague on the livestock, what did they discover? (9:7)

1. **Not even one of the animals of the Israelites died.**
2. The Egyptian livestock were fine.
3. The Israelites had no livestock.

3. What word describes Pharaoh's heart after the plague on the livestock? (9:7)

1. Nervous
2. **Hard**
3. Sad

4. What would the soot that Moses threw become? (9:9)

1. A fine mist over the land
2. A fine cloud over the land
3. **A fine dust over the whole land**

5. What did the Lord tell Moses to say to Pharaoh after the plague of boils? (9:13-14)

1. "Let my people go."
2. "This time I will send the full force of my plagues against you and against your officials and your people."
3. **Both answers are correct.**

6. What did the officials who feared the Lord do when they heard a plague of hail was coming? (9:19-20)

1. They told their slaves to keep working.
2. **They brought their slaves and livestock inside.**
3. They sent their slaves to the Nile River.

7. Where did it not hail? (9:26)

1. **Goshen**
2. Egypt
3. Both answers are correct.

8. What did Pharaoh say before the hail stopped? (9:27)

1. "My magicians will make this hail stop."
2. **"I have sinned. The LORD is in the right."**
3. "I will pray to my gods to make this hail stop."

9. What did Pharaoh ask Moses to do? (9:28)

1. Stop the storm
2. **Pray to the Lord to stop the storm**
3. Get the Israelites to stop the storm

10. After the hail stopped, what did Pharaoh do? (9:34-35)

1. He sinned again.
2. He would not let the Israelites go.
3. **Both answers are correct.**

BIBLE QUIZ REVIEW QUESTIONS—EXODUS

LESSON 8—QUESTIONS FOR BLUE LEVEL REVIEW

1. What distinction did the Lord make between the livestock of Israel and Egypt? (9:4, 6)

1. He made no distinction.
2. **The Egyptian livestock died, and the Israelite livestock lived.**
3. The Egyptian livestock got sick, and the Israelite livestock stayed healthy.
4. The Bible does not say.

2. After the plague on the livestock, what did Pharaoh's investigation reveal? (9:7)

1. That Moses and Aaron had died
2. That only some of the Egyptian livestock had died
3. That the Israelite farmers would sell Pharaoh some livestock
4. **That none of the Israelite animals had died**

3. What happened when Moses tossed soot into the air in front of Pharaoh? (9:10-11)

1. Festering boils broke out on men and animals.
2. The magicians couldn't stand before Moses because of their boils.
3. Boils were on all the Egyptians.
4. **All of the above**

4. What did the Lord direct Moses to tell Pharaoh after the plague of boils? (9:13-14)

1. "Let my people go to Goshen."
2. **"If you don't let my people go, I will send the full force of my plagues against you."**
3. "Let my people worship me every day in Egypt."
4. "Let my people go, or I will send your enemies against you."

5. Why did the Lord say he had raised up Pharaoh? (9:16)

1. "For this very purpose"
2. "That I might show you my power"
3. "That my name might be proclaimed in all the earth"
4. **All of the above**

6. What plague did the Lord say He would send after the plague of boils? (9:18)

1. **"The worst hailstorm that has ever fallen on Egypt"**
2. "The worst flood that has ever come on Egypt"
3. "A huge cloud of grasshoppers"
4. "A terrible tornado"

7. Before the hail, who hurried to bring their slaves and livestock inside? (9:20)

1. Moses and Aaron
2. **Officials of Pharaoh who feared the Lord**
3. The Israelite women
4. All of the above

8. Where did it not hail? (9:26)

1. **Goshen**
2. Egypt
3. Midian
4. Canaan

9. What did Moses say he would do when Pharaoh asked him to pray to the Lord to stop the hail? (9:29)

1. He would raise his staff, and the hail would stop.
2. He would pray, and the Lord would send the storm out to sea.
3. He would shout to the sky, and the hail would stop.
4. **He would spread out his hands in prayer to the Lord, and there would be no more hail.**

10. What was Pharaoh's response after the plague of hail? (9:28, 35)

1. **He broke his promise to let the people go.**
2. He finally let the people go.
3. He felt more loving toward the Israelites.
4. He said he was Pharaoh, and he did not have to obey the Lord.

Bible Studies for Children: Exodus
Bible Quiz Review Questions

BIBLE QUIZ REVIEW QUESTIONS—EXODUS

LESSON 9—QUESTIONS FOR RED LEVEL REVIEW

1. After the plague of hail, what did Moses do? (10:1)

1. Talked to the Israelites
2. **Went to Pharaoh with a message from the Lord**
3. Both answers are correct

2. What plague would cover the ground and devour what little the Egyptians had left? (10:4-5)

1. **Locusts**
2. Hail
3. Flies

3. What did the officials tell Pharaoh when they heard about the plague of locusts? (10:7)

1. "Let the people go."
2. "Do you not yet realize that Egypt is ruined?"
3. **Both answers are correct.**

4. When did the east wind bring the locusts to Egypt? (10:13)

1. **By the morning**
2. By the afternoon
3. By the evening

5. What happened because of the plague of locusts? (10:15)

1. **Nothing green was left in Egypt.**
2. Pharaoh let the Israelites go.
3. Both answers are correct.

6. How long did the darkness cover Egypt? (10:22)

1. Three weeks
2. **Three days**
3. Three months

7. Who had light during the plague of darkness? (10:23)

1. The Egyptians
2. **The Israelites**
3. Both answers are correct.

8. What was the last plague that the Lord would bring on Egypt? (11:1, 4-5)

1. **Death of the firstborn**
2. Hailstorms
3. Locusts

9. When would the last plague happen? (11:4-5)

1. At sunrise
2. In the middle of the day
3. **About midnight**

10. During the last plague, where would there be a loud wailing? (11:6)

1. In Goshen
2. **Throughout Egypt**
3. Both answers are correct.

BIBLE QUIZ REVIEW QUESTIONS—EXODUS

LESSON 9—QUESTIONS FOR BLUE LEVEL REVIEW

1. What was the Lord's message to Pharaoh after the plague of hail? (10:3-4)

1. "How long will you refuse to humble yourself before me?"
2. "Let my people go."
3. "If you refuse to let them go, I will bring locusts into your country tomorrow."
4. **All of the above**

2. Before the plague of locusts, whom did Pharaoh say could go to worship the Lord? (10:11)

1. **Only the men**
2. Only the men and livestock
3. Only the men, women, and children
4. The young, old, sons, daughters, flocks, and herds

3. From what direction did the wind bring the locusts to Egypt? (10:13)

1. North
2. South
3. **East**
4. West

4. How would the locusts affect Egypt? (10:5-6)

1. **They would cover the ground, devour what little the people had left, and fill their houses.**
2. They would fill the Egyptians' dishes and buckets and eat their food.
3. They would cover the buildings and get in their beds.
4. They would fill the wells and rivers.

5. What happened after the plague of locusts? (10:21-22)

1. A strong wind blew the locusts into Midian.
2. Only the men were allowed to leave.
3. **The plague of darkness came for three days.**
4. All of the above

6. What was unusual about the darkness? (10:21-23)

1. The darkness could be felt.
2. The Egyptians couldn't see anyone else for three days.
3. The Israelites had light where they lived.
4. **All of the above**

7. What did Moses tell Pharaoh they would need for their worship? (10:26)

1. **Their livestock**
2. Some wood
3. A load of stones
4. All of the above

8. What was the last plague on Pharaoh and Egypt? (11:1, 5)

1. Egypt would be dark for three months.
2. **Every firstborn son in Egypt and all the firstborn of the cattle would die.**
3. The Israelites would kill the firstborn sons of the Egyptians.
4. All of the above

9. When would the last plague begin? (11:4)

1. At sunrise
2. Around noon
3. At sundown
4. **Around midnight**

10. What would be heard throughout Egypt during the last plague? (11:6)

1. Total silence
2. Dogs barking
3. Loud laughing among the Israelites
4. **Loud wailing**

Bible Studies for Children: Exodus
Bible Quiz Review Questions

Download additional resources from *kidzfirstpublications.org*

BIBLE QUIZ REVIEW QUESTIONS—EXODUS

LESSON 10—QUESTIONS FOR RED LEVEL REVIEW

1. What animal was each Israelite man to choose for his family on the 10th day of the first month? (12:3)

1. A lamb
2. A cow
3. A horse

2. Where were the people to put the blood of the lamb? (12:7, 22)

1. On the ground in front of their houses
2. On the walls of their homes
3. On the tops and sides of their doorframes

3. What was the name of the meal the Israelites were to eat in haste? (12:11)

1. The Feast of Manna
2. The Lord's Passover
3. Both answers are correct.

4. Whom would the Lord strike down at midnight on Passover? (12:12)

1. All Egyptians
2. Every firstborn of men and animals
3. All Israelites

5. Where were the Israelites to stay while the Lord went through the land? (12:22-23)

1. In their houses
2. In their fields
3. The Bible does not say.

6. Why was there loud wailing in Egypt at midnight? (12:29-30)

1. "The Lord struck down all the firstborn in Egypt."
2. "There was not a house without someone dead."
3. Both answers are correct.

7. What did Pharaoh say the night the Lord passed through Egypt? (12:31-32)

1. "Go, worship the Lord as you have requested."
2. "Take your flocks and herds, as you have said, and go."
3. Both answers are correct.

8. How many people left Egypt? (12:37-38)

1. 60,000 Israelite men
2. About 600,000 Israelite men plus women, children, other people, and livestock
3. 6,000 men, women, and children

9. Why was the dough without yeast? (12:39)

1. They did not have time to prepare food.
2. They liked it that way.
3. They did not have any ovens.

10. How long did the Israelites live in Egypt? (12:40)

1. 1,000 years
2. 430 years
3. 430,000 years

BIBLE QUIZ REVIEW QUESTIONS—EXODUS

LESSON 10—QUESTIONS FOR BLUE LEVEL REVIEW

1. On the 10th day of the month, what was each Israelite man to take for his family? (12:3-5)

1. **A year-old lamb, either sheep or goat**
2. A year-old calf
3. A dove or pigeon
4. A pheasant or chicken

2. What were the Israelites to do with the sheep or goats they chose? (12:6-8)

1. Keep the animals as a reminder of God's faithfulness
2. **Roast and eat the meat and put the blood on the sides and tops of their doorframes**
3. Burn the animals completely on an altar
4. Take them along when they left Egypt

3. How were the Israelites to eat the Passover meal? (12:11)

1. With their cloaks tucked into their belts
2. With their sandals on and staffs in hand
3. In haste
4. **All of the above**

4. What was the Lord going to do when he passed through Egypt? (12:12)

1. Confront Pharaoh directly
2. Choose the sheep for each family
3. **Strike down every firstborn and judge all the gods of Egypt**
4. All of the above

5. Why would no destructive plague touch the Israelites? (12:13)

1. The blood would be a sign for them.
2. The Lord would see the blood.
3. The Lord would pass over their houses.
4. **All of the above**

6. What were the Israelites to do during the Feast of Unleavened Bread? (12:15-16)

1. Eat only fruits and vegetables
2. **Eat bread without yeast and do no work except to prepare food.**
3. Eat meat that had been sacrificed to the Lord
4. Hold a feast in honor of Pharaoh

7. Why did Pharaoh summon Moses and Aaron during the night? (12:31-32)

1. **He told them to leave, to take their flocks and herds with them, and to bless him.**
2. He ordered the guards to throw them in prison.
3. He told them they could never leave Egypt.
4. He told them to leave everything behind and just go.

8. What did the Israelites plunder from the Egyptians? (12:35-36)

1. Bread and water
2. Fruits and vegetables
3. **Gold, silver and clothing**
4. Only cattle

9. What happened after Pharaoh said the Israelites could go? (12:37-38, 42)

1. They traveled from Rameses to Succoth.
2. Many other people went with them.
3. "The LORD kept vigil that night to bring them out of Egypt."
4. **All of the above.**

10. How long did the Israelites live in Egypt? (12:40)

1. 500 years, to the very hour
2. **430 years, to the very day**
3. 800 years exactly
4. The Bible doesn't say.

BIBLE QUIZ REVIEW QUESTIONS—EXODUS

LESSON 11—QUESTIONS FOR RED LEVEL REVIEW

1. Why did God lead the Israelites around the Philistine country? (13:17)

1. **He did not want them to face war.**
2. Because it was a longer journey.
3. Both answers are correct.

2. How did the Lord guide the Israelites? (13:21)

1. With a pillar of cloud by day
2. With a pillar of fire by night
3. **Both answers are correct.**

3. Why did Pharaoh prepare his chariot for travel? (14:5-6)

1. He wanted to visit the Philistines.
2. **He planned to pursue the Israelites.**
3. Both answers are correct.

4. What did the Israelites see when they camped at Pi Hahiroth opposite Baal Zephon? (14:9-10)

1. **The Egyptians marching after them**
2. The Philistines fighting the Egyptians
3. Both answers are correct.

5. What did Moses say the Lord would do for the Israelites? (14:14)

1. Hide them from Pharaoh
2. Deliver them from the Philistines
3. **Fight for them**

6. What happened to the pillar of cloud that was in front of the Israelites? (14:19-20)

1. It moved over the Red Sea.
2. **It moved between the armies of Egypt and Israel.**
3. It became a pillar of fire that consumed Pharaoh.

7. What did the Lord do all night long? (14:21)

1. He drove the Egyptians back to Egypt.
2. **He drove the sea back with a strong east wind.**
3. Both answers are correct.

8. What was the sea like when the Israelites went through it? (14:22)

1. There was a wall of water on each side of them.
2. The ground was dry.
3. **Both answers are correct.**

9. What did the Egyptians say when the wheels came off their chariots? (14:25)

1. "Let's chase them on foot!"
2. **"The Lord is fighting for them against Egypt."**
3. Both answers are correct.

10. What did the Israelites see after the sea went back? (14:30)

1. Boats filled with Philistines
2. **Egyptians lying dead on the shore**
3. Wreckage of Egyptian chariots.

BIBLE QUIZ REVIEW QUESTIONS—EXODUS

LESSON 11—QUESTIONS FOR BLUE LEVEL REVIEW

1. Why did the Lord direct the Israelites to travel the desert road and then go back to the sea? (13:17, 14:2-3)

1. He was not sure which direction was best.
2. **He wanted them to avoid war with the Philistines and to make Pharaoh think they were confused.**
3. The Israelites needed more time to prepare.
4. They wanted to see the beach again.

2. Why did Moses take the bones of Joseph from Egypt? (13:19)

1. They had not buried the bones yet.
2. Pharaoh made him.
3. **Joseph made the sons of Israel swear an oath to carry his bones away from Egypt.**
4. There weren't enough graves in Egypt.

3. Who was in the pillar of cloud and pillar of fire? (13:21)

1. Moses
2. **The Lord**
3. An angel of the Lord
4. All of the above

4. What was the purpose of the pillar of cloud and fire? (13:21)

1. To protect the animals
2. To shade the people
3. **To guide the Israelites and give them light**
4. All of the above

5. What did Pharaoh do after the Israelites left Egypt? (14:5-6)

1. He made a treaty with the Philistines.
2. **He changed his mind and pursued the Israelites.**
3. He asked the Philistines to help him pursue the Israelites.
4. He never left Egypt again.

6. Who pursued and overtook the Israelites at Pi Hahiroth? (14:9)

1. Pharaoh's chariots
2. Pharaoh's horsemen
3. Pharaoh's troops
4. **All of the above**

7. What did Moses say when the Israelites saw the Egyptians marching after them? (14:10, 13)

1. "We must ask the Lord to leave Egypt and help us."
2. "Men! We must stand and fight."
3. **"Stand firm and you will see the deliverance the Lord will bring you today."**
4. "Do not worry, I asked the Lord to come from heaven and protect us."

8. What happened as the Egyptians approached? (14:19-22)

1. The pillar of cloud moved between Egypt and Israel.
2. The Lord drove the sea back with a strong east wind.
3. The people went through the sea on dry ground.
4. **All of the above.**

9. Why did the Egyptians say, "Let us get away from the Israelites! The Lord is fighting for them"? (14:25)

1. They were eager to get back home.
2. **The wheels of their chariots came off.**
3. Their horses were running wild.
4. They were tired.

10. After the sea went back, where were the Egyptians lying? (14:30)

1. **Dead on the shore**
2. Asleep in their beds
3. Sitting in their chariots
4. In the desert

BIBLE QUIZ REVIEW QUESTIONS—EXODUS

LESSON 12—QUESTIONS FOR RED LEVEL REVIEW

1. What did the Lord say would rain down for the people? (16:4)

1. Water
2. Bread
3. Both answers are correct.

2. On what day were the people to gather twice as much bread? (16:5)

1. The sixth day
2. The first day
3. The seventh day

3. Whom did Moses say the people were grumbling against? (16:8)

1. Moses
2. Aaron
3. The Lord

4. What did God say the people would eat at twilight? (16:12)

1. Bread
2. Meat
3. Nothing

5. What happened when people disobeyed and kept the bread overnight? (16:20)

1. It began to smell.
2. It was full of maggots.
3. Both answers are correct.

6. What happened to the bread when the sun grew hot? (16:21)

1. It melted away.
2. It turned into quail.
3. Both answers are correct.

7. What did the people do on the seventh day? (16:27, 30)

1. They rested.
2. Some people tried to gather bread, but there was none.
3. Both answers are correct.

8. After God gave them food, for what did the Israelites ask? (17:2)

1. Shade
2. Water
3. Both answers are correct.

9. Without water, what did the Israelites think would happen? (17:3)

1. They would die of thirst.
2. Their children and livestock would die of thirst.
3. Both answers are correct.

10. What did the Lord say would happen when Moses struck the rock? (17:6)

1. Blazing fire would come out.
2. Water would come out.
3. Both answers are correct.

BIBLE QUIZ REVIEW QUESTIONS—EXODUS

LESSON 12—QUESTIONS FOR BLUE LEVEL REVIEW

1. Why were the Israelites grumbling against Moses and Aaron? (16:2-3)

1. They thought they were going the wrong direction.
2. **They said Moses and Aaron would starve them all to death.**
3. They heard that Egyptians were coming to take them back to Egypt.
4. All of the above

2. Where did the Israelites say they ate all the food they wanted? (16:3)

1. **In Egypt**
2. At their festivals
3. By the Red Sea
4. All of the above

3. What did the Lord say he would do when the people complained about having no food? (16:4)

1. He would make wheat grow in the desert.
2. **He would rain down bread.**
3. He would multiply the bread they had.
4. All of the above

4. How much manna did each Israelite gather? (16:16-18, 21)

1. Enough for all his neighbors
2. Enough for the week
3. Enough for three days
4. **As much as he needed**

5. What did the Lord say about the bread he provided? (16:16, 19, 22)

1. The people were to only collect as much as they needed for that day.
2. They were to keep none overnight except on the sixth day.
3. They were to gather twice as much on the sixth day.
4. **All of the above**

6. What happened when some people disobeyed Moses and kept part of the bread until morning? (16:20)

1. **It was full of maggots and began to smell.**
2. It dried up and became hard.
3. It disappeared.
4. It turned to clay.

7. What did the Lord say about gathering bread on the seventh day? (16:29)

1. "Those people will find bread but no quail."
2. **"Everyone is to stay where he is on the seventh day."**
3. "I will send snakes to kill them."
4. None of the above

8. What was the second thing the Israelites complained about? (17:1-2)

1. They wanted to go a different direction.
2. They did not like to move from place to place.
3. **There was no water to drink.**
4. All of the above

9. How did the Lord provide water for the people's thirst? (7:5-6)

1. He told Moses to walk ahead with some of the elders.
2. Moses was to strike the rock at Horeb.
3. Water would come out of the rock.
4. **All of the above**

10. Why did Moses call this place Massah and Meribah? (17:7)

1. **Because the Israelites quarreled and tested the Lord**
2. Because the Israelites got lost
3. Because the Israelites found food and water
4. Because the Israelites started back to Egypt

BIBLE QUIZ REVIEW QUESTIONS—EXODUS

LESSON 13—QUESTIONS FOR RED LEVEL REVIEW

1. Where did the people camp when they entered the Desert of Sinai? (19:2)

1. **In front of the mountain**
2. By the river
3. In the jungle

2. Where did Moses go when they arrived at the Desert of Sinai? (19:3)

1. He stayed with the people.
2. **He went up to God, who called to him from the mountain.**
3. Both answers are correct.

3. How did the Lord say he carried the Israelites from Egypt? (19:4)

1. **On eagles' wings**
2. On horses' backs
3. On turtles' shells

4. At the mountain, how did the Lord want the Israelites to act? (19:5)

1. To sacrifice a lamb
2. **To keep his covenant and to fully obey him**
3. To celebrate the Egyptian's deaths.

5. What would the Israelites become if they obeyed the Lord? (19:5-6)

1. The Lord's treasured possession
2. A kingdom of priests and a holy nation
3. **Both answers are correct.**

6. At the mountain, what did the people say they would do? (19:8)

1. **Everything the Lord said**
2. They didn't say.
3. The Bible does not say.

7. What did the mountain look like when the Lord came down? (19:16)

1. There was thunder and lightning.
2. A thick cloud covered the mountain.
3. **Both answers are correct.**

8. What did the people do when they heard the loud trumpet blast? (19:16)

1. **They trembled.**
2. They laughed.
3. They ran away and never came back.

9. Whom did Moses go down the mountain to get? (19:24)

1. One man from each family
2. **Aaron**
3. Both answers are correct.

10. What warning did the Lord give the people? (19:24)

1. **Not to force their way up to see the Lord.**
2. Make sure only the elders came up to see the Lord.
3. Both answers are correct.

Bible Studies for Children: Exodus
Bible Quiz Review Questions

Download additional resources from *kidzfirstpublications.org*

BIBLE QUIZ REVIEW QUESTIONS—EXODUS

LESSON 13—QUESTIONS FOR BLUE LEVEL REVIEW

1. What happened when the Israelites came to the Desert of Sinai? (19:2)

1. The manna and quail stopped coming each day.
2. Moses, Aaron, and their sister went up the mountain of God.
3. The people camped in front of the mountain.
4. All of the above

2. What message from the Lord was Moses to give the Israelites? (19:3-4)

1. "You saw what I did in Egypt."
2. "I carried you on eagles' wings."
3. "I brought you to myself."
4. **All of the above**

3. What did the Lord say the Israelites would be to Him? (19:5-6)

1. A Holy Nation
2. A Kingdom of Priests
3. A Treasured Possession
4. **All of the above**

4. What was the people's response when they heard what the Lord had said about them? (19:8)

1. They complained about eating manna and quail.
2. **They said they would do everything the Lord said.**
3. They would obey the Lord if He led them out of the desert.
4. All of the above

5. Where did Moses lead the people to meet with God? (19:17)

1. They went to the river.
2. They stood by their tents.
3. They went out into the desert.
4. **They stood at the foot of the mountain.**

6. What happened when the Lord descended on the mountain? (19:16, 18)

1. There was a loud trumpet blast.
2. Smoke billowed up from it.
3. The mountain trembled violently.
4. **All of the above**

7. About what did God tell Moses to warn the people so that they wouldn't perish? (19:21)

1. Not to eat yeast ever
2. **Not to force their way through to see him**
3. Not to take anything with them from Egypt
4. Not to cross the Red Sea

8. What was the warning the Lord gave Moses? (19:23)

1. If people came too close, the lightning would strike them.
2. Moses should bathe in the river before going up the mountain.
3. Nobody, including Moses, must go up the mountain.
4. **There must be limits around the mountain, and set it apart as holy.**

9. Why did the Lord send Moses down the mountain? (19:24)

1. To bring up his sister
2. To bring up the offerings
3. **To bring up Aaron**
4. All of the above

10. What did Moses say when he went down to the people? (19:25)

1. **He told them everything the Lord said.**
2. He told them to be patient and wait.
3. He told them to get ready to leave.
4. He told them how to prepare for the sacrifice.

BIBLE QUIZ REVIEW QUESTIONS—EXODUS

LESSON 14—QUESTIONS FOR RED LEVEL REVIEW

1. What did the Lord do for the Israelites? (20:1-2)

1. **Brought them out of Egypt**
2. Let them stay in Egypt
3. Both answers are correct.

2. How many gods could the Israelites have before the Lord? (20:3)

1. One
2. **None**
3. Both answers are correct.

3. What were the Israelites not to misuse? (20:7)

1. **The Lord's name**
2. The Tabernacle
3. Their sacred tools

4. How were the Israelites to remember the Sabbath day? (20:8)

1. **By keeping it holy**
2. By having a feast
3. By playing games

5. How many days were the Israelites to work in a week? (20:9)

1. Seven days
2. **Six days**
3. Two days

6. What day did the Lord bless and make holy? (20:11)

1. **The Sabbath**
2. Every day
3. The third day of the week

7. Why should the Israelites honor their fathers and mothers? (20:12)

1. So that they may eat healthier
2. **So that they would live long in the land God was giving them**
3. So that they will stay out of trouble

8. What did God say about murder and stealing? (20:13, 15)

1. He said it was OK sometimes.
2. He said that everyone does these things.
3. **He said not to murder or steal.**

9. What did the mountain of God look like? (20:18)

1. **The mountain was in smoke**
2. The mountain looked normal.
3. Both answers are correct.

10. When God spoke to them, what did the people do? (20:18-19)

1. They stayed at a distance.
2. They asked Moses to speak to them for God.
3. **Both answers are correct.**

BIBLE QUIZ REVIEW QUESTIONS—EXODUS

LESSON 14—QUESTIONS FOR BLUE LEVEL REVIEW

1. Out of which land did God bring the Israelites? (20:2)

1. The land of the Philistines
2. The land of Jerusalem
3. **The land of slavery**
4. All of the above

2. Before whom should the Israelites have no other gods? (20:3)

1. **Before the Lord their God**
2. Before Moses
3. Before Aaron
4. Before Pharaoh

3. In what form were the Israelites not supposed to make an idol? (20:4)

1. Anything in heaven
2. Anything above or beneath the earth
3. Anything in the waters below
4. **All of the above**

4. What should the Israelites do for six days before the Sabbath? (20:9)

1. **Labor and work**
2. Rest and relax
3. Eat and drink
4. Play and celebrate

5. After God created everything in six days, what did he do on the seventh day? (20:11)

1. He wrote the laws.
2. **He rested.**
3. He talked to Moses.
4. He named the plants and animals.

6. How were the Israelites to treat their fathers and mothers? (20:12)

1. Not listen to them
2. Sometimes listen to them
3. **Honor them**
4. All of the above

7. What did God promise if the Israelites would honor their fathers and mothers? (20:12)

1. They would receive a blessing.
2. **They would live long in the land God was giving them.**
3. They would live forever.
4. They would receive an inheritance.

8. What should the Israelites not covet? (20:17)

1. Their neighbor's house
2. Their neighbor's wife
3. Their neighbor's ox or donkey
4. **All of the above**

9. Why did God come to test the Israelites? (20:20)

1. **To keep them from sinning**
2. To keep them from fighting each other
3. To make sure that they would hear
4. God thought they wouldn't listen

10. What fear would keep the Israelites from sinning? (20:20)

1. The fear of Moses
2. The fear of Aaron
3. **The fear of God**
4. All of the above

BIBLE QUIZ REVIEW QUESTIONS—EXODUS

LESSON 15—QUESTIONS FOR RED LEVEL REVIEW

1. Who did the Lord say should go up to see him? (24:1)

1. Moses, Aaron, Nadab, Abihu
2. The seventy elders
3. **Both answers are correct.**

2. Could everybody approach the Lord? (24:2)

1. Yes
2. **No**
3. The Bible does not say

3. What did the people say when they heard all the Lord's words and laws? (24:3)

1. **"Everything the LORD has said we will do."**
2. "We don't want to obey the LORD."
3. Both answers are correct.

4. What did Moses send the young Israelite men to do? (24:5)

1. To go look for water
2. To collect manna for the day
3. **To offer burnt offerings**

5. Who did Moses, Aaron, Nadab, Abihu, and the seventy elders see when they went up the mountain? (24:9-10)

1. No one
2. **The God of Israel**
3. Both answers are correct.

6. To whom were the tablets, law and commands going to be given? (24:12)

1. Joshua
2. **Moses**
3. Both answers are correct.

7. Who was Moses' aide? (24:13)

1. **Joshua**
2. Aaron
3. Nadab

8. On what day did the Lord call to Moses from within the cloud? (24:16)

1. The first day
2. The sixth day
3. **The seventh day**

9. What did the top of the mountain look like to the Israelites? (24:17)

1. **Like a consuming fire**
2. Like it was raining
3. Like it was snowing

10. How long did Moses stay on the mountain? (24:18)

1. 7 days and nights
2. **40 days and nights**
3. 4 days and nights

BIBLE QUIZ REVIEW QUESTIONS—EXODUS

LESSON 15—QUESTIONS FOR BLUE LEVEL REVIEW

1. Who was to come with Moses up the mountain to worship? (24:1-2)

1. The seventy elders only
2. Aaron, Nadab, Abihu, and the seventy elders
3. The young Israelite men
4. All of the above

2. Who was to approach the Lord while the others worshiped at a distance? (24:1-2)

1. Aaron, Nadab, and Abihu
2. The seventy elders
3. Moses
4. All of the above

3. What did Moses do when he got up early in the morning after telling the people what the Lord had said? (24:4)

1. He put up a special tent.
2. He caused a great feast to be prepared.
3. He built an altar at the foot of the mountain.
4. All of the above

4. Where did the young Israelite men sacrifice the young bulls? (24:4-5)

1. In the middle of the camp
2. On the mountain
3. On the altar Moses built at the foot of the mountain
4. Just on the outside of camp by the desert

5. How many times did the people say they would do everything the Lord had said? (24:7)

1. One time
2. Two times
3. Three times
4. Four times

6. What did Moses sprinkle on the altar and the people? (24:6, 8)

1. Blood
2. Water
3. Manna
4. Milk

7. Who read the Book of the Covenant to the people? (24:7)

1. Aaron
2. Moses
3. God
4. The elders

8. What happened to the leaders when they saw God on the mountain? (24:11)

1. They were blinded.
2. They ate and drank.
3. They fell asleep.
4. They sang and prayed.

9. What was the Lord going to give Moses when he went up the mountain with Joshua? (24:12-13)

1. A new staff
2. The ability to do more miracles
3. Tablets of stone with the law and commands
4. All of the above

10. What happened when Moses entered the cloud on the mountain? (24:14, 17-18)

1. He stayed for forty days and nights.
2. The Israelites saw what looked like a consuming fire on the top of the mountain.
3. The elders were to wait for Joshua and Moses.
4. All of the above

BIBLE QUIZ REVIEW QUESTIONS—EXODUS

LESSON 16—QUESTIONS FOR RED LEVEL REVIEW

1. What were the Israelites to bring the Lord? (25:1-2)

1. Manna
2. An offering
3. Both answers are correct.

2. What were some of the offerings the people were to bring? (25:3-6)

1. Gold and silver
2. Goat hair and olive oil
3. Both answers are correct.

3. Where was the Lord planning to dwell? (25:8)

1. In Egypt
2. On the mountain away from the people
3. Among them

4. What was the name of the sanctuary the people were to make for the Lord? (25:8-9)

1. The Tabernacle
2. The Resting Place
3. God's House

5. How would Moses and the people know how to make the Tabernacle and the things that went in it? (25:9)

1. Moses would create the pattern.
2. The Lord would show them the pattern.
3. Both answers are correct.

6. What was the ark to be made of? (25:10)

1. Stone
2. Bricks
3. Acacia wood

7. What would the ark of the covenant be covered with? (25:11)

1. Silver
2. Bronze
3. Gold

8. How would the ark be carried? (25:14)

1. With poles
2. On a cart
3. With people's hands

9. Where on the ark's cover were the cherubim supposed to be? (25:18)

1. The middle
2. The ends
3. The Bible does not say.

10. What were the people to put in the ark? (25:21)

1. The Testimony
2. Objects from Egypt as reminders of how God rescued them
3. Both answers are correct.

BIBLE QUIZ REVIEW QUESTIONS—EXODUS

LESSON 16—QUESTIONS FOR BLUE LEVEL REVIEW

1. Who was to bring an offering to the Lord? (25:1-2)

1. The seventy elders
2. Each man whose heart prompted him to give
3. Only Aaron and his sons
4. Everybody was required to give something.

2. What did the Lord want the people to do with all the things they gave? (25:8)

1. Make a monument to always remember what he did for them in the desert.
2. Make a statue of what the elders saw when they were on the mountain.
3. Make a sanctuary for him to dwell in
4. All of the above

3. How would the people know what the Tabernacle and its furnishings should look like? (25:9)

1. Moses and Aaron would create the plan.
2. The Lord would show them the pattern.
3. The elders of the people would design it.
4. They were to copy the pattern of an Egyptian temple.

4. What did the ark look like? (25:10-13)

1. It was made from acacia wood covered with gold and had rings on its four feet.
2. It was made of pure gold and had rings on the top of it.
3. It was gold and silver over acacia wood and had no rings.
4. It was gold with silver rings on the side of it.

5. Why did the ark need gold rings? (25:12-16)

1. Candles would be put in the rings as an offering.
2. Gold chains would be put in the rings to drag the ark.
3. People would hold the rings to carry the ark.
4. Poles would be put in the rings to carry the ark.

6. Where was the Testimony that God was going to give Moses to be put? (25:16)

1. In the ark
2. On the table
3. In a cave
4. On the mountain

7. What was placed on each end of the ark cover? (25:19-20)

1. Sacred bulls
2. Cherubim with their wings spread looking at each other.
3. Eagles with their wings folded up
4. None of the above

8. What was Moses to place on top of the ark? (25:21)

1. The cover
2. The ark of the Testimony
3. The jar of manna
4. Some gold from Egypt

9. How would Moses get the Testimony for the ark? (25:21)

1. God would give it to him.
2. It would appear in the morning.
3. Aaron would write it.
4. He already had it.

10. Where would the Lord meet with Moses and give his commands? (25:22)

1. Above the ark between the two cherubim
2. By the altar where the offerings were made
3. In the desert
4. In his dreams

BIBLE QUIZ REVIEW QUESTIONS—EXODUS

LESSON 17—QUESTIONS FOR RED LEVEL REVIEW

1. What was the table made of? (25:23-24)

1. Gopher wood
2. **Acacia wood**
3. Bronze

2. What was to be on the table at all times? (25:30)

1. Manna
2. **The bread of the Presence**
3. Both answers are correct.

3. What was the lampstand made of? (25:31)

1. Pure bronze
2. Pure silver
3. **Pure gold**

4. How were the people to set up the tabernacle? (26:30)

1. **According to the plan God showed Moses on the mountain**
2. According to the plan Moses showed the elders in Egypt
3. According to the plan Jethro showed Moses in Midian

5. What did the curtain separate? (26:33)

1. The ark of the Testimony from the bread of the Presence
2. **The Holy Place from the Most Holy Place**
3. Both answers are correct.

6. What was in the Most Holy Place? (26:34)

1. The ark of the Testimony
2. The atonement cover
3. **Both answers are correct.**

7. What were the altar utensils made of? (27:3-6)

1. Silver
2. **Bronze**
3. Gold

8. Who was to serve God as priests? (28:1)

1. Aaron, Nadab, and Abihu
2. Eleazar and Ithamar
3. **Both answers are correct.**

9. What were the priests to wear? (28:2-4)

1. **Sacred garments**
2. Golden sandals
3. Both answers are correct.

10. Which skilled men were to make the priests' garments? (28:3)

1. Those who made the Egyptian priests' clothes
2. **Those to whom the Lord had given wisdom in such matters**
3. Both answers are correct.

BIBLE QUIZ REVIEW QUESTIONS—EXODUS

LESSON 17—QUESTIONS FOR BLUE LEVEL REVIEW

1. What was to be on the table at all times? (25:30)

1. The bowl of virgin olive oil
2. **The bread of the Presence**
3. The bronze basin
4. The silver pitcher

2. What furniture was in the tabernacle? (26:33-35; 27:21; 30:6)

1. Only the ark of the Testimony
2. The ark and the atonement cover
3. The ark, the basin, and the altar of sacrifice
4. **The ark and its covering, the altar of incense, the lampstand, and the table**

3. What was overlaid on the altar of burnt offering? (27:1-6)

1. Gold
2. Silver
3. **Bronze**
4. All of the above

4. What surrounded the tabernacle? (27:9)

1. Curtains
2. Posts and bases
3. A courtyard
4. **All of the above.**

5. What separated the Holy Place from the Most Holy Place? (26:31, 33)

1. The ark of the Testimony
2. **A curtain**
3. The basin for washing
4. Gold lampstands

6. Who was to keep the lamps burning from evening till morning? (27:21)

1. Moses and Joshua
2. The leaders of the twelve tribes
3. The elders
4. **Aaron and his sons**

7. What would give Aaron and his sons dignity and honor? (28:2, 4)

1. Planning the tabernacle furnishings
2. Making the furniture for the tabernacle
3. **Sacred garments made especially for them**
4. Keeping the lamps burning

8. How did the priests get their sacred garments? (28:3-4)

1. The Lord gave skilled women the wisdom to make them.
2. Moses brought them out of Egypt.
3. **The Lord gave skilled men the wisdom to make them.**
4. God gave them to Moses on Mt. Sinai

9. Where was the bronze basin for washing placed? (30:18)

1. Between the lampstand and the table
2. **Between the Tent of Meeting and the altar**
3. Between the ark of the Testimony and the curtain
4. Between the altar of Burnt Offerings and the entrance

10. When were Aaron and his sons to wash with the water in the bronze basin? (30:19-21)

1. **Whenever they entered the Tent of Meeting or approached the altar**
2. Before they entered the courtyard
3. Whenever they entered the Tent of Presence
4. Whenever they completed their work

BIBLE QUIZ REVIEW QUESTIONS—EXODUS

LESSON 18—QUESTIONS FOR RED LEVEL REVIEW

1. When did the people ask Aaron to make gods for them? (32:1)

1. As soon as Moses went up the mountain
2. As soon as Moses was out of sight
3. **After Moses was gone a long time**

2. What did Aaron tell the Israelites to bring him? (32:2)

1. Their silver necklaces
2. **Their gold earrings**
3. Their bronze bracelets

3. What did Aaron build in front of the calf? (32:5)

1. **An altar**
2. Stairs
3. Both answers are correct.

4. What did the Israelites do after they presented offerings to the calf? (32:6)

1. They sat down to eat and drink.
2. They got up to indulge in revelry.
3. **Both answers are correct.**

5. Why did the Lord tell Moses to go down the mountain? (32:7)

1. Because Moses had completed his work
2. **Because the people had become corrupt**
3. Because Moses needed to rest

6. What did the Lord say the Israelites were quick to do? (32:8)

1. **Turn away from what he commanded**
2. Obey all of his commands
3. Both answers are correct.

7. Who did the Lord want to make into a great nation? (32:10)

1. Aaron
2. **Moses**
3. Joshua

8. What did Moses ask the Lord to remember? (32:13)

1. **The covenant he swore to Abraham, Isaac, and Israel**
2. Times in the past when the people obeyed
3. Both answers are correct.

9. When did Moses throw the tablets down? (32:19)

1. When he saw the calf
2. When he saw the dancing
3. **Both answers are correct.**

10. Who did Moses ask to come to him when he saw the people running wild? (32:26)

1. **Whoever is for the Lord**
2. Whoever is standing still
3. Whoever still has gold earrings

BIBLE QUIZ REVIEW QUESTIONS—EXODUS

LESSON 18—QUESTIONS FOR BLUE LEVEL REVIEW

1. What did the people ask Aaron to make? (32:1)

1. A new altar
2. A larger tent
3. Gods
4. All of the above

2. In what shape did Aaron make the idol? (32:4)

1. The shape of a serpent
2. The shape of a calf
3. The shape of the pyramids
4. The shape of Mount Sinai

3. How did the people celebrate the festival to the calf? (32:6)

1. They rose early.
2. They sacrificed and presented offerings.
3. They ate, drank, and indulged in revelry.
4. All of the above.

4. Who did the Lord want to destroy? (32:7-10)

1. Aaron and his sons
2. Only the Levites
3. All of the people
4. Joshua and Caleb

5. Why did Moses ask the Lord to remember His covenant? (32:7-8, 13)

1. To turn aside his fierce anger
2. To prevent mocking by the Egyptians
3. To save the people from disaster
4. All of the above.

6. What were the tablets that Moses had in his hands when he went down the mountain? (32:15-16)

1. Tablets of the prophecy
2. Tablets of the Testimony
3. Tablets of Abraham's covenant
4. Tablets of gold.

7. What did Moses do with the tablets when he saw the calf and the dancing? (32:19)

1. He gave them to Joshua to hold
2. He gave them to Aaron to read to the people
3. He threw them down
4. He took them back up the mountain

8. What did Moses do with the gold calf? (32:20)

1. He burned it.
2. He ground it into powder.
3. He mixed it with water and made the people drink it.
4. All of the above.

9. What did Moses say that Aaron had done? (32:21)

1. Brought destruction on the people
2. Delayed their entry into the Promised Land
3. Led the people into great sin
4. Taught the people an important lesson

10. What did Moses tell the people he would do for them? (32:30)

1. Try to make atonement for their sin
2. Try to find a shorter way to Canaan
3. Try to find more gold
4. All of the above.

BIBLE QUIZ REVIEW QUESTIONS—EXODUS

LESSON 19—QUESTIONS FOR RED LEVEL REVIEW

1. What did the Lord tell Moses to make? (34:1)

1. A new walking staff
2. **Two stone tablets**
3. Both answers are correct.

2. Where did the Lord tell Moses to go after making the tablets? (34:2)

1. **Mount Sinai**
2. Red Sea
3. The Israelite camp

3. Who came and stood with Moses on the mountain? (34:5)

1. Aaron
2. Joshua
3. **The Lord**

4. How did the Lord describe himself? (34:6-7)

1. The compassionate God
2. The gracious God
3. **Both answers are correct.**

5. What did the Lord declare that the people will see? (34:10)

1. The awesome works that Moses will do
2. **The awesome works that the Lord will do**
3. Both answers are correct.

6. What did the Lord tell Moses he was not to do? (34:12-14)

1. Not to make a treaty with those who live in the land
2. Not to worship any other god
3. **Both answers are correct.**

7. How many days did the Lord say the people should labor? (34:21)

1. Five days
2. **Six days**
3. Seven days

8. How long was Moses on the mountain? (34:28)

1. **Forty days and forty nights**
2. Four days and four nights
3. Fourteen days and fourteen nights

9. What happened to Moses's face after he spoke with the Lord? (34:29)

1. His face was young again.
2. His wrinkles were gone.
3. **His face was radiant.**

10. How did the Israelites respond when they saw Moses's radiant face? (34:30)

1. **They were afraid to go near him.**
2. They laughed at him.
3. They asked him to explain what had happened.

Bible Studies for Children: Exodus
Bible Quiz Review Questions

Download additional resources from kidzfirstpublications.org

BIBLE QUIZ REVIEW QUESTIONS—EXODUS

LESSON 19—QUESTIONS FOR BLUE LEVEL REVIEW

1. What did the Lord tell Moses to do before climbing Mt. Sinai? (34:1-4)

1. Pray for three days
2. **Chisel out two new stone tablets**
3. Do not eat or drink for three days
4. All of the above

2. How were the people to treat the mountain when Moses went up to present himself to the Lord? (34:2)

1. No one was to come with Moses.
2. No one was to be seen anywhere on the mountain.
3. No flocks or herds were to graze in front of the mountain.
4. **All of the above**

3. What did God say about himself when he met Moses on the mountain? (34:6-7)

1. He is compassionate and slow to anger.
2. He abounds in love and faithfulness.
3. He does not leave the guilty unpunished.
4. **All of the above**

4. What did Moses ask the Lord to do? (34:9)

1. Start a new line of people through Moses
2. **Forgive the people's sin and take them as his inheritance**
3. Punish the guilty with a plague
4. All of the above

5. What did the Lord say that the people would see? (34:10)

1. How beautiful is the work that the Lord will do for you
2. How amazing is the work that the Lord will do for you
3. **How awesome is the work that the Lord will do for you**
4. All of the above

6. What would happen to the Amorites, Canaanites, and Jebusites? (34:11)

1. **They would be driven out by the Lord.**
2. They would be killed with a plague.
3. They would live among the Israelites and learn to worship the Lord.
4. All of the above.

7. What did the Lord say the Israelites should be careful not to do with those who live in the land? (34:12)

1. Marry them
2. Talk with them
3. Live near them
4. **Make treaties with them**

8. What did the Lord tell Moses to write down while he was on the mountain? (34:27)

1. Instructions for building the tabernacle
2. **Instructions for the covenant he made with Moses and with Israel**
3. Instructions for defeating the enemies of Israel
4. Instructions for traveling to the Promised Land

9. What were the Israelites to do with the altars and sacred stones of those who lived in the land? (34:13)

1. Build God's altar over them
2. **Break them down and smash them**
3. Ignore them
4. Worship God on them

10. Why were Aaron and the Israelites afraid to come near Moses? (34:29-30)

1. Moses was angry.
2. Moses was blinded.
3. **His face was radiant.**
4. He was standing too close to the mountain.

BIBLE QUIZ REVIEW QUESTIONS—EXODUS

LESSON 20—QUESTIONS FOR RED LEVEL REVIEW

1. What was Moses to do on the first day of the first month? (40:1-2)

1. Set up the tabernacle
2. Set up the Tent of Meeting
3. **Both answers are correct.**

2. What was Moses to use to wash Aaron and his sons? (40:12)

1. Blood
2. **Water**
3. Both answers are correct.

3. Who were to serve as priests? (40:13-15)

1. **Aaron and his sons**
2. Moses and Joshua
3. Both answers are correct

4. What did Moses offer on the altar of burnt offering? (40:29)

1. Grain offerings
2. Burnt offerings
3. **Both answers are correct.**

5. Where did Moses place the basin of water? (40:30)

1. **Between the Tent of Meeting and the altar**
2. On top of the table in the tabernacle
3. Next to the ark of the Testimony

6. What did Aaron and his sons use the basin for? (40:31)

1. **To wash their hands and feet**
2. To wash grain offerings
3. Both answers are correct.

7. When did Aaron and his sons use the basin to wash? (40:32)

1. Whenever they entered the Tent of Meeting
2. Whenever they approached the altar
3. **Both answers are correct.**

8. Where did Moses set up the courtyard? (40:33)

1. In the middle of the tabernacle
2. **Around the tabernacle and altar**
3. Between the tabernacle and altar

9. What filled the tabernacle? (40:34)

1. **The glory of the Lord**
2. A fiery fog
3. Trumpet blasts

10. What was in sight of all the Israelites in all their travels? (40:38)

1. The spirit of Moses
2. **The cloud of the Lord**
3. Both answers are correct.

BIBLE QUIZ REVIEW QUESTIONS—EXODUS

LESSON 20—QUESTIONS FOR BLUE LEVEL REVIEW

1. Who was told to set up the tabernacle? (40:1-2)

1. Aaron
2. Moses
3. The Israelites
4. Aaron's sons

2. Where were Aaron and his sons to be washed? (40:12)

1. At the entrance to the Tent of Meeting
2. Inside the Tent of Meeting
3. Inside the courtyard
4. Outside the courtyard

3. What was required of Aaron before he could serve God as priest? (40:13)

1. He had to present himself to Moses.
2. He had to climb Mount Sinai.
3. He had to be dressed in the sacred garments, anointed, and consecrated.
4. He had to be baptized.

4. How were Aaron's sons prepared for anointing? (40:12, 14-15)

1. They were washed
2. They were dressed in tunics
3. They were brought to the Tent of Meeting
4. All of the above

5. What would the anointing of Aaron and his sons accomplish? (40:15)

1. They would be anointed into a secret club.
2. They would become best friends forever.
3. They would be anointed into a priesthood continuing for all generations.
4. They would never have to do unpleasant chores again.

6. How did Moses offer burnt offerings and grain offerings? (40:29)

1. In the same way he had done in Midian
2. With many songs and special dancing
3. As the Lord commanded him
4. With a troubled heart

7. What did Moses put in the basin at the Tent of Meeting? (40:30)

1. Water for drinking
2. Blood from the sacrifices
3. The bread of the Presence
4. Water for washing

8. Why could Moses not enter the Tent of Meeting? (40:35)

1. The glory of the Lord filled it.
2. He had no animal sacrifice.
3. God was angry with him.
4. All of the above

9. What was over the tabernacle? (40:38)

1. A covering
2. A cloud and fire
3. A thunderstorm
4. All of the above

10. What was in the sight of all the house of Israel during all their travels? (40:38)

1. The mountain of God
2. The Red Sea
3. The cloud of the Lord
4. The star of David

CERTIFICATE OF COMPLETION

presented to

Congratulations for successfully completing
Bible Studies for Children: Exodus

TEACHER

LOCATION

DATE

AWARD FOR EXCELLENCE

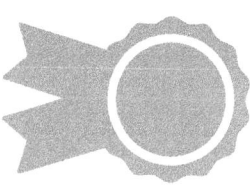

presented to

Great job! We recognize your outstanding achievement in
Bible Studies for Children: Exodus

_____ _____
TEACHER DATE

_____
LOCATION

ATTENDANCE SHEET

Write the children's names in the lines provided. Place an X in the column for each lesson the child attends. You may reproduce this attendance sheet if you need more lines.

BIBLE STUDIES FOR CHILDREN

NAME	1	2	3	4	5	6	7	8	9	10	11	12	13	14	15	16	17	18	19	20

CHILDREN'S QUIZZING SCORE SHEET

Basic quizzing uses only questions 1-15. Advanced quizzing uses 20 questions. Read the Official Rules and Procedures for complete instructions.

CHURCH/TEAM NAME:

ROUND 1

Child's Name	1	2	3	4	5	6	7	8	9	10	11	12	13	14	15	16	17	18	19	20	Total:

Team Bonus:

Team Total:

ROUND 2

Child's Name	1	2	3	4	5	6	7	8	9	10	11	12	13	14	15	16	17	18	19	20	Total:

Team Bonus:

Team Total:

ROUND 3

Child's Name	1	2	3	4	5	6	7	8	9	10	11	12	13	14	15	16	17	18	19	20	Total:

Team Bonus:

Team Total:

MEMORY VERSES FOR EXODUS—PROGRESS CHART

EVENT: _____ CHILD'S NAME: _____ SCORE _____

1 The LORD said, "I have indeed seen the misery of my people in Egypt. I have heard them crying out because of their slave drivers, and I am concerned about their suffering." Exodus 3:7

DATE MEMORIZED: ....

2 My shield is God Most High, who saves the upright in heart. Psalm 7:10

DATE MEMORIZED: ....

3 God said to Moses, "I AM WHO I AM. This is what you are to say to the Israelites: 'I AM has sent me to you.'" Exodus 3:14

DATE MEMORIZED: ....

4 Those who know your name trust in you, for you, LORD, have never forsaken those who seek you. Psalm 9:10

DATE MEMORIZED: ....

5 Moreover, I have heard the groaning of the Israelites, whom the Egyptians are enslaving, and I have remembered my covenant. Exodus 6:5

DATE MEMORIZED: ....

6 The earth is the LORD'S, and everything in it, the world, and all who live in it. Psalm 24:1

DATE MEMORIZED: ....

7 Know that the LORD has set apart his faithful servant for himself; the LORD hears when I call to him. Psalm 4:3

DATE MEMORIZED: ....

8 A person may think their own ways are right, but the LORD weighs the heart. Proverbs 21:2

DATE MEMORIZED: ....

9 Your right hand, LORD, was majestic in power. Your right hand, LORD, shattered the enemy. Exodus 15:6

DATE MEMORIZED: ....

10 The LORD is my strength and my defense; he has become my salvation. He is my God, and I will praise him, my father's God, and I will exalt him. Exodus 15:2

DATE MEMORIZED: ....

11 The LORD will fight for you; you need only to be still. Exodus 14:14

DATE MEMORIZED: ....

12 Who among the gods is like you, LORD? Who is like you—majestic in holiness, awesome in glory, working wonders? Exodus 15:11

DATE MEMORIZED: ....

13 Now if you obey me fully and keep my covenant, then out of all nations you will be my treasured possession. Although the whole earth is mine, you will be for me a kingdom of priests and a holy nation. Exodus 19:5-6

DATE MEMORIZED: ....

14 You shall have no other gods before me. You shall not make for yourself an image in the form of anything in heaven above or on the earth beneath or in the waters below. Exodus 20:3-4

DATE MEMORIZED: ....

15 You shall not misuse the name of the LORD your God, for the LORD will not hold anyone guiltless who misuses his name. Remember the Sabbath day by keeping it holy. Exodus 20:7-8

DATE MEMORIZED: ....

16 Honor your father and your mother, so that you may live long in the land the LORD your God is giving you. Exodus 20:12

DATE MEMORIZED: ....

17 You shall not murder. You shall not commit adultery. You shall not steal. You shall not give false testimony against your neighbor. Exodus 20:13-16

DATE MEMORIZED: ....

18 You shall not covet your neighbor's house. You shall not covet your neighbor's wife, or his male or female servant, his ox or donkey, or anything that belongs to your neighbor. Exodus 20:17

DATE MEMORIZED: ....

19 And he passed in front of Moses, proclaiming, "The LORD, the LORD, the compassionate and gracious God, slow to anger, abounding in love and faithfulness." Exodus 34:6

DATE MEMORIZED: ....

20 Then the LORD said, "I am making a covenant with you. Before all your people I will do wonders never before done in any nation in all the world." Exodus 34:10

DATE MEMORIZED: ....

Bible Studies for Children

Download additional resources from kidzfirstpublications.org

KIDZFIRST QUIZ EVENTS
GUIDELINES, RULES, AND PROCEDURES

KidzFirst Bible Studies and Quiz Events provide in-depth Bible study for children ages 6 through 12 years. This resource invites children to experience genuine discipleship through the study of God's transforming Word. Through *KidzFirst Bible Studies*, children learn about God, study his Word, and gain a saving knowledge of Jesus Christ. Children also learn to apply biblical teachings to actual life situations. *KidzFirst Bible Studies and Quiz Events* encourage children to grow in Christlikeness and to live in relationship with God.

KidzFirst Bible Studies and Quiz Events help children in the following ways:

- To desire to study the Bible
- To learn and develop Bible study habits
- To become familiar with God's holy Word
- To understand that God is the central character and hero of the Bible
- To understand the Bible as the story of God's redeeming love
- To begin a personal relationship with God through Jesus Christ
- To grow in wisdom, understanding, and Christlikeness
- To apply scripture to real life situations and reflect Christian attitudes during quiz events
- To celebrate God's Word and all that they have learned at quiz events

KidzFirst Bible Studies and Quiz Events are sponsored by the Church of the Nazarene. These are the official *KidzFirst Quiz Events: Guidelines, Rules, and Procedures* worldwide.

SECTION 1: OVERVIEW AND RESOURCES

1.1 SIX YEAR CYCLE

KidzFirst Bible Studies and Quiz Events follow a six-year cycle. Each year focuses on different books from the Bible. These books offer an overview of God's redemptive love for all creation. Together they provide a spiritual foundation and a chronology of God's relationship with humanity. Whenever possible, the quiz season follows the schedule for local area schools. The current cycle is as follows:

  2019-2020—*Bible Studies for Children: Genesis*

* 2020-2021—*Bible Studies for Children: Exodus*

  2021-2022—*Bible Studies for Children: Joshua, Judges, and Ruth*

  2022-2023—*Bible Studies for Children: 1 & 2 Samuel*

  2023-2024—*Bible Studies for Children: Matthew*

* 2024-2025—*Bible Studies for Children: Acts*

* Indicates a World Quiz year. The World Quiz is held every four years during the Church of the Nazarene General Assembly and Conventions.

1.2 BIBLE STUDY RESOURCES

- *The Holy Bible*, NIV 2011
- *KidzFirst Bible Studies* (20 Lessons)
- Review Questions for RED Level
- Review Questions for BLUE Level
- Memory Verse Activities
- Memory Verse Progress Chart
- Attendance Sheet

The Holy Bible, NIV 2011, is the primary resource for all English-language curriculum and events. In the USA and Canada, American English curriculum and resources are available from The Foundry Publishing at *www.gokidsquiz.com*. *KidzFirst Bible Studies and Quiz Events* resources are available online at *www.KidzFirstPublications.net* and in the Wesleyan Holiness Digital Library (*WHDL.org*) for use outside the USA and Canada.

1.3 QUIZ EVENT RESOURCES

- Official *KidzFirst Quiz Events: Guidelines, Rules, and Procedures*
- Memory Verse Sheets
- Event Memory Verse Progress Chart
- Event Questions
- Event PowerPoint Slides
- Score Sheets
- Awards and Certificates
- Quiz Box. A child uses a quiz box (or similar device) to answer questions during events. The quiz box contains four tab inserts that are numbered 1, 2, 3, and 4. The numbers represent possible answer choices. Participants pull one numbered insert to indicate the correct answer. Children can also use the quiz box to answer multiple-choice review questions in the classroom. The quiz box dimensions are 30 cm wide X 13 cm deep X 28 cm high. Quiz boxes may be purchased from The Foundry Publishing (*www.gokidsquiz.com*), or a local team may make their own. For instructions to make quiz boxes, visit *www.KidzFirstPublications.net*.

1.4 TIERED QUIZ EVENTS

See Section 2 for more details.

Quiz events provide children intentional opportunities to discover what they learn throughout a quiz event season. This guiding principal allows the children to celebrate God's Word and reinforces the children's knowledge and confidence.

A. Tiered quiz events encourage and effectively prepare children to participate in the World Quiz.

B. Leaders should organize and participate in tiered quiz events as often as practical, preferably between two or more churches. When children participate in smaller quiz events, they are better prepared psychologically, emotionally, and physically for a larger event.

C. The tiered event structure should reflect each context's organizational structure: regional, field, area, etc. Regional leaders should adjust this structure as needed.

   Tier 1: Invitational Practice Event(s)

   Tier 2: Zone Event

   Tier 3: District or National Event

   Tier 4: Field Event. In the USA and Canada, this refers to educational regions (fields).

   Tier 5: World Quiz and World Region Quiz Event

D. Each world region should conduct or designate at least one World Quiz qualifying event.

1.5 QUIZ PERSONNEL

See Section 3 for detailed leader responsibilities.

A. Structural Leadership

Quiz personnel should reflect each region's structure for tiered events. Leaders are encouraged to structure events in Tiers 1-4 according to their local contexts and structures: regional, fields, areas, etc. Regional children's ministry and quiz leaders should adjust personnel as needed. Each director promotes and provides support for Bible studies for children and a tiered quiz event.

Tier 1: Invitational Practice Event: Event Director. These events may be conducted by zone event directors or by local coaches.

Tier 2: Zone Event: Zone Quiz Director. The district quiz director determines the zone boundaries and responsibilities. Zones include multiple churches in a geographical area.

Tier 3: District or National Event: District or National Quiz Director. Districts may include multiple nations, requiring multiple national quiz directors. In large districts, district or national quiz directors are encouraged to group churches and child development centers into smaller zones and to recruit zone directors.

Tier 4: Field Event: Field Quiz Director. In the USA, this refers to the educational region's quiz director. The field's children's ministries coordinator may fill this position.

Tier 5: World Quiz: Global Quiz Coordinator and Regional Quiz Director. The regional quiz director position may be filled by the regional children's ministries director, who will work in tandem with the global quiz coordinator to host a World Quiz satellite event or an event for their world region.

B. Event Leadership

All events include the following positions.

- Local Coach(es)
- The Quizmaster
- The Judge
- The Head Scorekeeper
- Scorekeepers

1.6 CONNECTIONS AND SUGGESTIONS

You may send inquiries, suggestions, and ideas to the global quiz coordinator at:

Rev. Leslie M. Hart, Global Children's Quiz Coordinator
SDMI/Children's Bible Quiz Office
17001 Prairie Star Parkway
Lenexa, KS 66220

E-mail: *childquiz@nazarene.org*

Facebook: *https://www.facebook.com/groups/ChildrensBibleQuizzing/*

SECTION 2: QUIZ EVENTS

When the rules reference a local church or coach, they also apply to child development centers or other organizations and leaders that sponsor children who participate in a quiz event. When children participate in a quiz event, their desire to learn God's Word grows.

A. Quiz events celebrate the child and God's Word.

B. Quiz events operate in accordance with the *KidzFirst Quiz Events: Guidelines, Rules, and Procedures*. Quiz events that follow these rules prepare children to participate effectively in higher-level events.

C. Tiered quiz events should reflect each region's structure and context. Leaders are encouraged to structure events in Tier 1 through Tier 4 according to their local contexts and structures: regional, fields, areas, etc. Regional children's ministry and quiz leaders should adjust tiered events as needed.

D. Each world region will conduct at least one World Quiz qualifying event. Each region should choose the event tier in which the majority of children are able to participate for its World Quiz qualifying event.

2.1 TYPES OF QUIZ EVENTS

Tier 1: Invitational or Practice Events

Invitational or practice events involve two or more churches or teams. These optional events provide children the opportunity to practice prior to the Tier 2: Zone Event.

A. The district or national quiz director determines the geographical boundaries for groups to participate. See Section 2.1, Tier 2: The Zone Event A.

B. The district quiz director recruits a local coach or zone director to serve as the invitational event director for that zone. The invitational event director leads under the authority of the district quiz director.

C. The district quiz director determines the number of invitational (practice) events and which lessons to include at each event.

- Ideally, districts host four invitational events, one invitational event after every five lessons of the Bible study.

- An invitational event may include questions over five lessons or it may include all the lessons leading up to the event. For example, invitational event number one includes questions from lessons 1-5. Event number two may include questions from lessons 6-10 or questions from lessons 1-10. Also included are memory verses from the lessons that are included in each event.

- A district quiz director may choose to have fewer invitational events and evenly divide the 20 lessons of a study throughout the number of events that they choose to host.

D. The district quiz director determines and communicates the dates for the invitational events to all the event directors. All invitational events should happen on the same day. If the event director determines an exception is needed, the district quiz director's approval is required.

E. The invitational event directors select and communicate the time and locations of the invitational events to coaches and to the district quiz director. The coaches communicate the event schedules and locations to the children in their Bible study groups.

F. The district quiz director selects the invitational event questions from the review questions available in the Bible study books, or they may also write their own.

G. When appropriate, the district quiz director provides the event questions to the invitational event directors in a format that may be easily projected.

H. The quiz event will include an opportunity for the children to recite memory verses from each lesson that is included for that event. See Section 2.3.

I. Churches that are unable to participate in invitational events with other churches should conduct their own practice events.

Tier 2: The Zone Event

The Zone Event is the first official event and involves two or more nearby churches or teams in the same area or "zone." This event happens annually.

A. The district or national quiz director determines groups or "zones" of nearby churches located in the same general geographical areas across their district. If the district has established these sub-divisions in its organizational structure, the district quiz director may choose to follow these or establish new quiz event "zones" as needed.

B. The district or national quiz director recruits a local coach or event director to organize and lead each zone event. The zone event directors lead under the authority of the district or national quiz director.

C. The district or national quiz director determines and communicates the date for the zone event to all the zone event directors. All zone events should happen on the same day. Any exception requires the district quiz director's approval.

D. The zone event directors select and communicate the time and location of the event to coaches and to the district quiz director. The coaches communicate the event schedule and location to the children.

E. The official zone event covers all 20 lessons in a study and all the memory verses.

F. The official zone event questions are those authorized and distributed by the global coordinator. The district director is responsible to secure the official questions in presentation-ready format and to distribute them to the zone directors.

G. The zone event includes an opportunity for children to recite memory verses. See Section 2.3.

Tier 3: The District and National Event

The district event is the second official event and involves all churches and teams from a district. In the USA and Canada, this event provides the opportunity to qualify for the World Quiz. Some districts are multi-national and may hold national rather than district events. Tier 3 events happen annually and are conducted in the same manner.

A. The district or national event director determines the details of the event and leads under the authority of the global coordinator and regional or field director.

B. The district director selects and communicates the date, time, and location of the district event to all zone directors and coaches. Coaches communicate with the children and parents.

C. The district event includes all 20 lessons and memory verses in a study.

D. The official district event questions are those authorized and distributed by the global coordinator. The district director is responsible to secure the official questions in presentation-ready format for the district or national event.

E. This event includes an opportunity for children to recite memory verses. See Section 2.3.

F. From this event, children qualify to participate in the Tier 5 or World Quiz event and possible future events. The field or regional event director determines the qualification criteria for children to advance to Tier 4. The qualification for the World Quiz event is predetermined by the global coordinator. All qualification criteria will be communicated to district or national leaders prior to the event.

Tier 4: The Field Event

The field event includes the districts within a field. Children may qualify for the field event based upon their scores at the district or national event according to the field event director. This is an optional event according to the regional quiz director.

A. The field event director determines the details of the event and leads it under the authority of the regional coordinator.

B. The event director verifies participant qualifications, organizes, and leads the field event.

C. The event director selects and communicates the date, time, and location of the event.

D. The field event follows the district event guidelines.

E. The official field event questions are authorized and distributed by the global coordinator. The field director secures the official questions in presentation-ready format for the event.

Tier 5: The Regional Event and World Quiz Event

The regional event includes the fields or districts from a world region. Children will qualify for the regional or World Quiz event based upon their scores at the district event according to the regional or World Quiz event director.

The Regional Event

A. The regional quiz director determines the details of the regional event and leads it under the authority of the global coordinator and the regional children's director.

B. The regional quiz director verifies participant qualifications, organizes, and leads the regional event.

C. The regional quiz director selects and communicates the date, time, and location of the regional event.

D. The regional event follows the district event guidelines.

E. The official regional event questions are those authorized and distributed by the global coordinator. The regional quiz director requests and secures the official questions in presentation-ready format for the regional event one month in advance of the event.

The World Quiz Event

Once every four years, the International World Quiz is sponsored by the Church of the Nazarene. The event is traditionally celebrated in June during the conventions and General Assembly of the Church of the Nazarene. The global coordinator organizes and leads the World Quiz event. See Section 1.

A. The global coordinator determines and communicates the date, time, location, cost, qualification, registration, and procedures.

B. All world regions are encouraged to host satellite locations for the World Quiz event.

C. All satellite locations will be hosted by that region's leadership team in conjunction and cooperation with the global children's quiz coordinator.

D. The World Quiz and satellite events follow the district event guidelines.

E. Children qualify for the World Quiz and satellite events based upon the results of their participation at that year's district event or as determined by the regional director for that world region.

2.2 REGISTRATION

Children register to participate in quiz events at any level.

A. Local churches or coaches register every child to participate in each event throughout the quiz event season.

B. Children 6 to 12 years old may participate at any level, regardless of their academic grade. The district director must approve exceptions to these age limits.

C. Children who participate in youth Bible quiz events will not participate in a children's quiz event.

D. The event director determines the details of the registration process for an event. This includes any fees that are collected. All collected fees should be processed through an official account (such as a Nazarene church, a district, a field, or a regional office).

2.3 MEMORY VERSE RECITATION

Children are encouraged to recite memory verses at every red and blue level event.

A. The event director determines the method and manner used to quote the memory verses and how to recognize and reward success.

B. The event director designates no less than two scorekeepers or coaches to listen to children recite memory verses. A child will not recite memory verses to their own coach or parent without an additional "listener" present.

C. When a child is ready the listener will choose a scripture reference saying, for example, "Quote John 3:16." The child may be offered three chances to quote correctly the verse with the reference. The listener may only tell the child, "Your answer is correct," or "Your answer is incorrect. Would you like to try again?" If so, then "Quote John 3:16." the listener will not prompt the child by giving a hint or offering the first word or two. The child may not leave and return to try again.

D. Scorekeepers record the correctly quoted memory verses on the child's Event Memory Verse Progress Chart.

2.4 RED AND BLUE LEVEL QUIZ EVENTS

Children 6 to 12 years old may participate at either event level regardless of the academic grade level. The child's comprehension level is the primary consideration. Children recite memory verses at both red and blue level events. All events include printed questions and questions in presentation-ready format when possible and appropriate.

A. RED LEVEL

Red is the basic level. The red level event is for younger or beginning quizzers and for older quizzers who prefer this level. The red level questions generally apply to children from age six to eight years old. Red level events use the individual event method. See Section 3.1.

1. At the start of the season, the district director determines if red level events consist of two or three games.
2. A red level game consists of 15 questions.
3. Red level questions offer three multiple-choice answers.
4. The quiz master clearly articulates and audibly reads questions.
5. When possible, the event director visibly projects or posts the questions.
6. The children recite memory verses at all red level events. See Section 2.3.
7. See Section 5 for red level question details.

B. BLUE LEVEL

Blue is the advanced level. The blue level event is for older or experienced quizzers and younger children who desire a greater challenge. The blue level questions generally apply to children from age 9 to 12 years old. Blue level events offer three opportunities for participation. Children may choose to participate as an individual, on a team, or in a combination method. See Section 3.

1. Individual Participation:
    a) At the beginning of the quiz season, the district director determines if blue level events consist of two or three games.
    b) A blue level game consists of 20 questions divided into four rounds. Each round consists of five questions followed by a bonus question. See Section 6: Bonus Questions
    c) Blue level questions offer four multiple-choice answers.
    d) The quiz master clearly articulates and audibly reads questions.
    e) When possible, the event director visibly projects or posts questions.
    f) The children recite memory verses at all blue level events. See Section 2.3.
    g) See Section 5 for blue level question details.
2. Team Participation:
    a) A team consists of four or five children, preferably from the same church. At

the beginning of the quizzing season, the district director announces the number of children required to form a team for that season. If individual churches do not have enough children to form a team, they may combine to form a team.

b) After every fifth question, a bonus question is offered to the teams who qualify. See Section 6 for bonus question details.

c) Bonus questions provide the opportunity for teams to earn additional points and do not affect individual scores.

2.5 WHEN TO SWITCH BETWEEN RED LEVEL AND BLUE LEVEL

A. During a quiz event, children remain in either the red or the blue level until that event is complete.

B. Between Tier 1 events, a child may switch between red and blue levels. This often helps leaders and children to determine the most appropriate quiz level for the child.

C. At the Tier 2 event, each child permanently registers for the remainder of the season for either the red level or the blue level. The child must remain at the same level as they progress from a Tier 2 event and beyond.

2.6 AWARD LEVELS

At KidzFirst Bible Study Quiz Events, every child has an opportunity to answer every question and to receive recognition for every correct answer.

A. When scores are tied, the tie is never broken.

B. Children and teams do not compete against each other. They participate to reach an award level. All children and teams who reach the same award level receive the same award. The goal is for all participants and teams to achieve the highest award level.

C. Recommended award levels:
- Bronze Award = 70-79% correct
- Silver Award = 80-89% correct
- Gold Award = 90-99% correct
- All Star Award = 100% correct

D. Event directors may add recognition for participation, additional awards, or adjust award level percentages. Event directors will fairly apply any additions or adjustments. Prior to the event, the director will announce the award levels to all participants and teams.

E. Districts may choose to award a traveling trophy to the top blue level team. The top team receives the trophy. The trophy resides with the top team until the next event. The trophy returns to each event and is available for the next winner. See Section 11.2.

2.7 CHILDREN WITH SPECIAL NEEDS

God loves and celebrates every child. When possible, children with special needs and disabilities may participate in events. It may be possible for the event director to make reasonable modifications and accommodations under the *KidzFirst Quiz Event: Guidelines, Rules, and Procedures*, but it is not required.

A. The event director will exercise caution to protect the integrity of quiz events. The strategic use of modifications and accommodations to achieve unfair advantage is prohibited.

B. In advance of an event, a coach must declare the special needs of a child and request a modification or accommodation.

C. The event director decides what, if any, accommodations or modifications to make.

D. The existence of accommodations or modifications at one event does not guarantee the same accommodations will be made at future events.

SECTION 3: EVENT METHODS

The district director selects either the individual event method or the combination event method for blue level events.

3.1 INDIVIDUAL EVENT METHOD

In this event method, all children participate as individual participants.

A. Each child's score is separate from all other scores.

B. Children from the same church may sit together, but there are no teams in the individual method and scores are not combined.

C. There are no bonus questions or bonus points for individual participants.

D. The individual method is the only method used for red level events.

3.2 TEAM EVENT METHOD

In this event method, all children participate in teams.

A. In this method, churches may send teams to a blue level event or special event for teams only.

B. The district director determines the number of participants needed to form a team. All teams must have the same number of members. The recommended number per team is four or five.

C. In this method, the individual scores of all team members are combined for a team score.

D. Bonus questions may be used. See Section 6 for details.

3.3 COMBINATION EVENT METHOD

The combination event method combines individual and team methods.

A. In this method, churches may send to an event:
   - Individual participants only
   - Teams only
   - Individual participants and teams

B. The district director determines the team guidelines. See Section 3.2 (B).

C. Children who are not members of a team participate as individual quizzers.

D. In this method, each child's score is counted individually. Additionally, the individual scores of all team members are combined for a team score.

E. Only teams can qualify for bonus questions. See Section 6.

SECTION 4: EVENT PERSONNEL RESPONSIBILITIES

4.1 TIER 5: GLOBAL QUIZ COORDINATOR

This person serves through the Global Ministry Center of the Church of the Nazarene. This position provides support and encouragement for Bible study and quiz events worldwide. The global coordinator is responsible for the following:

A. To be accountable to the Global SDMI Director.

B. To recruit a Bible quiz advisory council, solicit feedback from council members, resolve disputes, and accept suggestions to improve *KidzFirst Bible Studies and Quiz Events*.

C. To serve as the event director for the World Quiz event according to the official *KidzFirst Quiz Events: Guidelines, Rules, and Procedures*.

D. To support and communicate with regional Bible quiz directors and regional children's ministry directors as they promote and organize Bible studies and quiz events on their region.

E. To connect regional directors to available resources and training.

F. To encourage and collaborate with regional directors to conduct satellite locations for participation in the World Quiz event.

G. To make decisions and solve interpretation disputes of the official *KidzFirst Quiz Events: Guidelines, Rules, and Procedures*.

H. To maintain a database of district and regional contact information and district and regional events statistical information.

I. To provide questions in presentation-ready format for the Tier 2, 3, 4 and 5 events. See Section 5.2 (A), (B).

J. To review the official *KidzFirst Quiz Events: Guidelines, Rules, and Procedures* at least annually, update as needed, and communicate updates through the following websites:
- www.WHDL.org
- www.gokidsquiz.com
- www.KidzFirstPublications.net
- www.Nazarene.org

K. To review KidzFirst Bible Study and Quiz Event materials and update as needed.

4.2 TIER 5: WORLD REGION QUIZ DIRECTOR

The regional quiz director is responsible for the following:

A. To be accountable to the global coordinator and regional children's ministries director.

B. To recruit an assistant to provide continuity of leadership in collaboration with the regional children's ministries coordinator and global children's quiz coordinator.

C. When possible, to organize and to lead a regional leadership team.

D. To maintain a database of contact information of field directors on the region and statistical information of the field and regional events.

E. To promote biblical literacy and discipleship through the use of *KidzFirst Bible Studies for Children*.

F. To encourage leaders and train leaders when possible.

G. To serve as that world region's event director and to plan and conduct the regional event in accordance with the official *KidzFirst Quiz Events: Guidelines, Rules, and Procedures*.

  1. To plan and communicate qualifications for participation, registration, procedures, event awards, and supplies.

  2. To recruit assistants for specific assignments from field, district, and national directors, coaches, and other workers as needed for the event. See Section 2.1 Tier 5 and 1.5 (B).

H. To maintain ethical standards and properly account for any and all related fees and expenses. All collected fees should be processed through an official account (such as a Nazarene church, a district, a field, or a regional office).

I. To communicate the final date and location of the regional event to the regional children's ministries director, global coordinator, and field directors. The field directors communicate with district and national directors, who communicate with coaches. Coaches communicate with participants.

J. To request and obtain the official event questions in presentation-ready format from the global coordinator.

K. To request and distribute official event questions to the field, national, and district directors in a timely way.

L. To annually report to the global coordinator the results of the regional event and other quiz events on the region.

M. To make decisions and solve problems within the *KidzFirst Quiz Events: Guidelines, Rules, and Procedures*.

N. To contact the global coordinator for assistance as needed and to report errors and suggest changes to the official *KidzFirst Quiz Events: Guidelines, Rules, and Procedures*.

4.3 TIER 4: FIELD QUIZ DIRECTOR

The field quiz director is responsible for the following:

A. To be accountable to the regional quiz director and the field children's ministries director.

B. To recruit an assistant to provide continuity of leadership in collaboration with the regional quiz director and the field children's ministries director.

C. To determine national or district participation and to appoint national or district directors.

D. When possible, to organize and to lead a field leadership team.

E. To maintain a database of contact information of national and district directors and statistical information on the field events, including churches, teams, and participants.

F. To annually report this information to the regional and global coordinators.

G. To serve as the field event director and to plan and conduct the event according to the official *KidzFirst Quiz Events: Guidelines, Rules, and Procedures*.

  1. To plan and communicate qualifications for participation, registration, procedures, event awards, and supplies.

  2. To recruit assistants for specific assignments from district and national directors, coaches, and other workers as needed for the event.

  3. To communicate the final date, location, and other details of the event to the regional, national, and district directors and coaches. See Section 2.1 Tier 4 and Section 1.5 Tier 4.

H. To follow ethical standards and properly account for related fees and expenses. All collected fees should be processed through an official account (such as a Nazarene church, a district, a field, or a regional office).

I. To regularly communicate with national and district directors and coaches.

J. To encourage churches in the nations and the districts to participate in *KidzFirst Bible Studies and Quiz Events*.

K. To promote biblical literacy and the use of *KidzFirst Bible Studies and Quiz Event* materials as a primary discipleship resource.

L. To train and provide resources when possible.

M. To request official event questions from the regional director well in advance of the event.

N. To distribute official national and district event questions in presentation-ready format to directors in a timely way.

O. To solve problems and make decisions in accordance with the official *KidzFirst Quiz Events: Guidelines, Rules, and Procedures*.

P. To contact the regional quiz director for assistance as needed and to report errors and suggest changes to the official *KidzFirst Quiz Events: Guidelines, Rules, and Procedures*.

4.4 TIER 3: DISTRICT OR NATIONAL QUIZ DIRECTOR

The district or national quiz director is responsible for the following:

A. To be accountable to the field children ministries coordinator, field quiz director, and district or national children's ministries director.

B. To recruit an assistant to provide continuity of leadership in collaboration with the field and district director.

C. To determine boundaries of the zone, to appoint zone directors, to organize the zone directors into a leadership team, and to lead that team.

D. To select and communicate the dates for the official zone event.

E. To appoint invitational event directors.

F. To select and communicate dates for invitational events.

G. To maintain a database of contact information for zone directors and local coaches on the district and statistical information on the district and zone events, churches, teams, and participants.

H. To annually report this information to the field or regional director and the global coordinator.

I. To serve as the event director for the district or national event and to plan and conduct the event according to the official *KidzFirst Quiz Events: Guidelines, Rules, and Procedures*.

   1. To plan and communicate qualifications for participation, registration, procedures, event awards, and supplies.

   2. To recruit assistants for specific assignments from district and national directors, coaches, and other workers as needed for the event.

   3. To communicate the final date, location, and other details of the event to the field and zone directors and coaches. See Section 2.1 Tier 3, and 1.5 Tier 3.

J. To follow ethical standards and properly account for all related fees and expenses. All collected fees should be processed through an official account (such as a Nazarene church, a district, a field, or a regional office).

K. To regularly communicate with zone directors, coaches, and churches.

L. To encourage churches on the district to participate in *KidzFirst Bible Studies and Quiz Events*.

M. To promote biblical literacy and the use of *KidzFirst Bible Studies and Quiz Events* materials as a primary discipleship resource.

N. To train and provide resources as possible.

O. To request official event questions from the regional or global coordinator well in advance of the district and zone events.

P. To distribute official zone event questions in presentation-ready format to zone event directors in a timely way.

Q. To create all questions for the invitational events and distribute these to event directors across the district.

R. To solve problems and make decisions in accordance with the official *KidzFirst Quiz Events: Guidelines, Rules, and Procedures*.

S. To contact the field or regional quiz director for assistance as needed and to report errors and suggest changes to the official *KidzFirst Quiz Events: Guidelines, Rules, and Procedures*.

4.5 TIER 2: ZONE QUIZ DIRECTOR

The zone quiz director may also serve as the invitational event director. This person is responsible for the following:

A. To be accountable to the district quiz director.

B. To recruit an assistant to provide continuity of leadership in collaboration with the district quiz director.

C. To organize the coaches in their zone into an event leadership team and lead that team.

D. To maintain a database of contact information for coaches in the zone and statistical information on the zone event, churches, teams, and participants.

E. To annually report this information to the district director.

F. To serve as the event director for the zone event and to plan and conduct the event according to the official *KidzFirst Quiz Events: Guidelines, Rules, and Procedures*.

  1. To plan and communicate qualifications for participation, registration, procedures, event awards, and supplies.

  2. To recruit assistants for specific assignments from coaches and other workers as needed for the event.

  3. To communicate the final date, location, and other details of the events to the district directors and coaches. See Section 2.1 Tier 2, and 1.5 Tier 2.

G. To follow ethical standards and properly account for all fees and expenses. All collected fees should be processed through an official account (such as a Nazarene church, a district, a field, or a regional office).

H. To regularly communicate with coaches to promote the event and to share information from the district director.

I. To encourage all churches in the zone to participate in *KidzFirst Bible Studies and Quiz Events*.

J. To promote biblical literacy and the use of *KidzFirst Bible Studies and Quiz Event* materials as a primary discipleship resource.

K. To train and to provide resources to local coaches as needed.

L. To keep the district director informed of event details.

M. To request official zone and invitational event questions from the district director well in advance of the invitational events.

N. To solve problems and make decisions in accordance with the official *KidzFirst Quiz Events: Guidelines, Rules, and Procedures*.

O. As needed, to contact the district director for assistance and to report errors or suggest changes to the official *KidzFirst Quiz Events: Guidelines, Rules, and Procedures*.

4.6 TIER 1: INVITATIONAL QUIZ DIRECTOR

This position may be served by the zone director. The invitational quiz event director is responsible for the following:

A. To be accountable to the district quiz director.

B. To recruit an assistant to provide continuity of leadership in collaboration with the district quiz director.

C. To organize the coaches and workers in their zone into an event leadership team and lead that team.

D. To maintain a database of contact information for coaches in the zone and statistical information on the invitational events, churches, teams, and participants.

E. To annually report this information to the district director.

F. To serve as the event director for the invitational events and to plan and conduct the invitational events according to the official *KidzFirst Quiz Events: Guidelines, Rules, and Procedures*.

  1. To plan and communicate qualifications for participation, registration, procedures, event awards, and supplies.

  2. To recruit assistants for specific assignments from coaches and other workers as needed for the event.

  3. To communicate the final dates, locations, and other details of the events to the district director and coaches. See Section 2.1 Tier 1, and 1.5 Tier 1.

G. To follow ethical standards and properly account for all fees and expenses. All collected fees should be processed through an official account (such as a Nazarene church, a district, a field, or a regional office).

H. To regularly communicate with coaches to promote events and to share information from the district director.

I. To encourage all churches in the zone to participate in *KidzFirst Bible Studies and Quiz Events*.

J. To promote biblical literacy and the use of *KidzFirst Bible Studies and Quiz Event* materials as a primary discipleship resource.

K. To train and to provide resources to local coaches as needed.

L. To keep the district director informed of event details.

M. To request invitational event questions from the district director well in advance of the invitational events.

N. To solve problems and make decisions in accordance with the official *KidzFirst Quiz Events: Guidelines, Rules, and Procedures*.

O. As needed, to contact the district director for assistance, and to report errors or suggest changes to the official *KidzFirst Quiz Events: Guidelines, Rules, and Procedures*.

4.7 COACH

The coach is recruited by the local church leadership and is responsible for the following.

A. To be accountable to the local church leader.

B. To create a leadership team from local church leaders to promote *KidzFirst Bible Studies and Quiz Events*, to plan and conduct Bible studies, and to prepare for quiz events.

C. To follow ethical standards in all matters and properly account for any fees collected. All collected fees should be processed through an official account (such as a Nazarene church, a district, a field, or a regional office).

D. To encourage children to participate in *KidzFirst Bible Studies and Quiz Events*.

E. If the group is unable to participate in invitational events, to conduct practice quiz events that will prepare children for upcoming events.

F. To organize and lead children's Bible studies using the *KidzFirst Bible Studies* curriculum.

G. During a quiz event, to call a timeout as allowed in the procedures authorized by the district director. See Section 8.

H. To challenge a question during an event. See Section 9.

I. To recruit event assistants and scorekeepers as needed.

J. To promote biblical literacy and the use of *KidzFirst Bible Studies for Children and Quiz Event* materials as a primary discipleship resource in their local congregation.

K. To create and maintain a database of participant and parent contact information.

L. To communicate with parents regularly, to promote events, and to share information from the district and zone director.

M. To support and participate in opportunities to train and gain resources.

N. To provide to the zone director current contact and statistical information.

O. To follow these official *KidzFirst Quiz Events: Guidelines, Rules, and Procedures* and to contact the zone director or district director with questions.

P. To contact the zone or district director to report errors or suggest changes to the official *KidzFirst Quiz Events: Guidelines, Rules, and Procedures*.

4.8 QUIZMASTER

The Quizmaster is recruited by the event director and is responsible for the following.

A. To read the event questions, including bonus questions. See Section 5.3.

B. To follow these official *KidzFirst Quiz Events: Guidelines, Rules, and Procedures*.

C. To refer to the official *KidzFirst Quiz Events: Guidelines, Rules, and Procedures* for authority in the event of a conflict and to collaborate with and support the decisions of the judge.

D. To serve as judge if needed. See Sections 4.9.

E. To call a timeout as needed.

4.9 JUDGE

The judge is recruited by the event director. In the event there is no judge, the quizmaster fills this role. The judge is responsible for the following:

A. To evaluate the validity of all challenges based on the scripture reference and to respond to challenges according to Sections 9.4 and 9.5.

B. To collaborate with the quizmaster or event director to address challenges, as needed.

4.10 HEAD SCOREKEEPER

The head scorekeeper is recruited and appointed by the event director. The head scorekeeper is responsible for the following:

A. To provide the resources and supplies to keep score for each event in cooperation with the event director.

B. To set the ratio of quizzers to scorekeepers and define the number of scorekeepers that each church must provide in collaboration with the district director.

C. To meet with and instruct the scorekeepers regarding these official *KidzFirst Quiz Events: Guidelines, Rules, and Procedures* prior to the start of the event. See Section 7.

D. To oversee the scorekeepers.

E. To tally the scores of each game and relay this information to the event director.

F. To resolve disputes about scores.

G. To provide instructions on how to keep team scores.

H. To determine any adjustment to the score criteria after a challenge has been resolved. See Section 9.7 (B).

4.11 SCOREKEEPER

A. Coaches are responsible to recruit an adequate number of scorekeepers for each event. The head scorekeeper and district director set the ratio of quizzers to scorekeepers. This defines the number of scorekeepers that each church must provide. For example, if the ratio is one scorekeeper for every three quizzers, a church with seven quizzers must provide three scorekeepers. Two scorekeepers from the same church will not score their team together.

B. Coaches may also serve as scorekeepers.

C. Churches that fail to provide the required number of scorekeepers may be required to decrease the number of children who participate so that they comply with the ratio set by the district director. In that case, the coach chooses which children participate.

D. The scorekeeper is responsible for the following:

   1. To use the official score sheet to mark the individual and team answers.

   2. To use the method to record correct answers and tabulate scores as instructed by the head scorekeeper. See Section 7.

   3. To listen to bonus question answers and award team points.

   4. To work in pairs when possible and compare scores after every 5th question in order to

assure that the two scorekeepers agree on the total to that point.

SECTION 5: EVENT QUESTIONS

5.1 HOW TO OBTAIN OFFICIAL EVENT QUESTIONS

A. The global coordinator creates questions for Tier 2, 3, 4, and 5 events and distributes them to registered regional, field, and district event directors. To register, leaders will submit a question request form. The form may be requested by email (childquiz@nazarene.org).

B. The regional director and field event director are the only persons authorized to obtain a copy of the official questions for a regional or field quiz event.

C. The district or national director obtains a copy of the official questions for the zone and district or national events.

D. The district director will distribute the official zone questions to the zone directors prior to the zone event.

E. The district director will create and distribute copies of the invitational event questions to the event directors prior to the invitational events.

F. The global coordinator annually emails order forms for official questions by December. District and regional directors should contact the global coordinator at childquiz@nazarene.org to update changes to their e-mail address. Official questions will be sent in January.

5.2 RED AND BLUE LEVEL EVENT QUESTIONS

A. Source and Nature of Red Level Questions

1. Red Level Tier 1 and Tier 2 events (Invitational and Zone) use the review questions from each lesson. Review questions are available at www.KidzFirstPublications.net and in the KidzFirst *Bible Studies for Children* books. If a book is not available, an event director may create their own questions.

2. Tier 3 events (district or national) use the review questions, reworded review questions, or memory verses. This approach provides a greater challenge than previous tier events.

3. Tier 4 and 5 (regional and world) event questions are a combination of review questions, reworded questions, new questions, and memory verses.

4. All events include opportunities to recite memory verses. See Section 2.3.

B. SOURCE AND NATURE OF BLUE LEVEL QUESTIONS:

1. Blue Level Tier 1 and 2 events use the review questions from each lesson available at KidzFirst publications.net and in the back of the *Kidzfirst Bible Studies for Children* books. If a book is not available, an event director may create their own questions. These events also offer reworded review questions, new questions, and memory verses.

2. Tier 3 events use the review questions, reworded review questions, new questions, or memory verses.

3. Tier 4 and 5 events use the review questions, reworded review questions, new questions, or based on memory verses.

4. All events include opportunities to recite memory verses. See Section 2.3.

5. Bonus questions shall include memory verses.

5.3 HOW TO READ AND PROJECT EVENT QUESTIONS

A. The quizmaster reads the question and all answer choices twice. After the quizmaster reads the second time, he or she will call the children to respond. The quizmaster never reads questions once.

- The quizmaster says, "QUESTION" and then reads the question and all answer choices.
- The quizmaster repeats this sequence.
- The quizmaster says, "ANSWER," which prompts the participants' to respond.

Example: The quizmaster says, "**QUESTION: What did Mary name her baby? Answer number one, Joseph. Answer number two, John. Answer number three, Jesus.**" The quizmaster briefly pauses and starts again and says, "**QUESTION: What did Mary name her baby? Answer number one, Joseph. Answer number two, John. Answer number three, Jesus.**" The quizmaster briefly pauses and calls for the answer and says, "**ANSWER.**" The children then indicate their answer choice.

B. The quizmaster may read a question a third time for especially difficult or long questions or if a mistake was made when the question was initially read. However, this practice should be the exception, and the participants should be notified of a third repeat in advance to avoid premature responses after the second question and answer sequence.

C. After the answers are indicated, the quizmaster pauses and watches for the scorekeepers to record all the scores. When the scores are recorded, the quizmaster instructs the children to return their answers.

D. For bonus questions, the quizmaster instructs the team representatives who will answer the bonus question for each team to stand and all the other children to place their hands in their laps. The quizmaster reads the question two times. The child who is ready to answer the bonus question steps to the scorekeepers and quietly gives their answer. The child speaks carefully and quietly so that they do not reveal their answer to other teams. When everyone completes their answer, the quizmaster asks the scorekeepers to raise their hand to reveal who correctly answered. The quizmaster affirms the correct answer or invites a participant to share the correct answer.

E. When possible, use PowerPoint or other visual media to project questions onto a screen that is visible to all quizzers for red and blue level events.

F. The projected presentation will only include the questions. All answers will be read.

SECTION 6: BONUS QUESTIONS

6.1 THE USE OF BONUS QUESTIONS

The team and combination event methods use bonus questions. Only teams that qualify may answer a bonus question. See Section 6.2.

A. A bonus question opportunity occurs after a five-question round.

B. There are four rounds in each twenty-question game. A bonus question is offered after every fifth question, i.e. after questions 5, 10, 15 and 20.

C. The content of bonus questions includes memory verses.

D. Correctly answered bonus questions add points to a team's final score.

6.2 HOW TO QUALIFY FOR A BONUS QUESTION

A. A team qualifies to answer a bonus question after each round of five questions. To qualify, a team cannot have more incorrect answers during the round than the total number of team members.

B. A four-member team will qualify with four or fewer incorrect answers during that round. A five-member team will qualify with five or fewer total incorrect answers.

C. The incorrect answers may occur through different children or the same child.

Examples of a Bonus Qualified Four-Member Team *

Name	1	2	3	4	5
John	5	0	5	5	5
Mary	5	5	5	5	5
Peter	5	5	0	5	5
Mark	0	5	5	0	5
Team Bonus					*

Name	1	2	3	4	5
John	5	0	0	0	0
Mary	5	5	5	5	5
Peter	5	5	5	5	5
Mark	5	5	5	5	5
Team Bonus					*

Examples of a Bonus Qualified Five-Member Team *

Name	1	2	3	4	5
John	5	5	5	5	5
Mary	5	0	5	5	0
Peter	0	5	5	5	5
Michael	5	5	5	0	5
Mark	5	5	0	5	5
Team Bonus					*

6.3 HOW TO ANSWER A BONUS QUESTION

A. The district director determines the way children answer bonus questions.

B. Prior to the reading of the bonus question, the coach selects a team member to answer the bonus question. They may choose the same child to answer several or all bonus questions or select different children for each bonus question.

C. Traditionally, the child goes to the scorekeepers and quietly gives the answer. The child speaks carefully and quietly so that they do not reveal their answer to other teams. See Section 5.3 (D).

6.4 HOW TO SCORE A BONUS QUESTION

A. The scorekeepers assign the points for a correct answer to a bonus question to the team's score, not to the individual child's score.

B. The scorekeepers record bonus points on the "Team Bonus" row on the score sheet. See the * in the examples in Section 6.2.

C. The scorekeepers add all bonus points to the combined individual team members' scores for the total Team score.

D. The district director determines how bonus points are scored. See Section 7.

SECTION 7: HOW TO SCORE

7.1 POINT SYSTEM

At the start of the quiz season, the district director selects option A or B and communicates the method to score to all event directors.

Option A: Five Points

A. The scorekeeper awards five points to each participant for each correct answer

B. The scorekeeper awards five points to each team for each correct bonus answer (blue level only). Remember, the individual does not receive an additional five points for a correct answer to a bonus question.

> Example 1: If a child correctly answers 20 questions in a blue level game, the child earns a total of 100 points. Extra points are not awarded for perfect rounds.

> Example 2: If every member of a four-person team correctly answers 20 questions in a blue level game and the team answers four bonus questions correctly, the team earns a total of 420 points.

C. Red level events include only 15 questions per game, no teams, no bonus questions, and result in lower scores than blue level events.

> Example 1: If a child answers 15 questions correctly in a red level game, the child earns a total of 75 points. Extra points are not awarded for perfect rounds.

Option B: One Point

A. The scorekeeper awards one point per correct answer

B. The scorekeeper awards one point per correct bonus answer (blue level only).

> Example 1: if a child answers 20 questions correctly in a blue level game, the child earns a total of 20 points. Extra points are not awarded for perfect rounds.

> Example 2: If every member of a four-person team answers 20 questions correctly in a blue level game and the team answers four bonus questions correctly, the team earns a total of 84 points.

C. Red level events include only 15 questions per game, no teams, no bonus questions, and result in lower scores than blue level events.

> Example 1: If a child answers 15 questions correctly in a red level round, the child earns a total of 15 points. Extra points are not awarded for perfect rounds.

7.2 TIE SCORES

A. Never break scores that are tied.

B. All individuals and teams that achieve the same score receive the same recognition, the same award, and the same opportunity for advancement to the next event level.

7.3 SCORE SHEETS

Free downloadable score sheets are available from KidzFirstPublishing.net or www.gokidsquiz.com.

7.4 HOW TO MARK A SCORE SHEET

A. The district director determines the method to be used by all scorekeepers.

B. The district director communicates this to all the event directors prior to the start of the quiz event season.

C. The district director determines the symbols that will be used to mark correct and incorrect answers on the score sheets.

D. All scorekeepers use the same method and symbols to insure the correct tabulation of scores.

SECTION 8: TIMEOUTS

8.1 NUMBER OF TIMEOUTS

A. The event director determines the number of timeouts that each church may use during a game.

B. Each church receives the same number of timeouts, regardless of the number of individual quizzers or teams from that church. For example, if the event director decides to give one timeout, each church receives one timeout.

C. The event director determines if an automatic timeout is given during a game and when the timeout occurs.

8.2 WHO MAY CALL A TIMEOUT

A. The coach is the only individual who may call a timeout for a team.

B. The event director or quizmaster may call a timeout at any time for any reason.

8.3 LENGTH OF TIMEOUTS

A. The event director determines the maximum duration of a timeout.

B. Prior to the start, the event director communicates to the coaches the length of a timeout.

SECTION 9: CHALLENGES

BASIC RULE: Challenges are the exception and not the normal practice at any event.

9.1 WHO ISSUES A CHALLENGE

A. Only the coach may issue a challenge.

B. If an individual other than the coach attempts to issue a challenge, that challenge is automatically ruled invalid and not considered.

9.2 WHEN TO ISSUE A CHALLENGE

The event director decides when a challenge may be issued.

A. The coach may use a timeout to issue a challenge.

B. The coach may issue a challenge at the conclusion of a five-question round, that is to say immediately after the 5th, 10th, 15th, or 20th question.

C. The coach may issue a challenge at the conclusion of a game, immediately after the last question.

D. Challenges are never accepted on a previous game after the next game begins. If a coach issues a challenge on a question in game one after game two begins, the challenge is invalid.

9.3 HOW TO ISSUE A CHALLENGE

A. At the start of the quiz season, the district director determines and communicates to all event directors the preferred method to issue a valid challenge.

1. The challenge may be written or verbal.

2. The coach may raise their hand to indicate the challenge and wait until the appropriate time to specifically explain. See Section 9.2.

3. The coach may approach the quizmaster to verbally discuss the reason for the challenge.

4. The coach may provide a written explanation to the quizmaster.

B. Prior to the start of an event, the event director explains who, when, and how a coach may issue a challenge.

9.4 CHALLENGE PROCEDURES

When a coach appropriately issues a challenge, these steps will be followed.

A. The judge determines if the challenge is valid or invalid according to Section 9.1 and 9.5. The judge may choose to consult with the quizmaster and the event director.

B. If the challenge is invalid, the judge announces that the challenge is invalid, and the event continues.

C. If the reason given is valid, the event director (or quizmaster in the absence of the event director) may choose one of the following:

   1. To eliminate the question. The result is that a 20-question game becomes a 19-question game. The result will impact the scores and the award criteria. Event leaders will always give children the best advantage to raise their scores.

   2. To replace the question. The quizmaster asks all participants a new question. All the answers are replaced with the answers to the new question.

   3. To award the point(s) for the challenged question to all participants as if they had answered correctly.

   4. To allow children who correctly answered the challenged question to keep their points and offer an alternative question to children who gave an incorrect answer.

D. If more than one person challenges the same question, the event director or quiz master selects one coach to explain the reason for the challenge.

E. After a decision has been made, another person may not challenge the same question.

9.5 *A Valid Challenge*

A. A challenge is valid for only one reason: the answer identified as correct is not correct according to the Scripture sited by the Bible reference.

B. Challenges issued for any other reason are invalid.

C. Challenges are only valid when made by the coach.

D. Invalid challenges are never considered. Invalid challenges disrupt the event and cause children to lose concentration. When someone consistently makes invalid challenges, it can be divisive.

E. Examples of common invalid challenges include:

   1. The correct answer is inconsistent with Bible references other than the Bible reference given for that question.

   2. A question is too difficult or poorly worded.

   3. Someone other than a coach makes a challenge.

9.6 LOSS OF CHALLENGE PRIVILEGES

A. The event director (or the quizmaster in the absence of the event director) has the authority to remove the privilege to challenge a question from any individual who abuses this privilege.

   1. The privilege to challenge may be removed if an individual consistently makes invalid challenges that disrupt the event.

   2. The privilege to challenge may be removed if an individual continues to argue after a decision has been made.

B. The individual's challenge privilege will be lost for the remainder of that event and possibly for future events.

9.7 THE EFFECT OF A CHALLENGE ON SCORES

A. If the team or combination event method is used, a challenge may change an individual quizzer's score and therefore affect the team's ability to qualify for a bonus question. See Section 3.2 and 3.3.

B. If a question is eliminated, the head scorekeeper determines if the award criteria needs to be adjusted and makes necessary changes. See Section 9.4 (C).

C. Resolve all challenge decisions before scores are declared final and awards are presented.

SECTION 10: ETHICS

10.1 EVENT ETHICS

The event director shall maintain order and conduct quiz events with the highest ethical standards.

A. Workers' Conduct and Attitudes

1. All coaches and event officials will display a respectful, Christlike attitude and demeanor.

2. Coaches will privately and discreetly discuss challenges and disputes.

3. The event director's decisions are final. Coaches and parents must respectfully and gracefully accept the final decision, even if they disagree.

4. Coaches and event officials will relay all decisions to quizzers and others without details or personal opinions.

5. The attitudes of coaches and event officials will reflect a spirit of Christlikeness, cooperation, and encouragement.

B. Disqualification for Behavior Prior to an Event

Events within a tier use the same questions. It is not appropriate for children, parents, or coaches to have access to event questions prior to an event, whether by attendance at other events or communication with anyone who attends other events.

1. A person(s) may be disqualified from participation if they gain prior access to event questions through any method.

a. If a coach or assistant attends another event, the district director may decide to disqualify participants connected with that person.

b. If a parent or child attends another event, the district director may decide to disallow participation by that child or that parent's child.

2. The district director will decide if any participant is disqualified.

C. Disqualification for Behavior During an Event

1. Leaders will provide graceful and progressive steps to help teach younger children to recognize and to resist the temptation to cheat. See Section 10.2.

2. Cheating will result in serious consequences. When someone is disqualified for cheating, he or she will not receive awards or continue to participate.

10.2 PROCEDURE TO INVESTIGATE A PERSON WHO CHEATS

The district quiz director determines the procedure to follow in the event that a child or an adult cheats at an event. At the start of the season, the district director communicates to all event directors and coaches the district's policy and procedure if someone cheats. Before someone is accused, it is important to have evidence or a witness.

A. The event director should be notified if someone suspects a person is cheating.

B. The event director will notify the judge to observe all participants. After several questions, if the judge does not see someone cheating, the quiz will continue.

C. If the judge sees someone cheat, he or she will describe it to the event director.

D. The event director will call a timeout and explain the problem to the child's coach. The coach will talk privately with the child and explain the consequences if he or she continues to cheat. The coach will ask the child if they understand the problem and if the child knows how to correct the behavior.

E. The judge, event director, and coach will watch to see if the child continues to cheat.

F. If a child continues to cheat, the judge will tell the coach that the child's score will be disqualified.

G. If a scorekeeper cheats, the event director will follow the same steps. If the person continues to cheat, the director will ask the scorekeeper to leave, and he or she will appoint a new scorekeeper.

H. If an adult in the audience cheats, the event director will privately ask the adult to stop. If the behavior continues, the event director will ask the person to leave the event.

SECTION 11: FINAL DECISIONS

11.1 AWARD DECISIONS

A. The quizmaster and scorekeepers should be certain that all final scores are accurate and challenge decisions are completed prior to the award presentation.

B. An individual award is never taken from a child after the awards are presented. If a mistake is made, children may receive a higher award but never a lower award.

C. Team awards are never taken from a child after the awards are presented. See the previous point B. The only exception is a rotating team trophy. See Section 11.2.

11.2 DISTRICT ROTATING TEAM TROPHY

A. A team trophy that rotates among top teams is an optional award. This is given to the top team on a zone at Tier 1 and Tier 2 events. The top team returns the award at the next event. The winner of that event will receive the award to celebrate with their church. See Section 2.6 (E).

B. If there is a mistake in the score tabulation, the team that incorrectly received the trophy shall return the trophy immediately so that it may be presented to the appropriate team.

C. The coach is responsible to help children to understand that they did not earn the trophy and that the right thing to do is to return the trophy to the winner.

11.3 UNRESOLVED ISSUES AND QUESTIONS

Consult with the global coordinator for unresolved issues and questions.

SECTION 12: SCOPE OF PARTICIPATION

The Church of the Nazarene is the official sponsor of *KidzFirst Bible Studies and Quiz Events*. It welcomes participation by other denominations and non-denominational Christian groups. It encourages participation in the following ways.

12.1 INDEPENDENT USE

Everyone is welcome to use the *KidzFirst Bible Studies and Quiz Events* materials. Other denominations that want to provide a *KidzFirst Bible Studies and Quiz Events* program may adapt these guidelines, rules, and procedures and follow their own organizational structure.

12.2 HOW TO PARTICIPATE IN A NAZARENE EVENT

If other denominations and non-denominational groups want to participate with a Nazarene Church, or quiz event, they should contact the district director.

1. The district director will assign the church or group to a zone.
2. Churches or groups in this situation will agree to follow these official Event Guidelines, Rules and Procedures.

THE STORY BEHIND KIDZFIRST BIBLE STUDIES FOR CHILDREN AND QUIZ EVENTS

The Kids Reaching Kids Mission Offering Project is designed to encourage children to give sacrificially to meet the needs of other children. Aptly named, it focuses on Kids… Reaching… Kids. Kids Reaching Kids challenges children, churches, districts, fields and regions, to meet children's needs in every world region.

Mentally through education to enrich children's minds.

Physically through compassion to meet children's basic needs.

Spiritually through evangelism to reach children for Christ.

Socially through discipleship to strengthen children's faith.

This biblical approach is modeled on the life of Jesus. Luke 2:52 reveals how Jesus' life was shaped in a holistic fashion. Jesus grew in wisdom(mentally) and stature(physically), and in favor with God(spiritually) and men (socially).

Each year a project is chosen that addresses a vital need of children across the globe. The proceeds are available for a variety of ministries with children in all six Nazarene world regions. For more information about Kids Reaching Kids, visit *https://www.usacanadaregion.org/ministry/childrens-ministry/kids-reaching-kids* or *https://nazarene.org/who-we-are/organization/ministries/sdmi/kids-reaching-kids*

The D-Code Challenge: Bible Quizzing – Unlocked, Unlimited, and Understood

In 2008-2009, the Kids Reaching Kids Mission Offering Project, the D-Code Challenge, raised funds for the translation, production and distribution of Children's Bible Quizzing materials.

The book you are holding originated from materials produced by The Nazarene Publishing House. It was translated into Global English, French, Korean, Portuguese, and Spanish through Children's Ministries International, Global Nazarene Publications, and a team of translators around the world.